THE STEREOTYPE OF THE SINGLE WOMAN

IN AMERICAN NOVELS

THE STEREOTYPE OF
THE SINGLE WOMAN
IN AMERICAN NOVELS

A Social Study
with Implications for the
Education of Women

by DOROTHY YOST DEEGAN

OCTAGON BOOKS

A DIVISION OF FARRAR, STRAUS AND GIROUX

New York   1981

Reprinted 1969
by permission of Dorothy Yost Deegan

Second Octagon printing 1975
Third Octagon printing 1981

OCTAGON BOOKS
A DIVISION OF FARRAR, STRAUS & GIROUX, INC.
19 Union Square West
New York, N.Y. 10003

LIBRARY OF CONGRESS CATALOG CARD NUMBER: 69-16754
ISBN 0-374-92090-7

Manufactured by Braun-Brumfield, Inc.
Ann Arbor, Michigan
Printed in the United States of America

PI LAMBDA THETA, National Association for Women in Education, has for some years been actively engaged in the study of women's professional problems. In 1935 the Association sponsored a survey of the research already accomplished in this field, and since then has granted Awards to fourteen research studies, most of them in this field of investigation. Pi Lambda Theta takes pride in acknowledging *The Stereotype of the Single Woman in American Novels* as the recipient of the 1947 Award granted from the Ella Victoria Dobbs Fellowship Fund.

TO MY LITTLE DAUGHTER

ELLEN MARGARET

FOREWORD

*Our stereotyped world is not necessarily the world we should
like it to be. It is simply the kind of world we expect it to be.*

WALTER LIPPMANN, Public Opinion

THIS study is a pioneer venture. It uses American novels for
their sociopsychological content rather than for their literary values, the underlying assumption being that literature
is a sensitive medium which both creates and reflects attitudes of society.

In forging its way through unexplored areas, the investigation met with two major difficulties: first, with regard to
its subject matter; and second, in its methodology. It deals
with a subject so charged with emotion, so vital, so personal,
and so clothed in prejudicial stereotype, that it has been difficult to consider it an appropriate subject for scholarly research.

The author's increasing interest in the problem of the
single woman and her work on this study have been temp-
ered at many points by the attitudes expressed by "intelligent people" toward her undertaking. She remembers—still
with something of shock and surprise—the query of one
professor of wide reputation who asked with a chuckle,
"What is it you want to do—write a guidebook for the old
maid?" It is less than likely that anyone in a university setting
would have challenged "the quality of the concepts" or
thought it strange if the investigation had proposed to deal
with problems of marital adjustment, or problems of the
young child, the adolescent, the middle-aged, or the senile.
Any of these subjects would have produced an entirely respectable study. But the single woman—the "old maid"—

was she and her plight—well—quite dignified enough for research?

If this investigation can bring out into the clear light of understanding and into the realm of the articulate some of the aspects of this deeply human problem so long clouded in prejudice and taboo, if it can ever so slightly change the attitude of society from one which imposes frustration to one which will liberate the spirit of the woman who must live her life without marriage, it will have amply achieved its purpose.

The second difficulty arose over the fact that the study is an interfield investigation of a kind much favored in theory but exceedingly difficult in execution. In breaking down and cutting across the boundaries of several academic departments, it presented a knotty problem in methodology. Its material is literature, its approach is both sociological and psychological, but its emphasis is upon the individual and her adjustment in present-day society. It is in its emphasis that the study yields its implications for the education of women.

Since it is a study in personnel and education, it follows accepted methods in educational research. It defines its terms precisely, if somewhat arbitrarily. It uses a sampling rather than the whole range of the American novel. Instead of giving a general treatment of its material, it attempts to fractionate certain sociopsychological elements in the lives of the single women of fiction. More specifically, it deals with the woman "thirty years of age or older," who has not married; it uses a fixed list of novels, the Dickinson list of "best books," and further reduces the sampling by applying certain criteria devised to make the material more appropriate to the subject under consideration. But it seeks to compensate for some of these limitations by offering some supplementary materials.

Though the study is patterned primarily along the lines of

educational research, it borrows from the methods of its kindred subject-matter fields in certain other respects. And since the study is a pioneer, which, it is hoped, may ease the way for other similar interfield studies, it may be useful to note briefly how and wherein it has made use of academic methods.

First, previous research has been cited, not only in its major field, but also in each of the several academic fields it borders upon: clinical psychology, sociology, and the "sociology of the American novel." Since only two earlier pieces of research have dealt specifically with the subject of the single woman, much of this academic background has been necessary and all of it has been useful in gaining an understanding of the complex nature of the problem.

Second, the analytic classification of factors in the lives of the fictive women has been preceded by a synthesis or developmental interpretation of the seven major characters. In its pattern this resembles the sociopsychological case study. Each narrative sketch is as complete as the material the novelist has furnished and is closely documented throughout.

Third, the study surveys much of the important fiction marginal to the central body of data. This includes an evaluation of single-woman characters in novels pruned out of the Dickinson list as well as an observation of other characters in other novels which Dickinson did not include. The study also surveys notable fiction which has appeared since 1935, the terminal point of the sampling. Furthermore, the findings are substantiated and the conclusions more deeply intrenched by comparing them with sociological facts reflecting the actual status of the single woman in American society.

The use of fiction as a social document is not without precedent. The chapter on previous research cites a number of academic studies built upon the pioneer work of Parrington in the sociology of American literature, all of which illustrate the use of fiction as a means and not an end—as a source of data on human experience.

Fiction has been used similarly in the field of student personnel work as well as in the allied fields of psychology and psychiatry. Courses in vocational guidance frequently refer to Morgan's *Vocations in Short Stories* and Lingenfelter's *Vocations in Fiction*, both designed to aid students in choosing vocations. The anthology, *Thicker than Water* by Wunsch and Albers, presents selected short stories dealing with typical problems of family life, implementing the interpretation Rosenblatt had made in *Literature as Exploration*, which sought to discover how "the experience and study of literature could foster a sounder understanding of life and nourish the development of balanced humane personalities." On the college level, *Psychology through Literature*, by Shrodes, Van Gundy, and Husband, states a fundamental concept: that implicit in literature are all the facts of psychology. Oberndorf, in his scholarly analysis of *The Psychiatric Novels of Oliver Wendell Holmes*, finds these novels (two of which appear in the present study) surprisingly sound and modern in their understanding of human behavior. All these books are not only worthy works in themselves, but illustrate a tendency in scholarly writing to utilize fiction in the attempt to solve human problems. In similar areas and in somewhat the same way, this study aims to be useful. The influence of social stereotypes in the choice of vocation suggests a live topic for informal discussion and future research. Furthermore, since it is allied with literature, sociology, psychology, as well as the general field of personnel, it might be used in conjunction with any of these in bringing greater insight into the varied aspects of one human problem—the problem of singleness as it pertains to women.

Stereotypes in and of themselves have been variously

called to attention. As long ago as 1922 Lippmann recognized stereotypes as an important element in public opinion. Since then stereotypes have been the subject of experimental research in studies made by Schoenfeld, Edwards, and others, with special emphasis upon racial, national, and political attitudes.

More closely related to this study is the recent investigation of how writers perpetuate stereotypes, made by the Columbia University Bureau of Applied Social Research at the instigation of the Writers' War Board. Examination of various media—the stage, motion pictures, radio, comic cartoons, the press, advertising copy, and fiction—strongly supported the assumption that white, Protestant Anglo-Saxons were more favorably presented in mass media than other elements in the American population. With regard to fiction specifically, it was found that the short story used the most stereotypes and was the worst offender while the novel ranked only second to the stage as the most liberal of all media in presenting minority characters sympathetically and honestly. One could hardly say this was true of the stereotype of the older single woman in the novel or of certain vocational "types" which this study has revealed.

For their advice and encouragement I am deeply indebted to Professors Ruth Strang and Edmund deS. Brunner, of Teachers College, Columbia University, who have jointly sponsored this investigation. I am also grateful to Professor Lennox Grey, of the Department of the Teaching of English and Foreign Languages, for his counsel and suggestions.

I wish to thank Professors Helen M. Walker and Ida A. Jewett, of Teachers College, for aid in special problems arising in connection with the research, and Professor Merle Curti, formerly of Teachers College and now at the University of Wisconsin, for directing my interest in the social and historical backgrounds of the study.

To all others—friends, neighbors, and members of my

family—who have encouraged me or borne with me while I was making this study, I offer my appreciation and my gratitude.

For permission to quote I am indebted to Rinehart & Company and to the author herself for material from Mary Roberts Rinehart's early mystery novel, *The Circular Staircase;* to Alfred A. Knopf for a summary description from Joseph Hergesheimer's *Mountain Blood;* and to Charles Scribner's Sons for the paragraph which introduces Mattie Silver in Edith Wharton's *Ethan Frome.* Mrs. Theodore Dreiser has been generous in permitting me to reproduce several portions of her late husband's novel, *Jennie Gerhardt.* Each of these works of fiction furnished a major character, and the study is enhanced by these quotations.

DOROTHY YOST DEEGAN

New York, New York
February 1, 1951

CONTENTS

5. What Do the Data Mean?

THE PROBLEM AND ITS SETTING

*The social meaning of singleness, outside of fertility, is in
the change of mental and spiritual values implied in development without sexual knowledge and emotionalization; singleness is harder or softer, differently ignorant and differently
wise . . . from marriage.*

DICKINSON and BEAM, The Single Woman

The Problem and Its Sociological Setting

SINCE early colonial days in America, single women have
gradually become a perceptible group in the population,
until today they are numbered in millions and comprise a
significant minority.

The fact that so many women—strong, healthy, attractive, and superior women—do not or cannot marry creates
a problem which is both sociological and psychological.
When great numbers of women do not marry and bear
children, it is a direct loss to society; if these women are less
efficient individuals by reason of the attitude of society toward them, it is an indirect loss. Their place in a society
founded upon monogamous marriage is one of far-reaching
importance, and their problem of personal adjustment, by
reason of deviating from that pattern, is beginning to be recognized as having unique components.

Much attention is being given currently to education for
home and family life, yet thousands of girls are facing the
possibility—in fact, the necessity—of living their lives without marriage. This situation would seem to justify a consideration of some of the problems a woman must face if she
does not marry. Furthermore, education is now investing
a great deal toward helping youth in the choice of a vocation. Choosing a vocation is a more complicated matter for

a girl than for her brother, since it is largely contingent upon whether she marries or not. She seldom can be sure, at the time she must make her choice of work, whether it is to be merely a way to earn her living until she marries or a career-for-life if she does not marry. If it is important to society and the individual to train for successful marriage and to aid in making a choice of vocation, it seems important also to consider some of the factors which make it difficult for a woman to live a satisfying and effective life if she remains single. If she is economically and emotionally independent, if she earns her own living and contributes to the care of dependents, she is performing a man's role in society. But a woman is not a man, and her social and psychological problems are uniquely her own.

Historically, the problem of the single woman in America has had an interesting evolution. There was no such problem in the early colonies nor along the frontier. Social history of the colonial period indicates that marriage was early and remarriage frequent and that many of the large families were made up of children of several different mothers. Life was difficult, and women were essential. As colonization moved westward, women were equally necessary on the frontier. The several efforts to transport groups of women into far outposts emphasize that need.

Under such conditions, one might presume that any woman who did not marry might possibly have been deserving of some degree of social censure. A few strong-minded women, to be sure, managed to remain single in the face of the urgent demand, among them remarkable "ancient maids" like Elizabeth Haddon, Elizabeth Poole, and Mistress Margaret Brent. But generally speaking, it may be said that marriage was universal and the single woman was not a reckonable factor in colonial and frontier society.

If, in that day, only the unattractive or the handicapped or the incompetent or the stanch-minded did not marry, certainly there are many women now who must remain single through no fault or shortcoming of their own. Has society recognized this change and revised its attitudes accordingly? This study sets up as its working hypothesis that it has not, that the stereotype of the single woman still persists even though her actual status has undergone tremendous change.

The secret of women's strength in the early days was that women were scarce. Much of their strength was merely "bargaining power." But this numerical equation, favorable to women and to marriage, was not to last. Other potent forces were soon to appear and to create a "problem of singleness." So many forces were at work simultaneously that one can hardly distinguish between what was cause and what was effect; but, generally speaking, everything that contributed to women's "independence" also contributed, directly or indirectly, to the increasing amount of singleness among them.

One momentous event to affect the numerical equation of the sexes and the personal lives of thousands of women in the United States was the Civil War. The war depleted the ranks of marriageable men. It created work for women outside the home. It gave the first impetus to the organization of women on a national scale. Following the war came the rapid development of large industrial centers, fed both by the energetic native youth from the rural and village districts and by the immigrant from many parts of the world. Presently, the population began to shift, with men predominating in one area and women in another. Not only did the rise of industry unbalance the sex-ratio; it also created an imbalance of wealth which created social caste and further barriers.

All these factors had a marked effect upon women. For the favored few of mounting fortunes, there was leisure and luxury; for the "lower classes," opportunity but unrest. Then followed the struggle to break down social barriers and the almost frantic seizing upon higher education to attain status, whereby children, especially daughters, could be "cultivated" to enhance the social prestige of the family. This social plowing prepared good soil for the European-born feminist philosophy which for decades inspired women of all classes literally to "fight for their right" of suffrage and the revision of certain archaic laws by which their lives had been governed. Add to these gradual but large-scale social forces the impact of two world wars, and the "problem of the single woman" assumes enormous proportions.

Sociologically, the problem of singleness among women affects the very fiber of society. Many factors are involved in the much discussed post-war social deterioration, but by no means the least of them is that numbers of women are denied the security and satisfactions of normal marriage and family life. Women are traditionally the conservators of the culture, and whenever the social fabric tends to weaken, one may venture to assume that something in the lives of women has relaxed its hold.

It is understandable that a culture such as that of the Western world which places so much emphasis upon the romantic aspects of marriage should express sympathy for the woman who must live her life without it. But regardless of her importance as an individual, or of what successful contribution she may have made, society still talks about her "failure to marry." Add this sense of failure to whatever biological frustration she may feel in not following the "normal" pattern of life, and her personal efficiency is almost certain to be affected. Some women seem to succeed in sublimating their energies and desires, but many, having been denied "the crowning experience of life" (to use another familiar phrase), take refuge in minor matters, attach undue importance to details, and lavish their affection on things and less-than-human creatures. They not infrequently take an inordinate interest in other people's affairs in a desperate effort to "fill the gap" in their own lives. By its attitude toward her, society places the single woman on the defensive and makes her into a supersensitive personality—thereby molding her into the very kind of person it criticizes her for being.

Regardless of how many other doors of opportunity may be opened to them, most women will continue to find marriage the best way of life. It is the most direct means of making their contribution to society as well as the most likely means of achieving happiness for themselves. The majority of women in each generation will marry. But to the others, society owes a more intelligent regard. They are not necessarily the undesirables. If "marriage is the first refuge of the incompetent," as someone has said, women who do not marry may often be superior to those who do. Yet, until such time as the public shall have clarified its aims and decided what it is educating its women for, there will continue to be some who are not physically or emotionally conditioned for marriage. Some women do not possess a strong drive toward motherhood. Some would not make successful partners in marriage if they did marry. (The increasing divorce rate would seem to indicate that many men and women are marrying who are not fit for marriage.) Many of those who remain single, as has been emphasized, are otherwise gifted women, capable of making a significant contribution to the larger welfare of society. The rights of these women must also be respected and defended, lest they be driven into marriage by a too-strong public opinion.

Society must regard the individual as an individual and in terms of potential worth. It must not estimate a woman's life merely on the basis of whether or not she has married. In a day in which more and more of the maternal role is being taken over by the community and the state, in which more of the task of rearing the young falls to the schools, in which health becomes a public responsibility and the

preparation of food a large-scale industry, in which hous-
ing becomes a community project instead of a one-family
provision—in such a world as the world of tomorrow will
be—there will be much work for all kinds of women. Single
women, free of the constant care and the enduring responsibilities of parenthood, are the ones who most appropriately
should turn their energies and resources to such endeavors as
these. There will be ample opportunity for those without
homes and families of their own to assume the increasingly
necessary role of mother-surrogate. At its best, it can be a
deeply satisfying role and one of vast social worth—if only
society will recognize it, dignify it, and appraise it more
highly.

Society's negative attitude expressed in the stereotype it
holds of its single women makes it extremely difficult to
explore the problems of singleness from the point of view
of the individual. It shuts off inquiry before it has begun.
In the face of a "rejecting" attitude, many women find it
extremely difficult to discuss matters pertaining to their
singleness. Even in these days when almost any human experience can be verbalized, many single women cannot bring
themselves to discuss this phase of their life.

This may partially explain why the problem of the single
woman, although it has been growing in size and complexity
for almost a century, has not been given the serious attention it deserves. As noted, only two earlier investigations
have dealt exclusively with the subject. One is a medical
study based upon anonymous case histories; the other deals
with the "old maid" in English life and fiction of the eighteenth century. This neglect of such an important social
problem is probably due to the fact that those most qualified
to deal with it were either too much concerned or too little.
For understandable reasons, single women themselves,
though largely comprising the feminine scholar-class, were
not able to see the problem with detachment and perspective.

Women who married early felt no further concern with the problem of the unmarried, were not highly enough trained to analyze it, or were simply too much occupied with their own families. Men have apparently not considered the subject quite appropriate to their talents.

The problem might be approached in a variety of ways. It may be studied as a medical problem, in the direction of which a beginning has been made. Psychological studies on the subject may be clinical or may move toward the domain of sociology. It can be considered a strictly sociological problem or it can be seen in terms of anthropological concepts. But whatever the approach, the element of social attitude, as expressed in the stereotype, will be an important factor. Social attitude may be glimpsed in literature in any form: the drama, the essay, and even in poetry, but fiction—novel-length fiction—probably offers the best media for detailed study.

Nowhere can social attitude be more easily recognized than in fiction; nowhere is the slow and subtle change in attitudes more readily observed. Fiction is one of the best sources of social data, being impersonal and detached from actual life, yet deeply personal in its connotative and empathizing qualities. Two reasons especially make it appropriate to study the attitudes of society toward the single woman as reflected in fiction. One is that much of the disapprobation associated with the "old maid" in England was carried to America through fiction. The word "spinster," meaning originally merely "a woman who spins," gradually came to be almost synonymous with the epithet "old maid," which from the beginning was a derogatory term. The latter, according to the scholarly study noted, can be traced to early Anglo-Saxon balladry, but appears in its most disparaging form in the English novels of the eighteenth century. And, as will be shown at a later point in this investigation, the earliest American novels were but feeble imitation of the English fiction formula. The second reason is that there is no material so familiar or so easily available either to the mature student who works on the academic level or the adolescent who wishes to understand more clearly his or her life in the making. Since fiction is being more and more widely utilized for studying social thought and action, it seems altogether appropriate to use it in exploring such a sensitive subject as the stereotype of the single woman in American life.

In considering this question and the problem it involves, one may casually refer to Hawthorne's weird study of "The White Old Maid," Mary E. Wilkins Freeman's drab tale of Louisa Ellis in "A New England Nun," or Edith Wharton's tragic women, Charlotte Lovell in "The Old Maid," and Lily Bart, heroine of *The House of Mirth*. Or perhaps one may turn to Zona Gale's *Miss Lulu Bett*, Edna Ferber's "Mother Knows Best," or Theodore Dreiser's memorable *Sister Carrie* and *Jennie Gerhardt*. One may also recall Katherine Mansfield's wistful little "Miss Brill," Guy de Maupassant's horrible account of "Miss Harriet," who threw herself into a well, or, if one has come upon the ultimate in decadence, William Faulkner's "A Rose for Emily"—Emily being Miss Emily Grierson, who kept the corpse of her lover in her canopied bed.

If these examples are, by any chance, representative of how the single woman appears in fiction on a larger scale, it is surely a pathetic portrait which emerges. Chekhov has pointed out that the function of literature is not to solve the problems of humanity but to state them more clearly. The problem of the single woman is a human problem which has seldom been stated at all—except by the creative writer.

From the viewpoint of education, it should be observed that the impressions which literature creates—in this case a stereotype—tend to etch themselves deeply in the mind and emotions of the reader, particularly the adolescent reader. Many adults will testify that certain books read during adolescence have had profound influence upon their later thought and behavior. It is probable also that a reader of any age is more impressed by narrative than by factual or expository writing. If a story can be made the vehicle of an idea, the idea will probably take a firmer hold upon the imagination than the mere fact or idea would otherwise do. The greatest teachers of mankind used the parable.

The present investigation interprets its findings and stresses its implications in terms of education, particularly the education of women. It is intended to be a dynamic study. It seeks to be sound as a work of reference, but the author is not content for it to stand as knowledge for its own sake. It is rooted in that philosophy of education which maintains that knowledge must be knowledge *for something;* that when a lamentable fact is brought to light by research, something should be done about it. Several generations may come and go before a change in social thought and action can be observed, but the illumination of a new area of fact should at least determine what direction that change should take.

The study which follows reveals substantial evidence of a derogatory social attitude toward women who do not marry, an attitude expressed in a stereotype which persists long after the actual facts have changed. The investigator believes that novels and novelists have, unwittingly, by repetition of certain fiction formulas, reinforced this attitude in the social mind. The findings show a marked discrepancy between the actual contribution which single women have made to American society and the composite portrait of them in American fiction. The obligation of education, therefore, the study concludes, is threefold: first, to inform and enlighten society of the facts concerning this important minority group; second, to clarify certain issues in the minds of those directly responsible for the education of women; and third, to enable the individual girl or woman to recog-

nize a basic truth of her existence amid the welter and confusion of social attitudes and pressures.

Previous Research

Highly critical research dealing exclusively with single
women in America is largely confined to one book—an
analysis based upon medical case histories. Another investigation resembles more nearly the present one, but it deals with
the single woman in English life and fiction of two centuries
ago.

In covering previous research, however, the writer has
gone far beyond the minimum requirement. In a pioneer
investigation of this kind it may be profitable to others to
mention some of the sources which have provided necessary
background. It may even be that an interfield study such
as this may have some obligation to lay a foundation structure in the several fields it borders upon even though it cannot be exhaustive in any one of them. For these reasons, brief
mention will be made of books which have been useful in a
general way, and this will be followed by an analysis of the
critical research.

Three books on women published within the last five years
have stirred considerable controversy. *The Psychology of
Women* by Helene Deutsch furnishes Freudian insight into
the normal psychic life of women and their normal conflicts.
Amram Scheinfeld's *Women and Men* gives a popular treatment of scientific data on heredity. The more recent book,
Modern Woman: the Lost Sex, by Ferdinand Lundberg and
Marynia F. Farnham reveals its central thesis in its title. It
is significant that these books use a variety of materials but
arrive at essentially the same conclusion: that the interplay
of biological, sociological, and psychological forces fashion
woman into a creature distinctly unlike man. She has proved
herself capable of doing a man's work but she loses more
than she gains if she tries to live a man's life. In women's

struggle to be "like men," they have created conditions and conflicts which make it difficult for them to attain their optimum adjustment.

Earlier interpretations also present searching analyses of women's problems. Esther Harding's *The Way of All Women* is the work of an English psychiatrist who holds the Jungian point of view. *The Case of Miss R* by Alfred Adler tells minutely the life story of a girl of Viennese background, while Olga Knopf here in America has brought the Adlerian theories to her discussion of *The Art of Being a Woman* and *Women on Their Own*. Karen Horney and Beatrice Hinkle show in much of their writing a keen understanding of the cultural as well as the individual aspects of woman's adjustment.

Three books written from different angles offer useful material of a more specialized kind. The symposium edited by Ira S. Wile on *The Sex Life of the Unmarried Adult* brings together facts concerning current sex practices. J. Bernan Wolfe's *A Woman's Best Years* and Grace Loucks Elliott's *Women after Forty*, the latter a popular version of an academic study, discuss problems of the climacteric.

Four small books deal exclusively with the single woman and are interesting in their widely different treatment. *The Single Woman and Her Emotional Problems* by Laura Hutton and *The Bachelor Woman and Her Problems* by Dame Mary Scharlieb are books by English writers who emphasize positive values in the single life. *The Single Woman* by Ruth Reed is a matter-of-fact volume of sound advice. Marjorie Hillis in her popular *Live Alone and Like It* brings wit and humor to the subject.

Several books have been especially useful in gaining a general perspective of literary and social history. Foremost among scholarly works which consider literature for its sociological significance is Vernon L. Parrington's three-volume *Main Currents in American Life*. Harry Hartwick's

The Foreground of American Fiction reveals the forces and fashions, the creeds and the trends reflected in the American novel since 1890. The critical work of Alfred Kazin, *On Native Grounds*, brings a new interpretation of the society which produced much of the fiction this investigation considers. *The Growth of American Thought* by Merle Curti shows the relation of the Feminist Movement to the larger ebb and flow of social thought and action. Ernest R. Groves in his social history of *The American Woman* points out striking regional differences in what he calls "the feminine side of a masculine civilization," but gives no explicit attention to the unique elements in the status of the single woman.

The critical research which follows—more appropriately called the previous research of this investigation—will be analyzed under three main headings: first, psychosexual studies conducted chiefly in a clinical setting; second, two groups of investigations which have a strictly sociological emphasis; and third, miscellaneous studies in what has been termed "the sociology of the American novel."

PSYCHOSEXUAL STUDIES

Five psychosexual investigations, the earliest published in 1929, yield results relevant to a study of single women. As has been said, only one deals exclusively with the subject, but each of the others includes a sizable group of single women as part of a larger study. All deal with essentially the same problem: the attempt to discover what effect, if any, certain practices or physical factors bearing upon sex life may have upon the development of personality.

The investigation which deals exclusively with the single woman was published by Dickinson and Beam in 1934.[1] Designated as a medical approach, and conducted under the auspices of the National Committee on Maternal Health, it is an attempt to ascertain the sex life of socially normal persons as revealed in medical case histories. It is a psychological study of personality, "describing the cost and meaning of the conflicts between biological function and social adaptation."

A larger study conducted five years earlier (1929) by Davis is only partly concerned with single women.[2] Although conducted chiefly from the sociologist's point of view, the aim of this questionnaire inquiry was to provide more adequate data as to both the physical and the mental facts of the sex life of the normal individual. The group of 1,200 single women who (out of 10,000 questioned) returned the questionnaire was composed of college graduates at least five years out of college, most of whom have achieved some distinction in professional fields.

Related to, and based upon, these earlier investigations was the more recent investigation by Strakosch,[3] in which the emphasis was placed upon psychopathic rather than upon normal individuals. The problem of this doctoral study, conducted in the Department of Psychology at Columbia University, was to discover whether or not the psychopathic group differed from a normal group with respect to specific overt sex practices.

Out of these three similar investigations, two general conclusions may have a bearing upon any subsequent investigation which deals with single women. The first concerns homosexuality and the second, the practice of masturbation.

Within the very limited scope of her study, Davis found a high relationship between homosexuality and high mental level plus educational attainment. Strakosch, however, clarifies the conclusion that Davis had reached:

It is not to be concluded that just because a girl goes to college she is more likely to indulge in homosexual behavior. It is rather that the close association of women in a college atmosphere and their relative isolation from heterosexual contacts afford more opportunity for homosexual reactions, in the sense that homosexual behavior is a "learned reaction." [4]

With regard to masturbation, certain of the findings may be worth noting. Dickinson and Beam reported that 60.9 per cent of the single women whose cases they studied had masturbated at some time. Davis reported a slightly higher percentage, 64.9 per cent. The data collected by Davis also showed that the majority of noncollege women had begun the practice before eleven years of age and the majority of college women, after the age of eighteen. Eighty-five of the Davis subjects reported that they began after twenty-six years of age. Strakosch found that the psychopathic girls had begun to masturbate in increasing numbers between the ages of fifteen and seventeen.

While these investigations emphasize that homosexual, autosexual, and certain heterosexual experiences, previously held to be abnormal practices, occur in the lives of normal women to a greater extent than has been assumed in the past, Strakosch concludes what the earlier investigations had implied, "that masturbation really has little differential effect on the development of the total personality." [5]

Directly in line with the work of Dickinson and Beam, Davis, and Strakosch are the two more recent clinical studies by Landis and his research associates. The first,[6] published in 1940, is a study of the growth and development of the emotional and sexual aspects of personality based upon physiological, anatomical, and medical information. It seeks answers to three questions: (1) What is the normal (average) pattern of psychological development? (2) How do deviations in this pattern affect the adult personality? (3) What are the characteristics of psychosexual development in different types of adult personalities?

This was a more extensive investigation than any which preceded it. It was made possible by financial assistance from the Committee for Research in the Problems of Sex, of the

National Research Council. Landis used seven different techniques but relied chiefly upon the controlled interview, supplemented by physical and psychiatric examinations.

Two of the conclusions of this investigation may profitably be observed in connection with the present study: first, "that personality structure is more fundamental than the psychological history"; and, second, that personality determines the history (style of life) "rather than the psychosexual history forming or determining the personality." [7] Furthermore, Landis found that "the weight of evidence inclines us to interpret the neurotic personality as a *style of life* which is consistent from a very early age." [8]

In his second and more recent study Landis [9] aimed to discover the effects of a handicap upon the emotional and psychosexual development in a special group of women. He used twenty-five cases each of four types of physical handicap: spastic paralysis, epilepsy, chronic heart disease, and orthopedic disability, all subjects having been handicapped since the age of thirteen or, presumably, prior to adolescence. By using the controlled interview, the investigators made an effort to get data on sex practices.

Quoting from the later investigation, the authors reemphasize the findings of the earlier work:

Our findings . . . do not indicate that psychosexuality (libidinal energy), any particular motive or emotion or combination of the same, any particular body form or deviation in body form, or any particular experience, of and by itself, is of sufficient importance to determine the particular form of personality development or style of reaction of any individual. . . . Rather we must seek the particular combination of forces which renders the particular type or style of personality reaction understandable.[10]

Of greater significance to the present investigation is the fact that their study presents an entirely new light on the importance of sex in the development of adult personality:

Some of these handicapped women were psychologically "neuter," in the sense that they never passed through the ordinary phases of sex development. There was no evidence that this was the result of repression, suppression, regression or frustration. This demonstrates that personality can and does develop without sex as the central, main, or most important instinctual or motivating force in the determination of adult personality.[11]

If the Landis investigations had developed their potential data to show differences between the single and married subjects, the research would have provided valuable material toward explaining factors which tend to make for singleness. Yet even with such data undeveloped, their findings suggest three problems for further clinical research: First, since the investigations find personality to be something more than the sum total of isolated factors, may not research profitably seek a constellation of psychosexual factors which may contribute to singleness? Second, if the "style of life" or personality pattern may be traced to factors recognizable at a very early age, may there not be factors identifiable at an earlier age of the girl child than has been generally believed —a psychological and emotional mind-set which may tend toward singleness in adult life? Third, since the study of handicapped women suggests that some of the subjects had grown to adulthood as sexually "neuter" individuals, may it be that in some women certain factors other than physical disability may combine to produce a pattern of personality which has little or no sex motivation toward marriage?

SOCIOLOGICAL INVESTIGATIONS

Analysis of sociological investigations brings to light impressive facts concerning single women. The analysis does not represent exhaustive research, nor does any one of the investigations which are analyzed deal with single women exclusively; but it is possible, nevertheless, to observe certain factors regarding the status of single women in America which are not widely known or understood, especially concerning eminence and economic dependency. Each analysis represents only a beginning in what might constitute a profitable problem for major research, but is here briefly summarized in order to illustrate the potential data and to furnish factual information which may be of value in interpreting the fiction with which this study deals.

The importance of single women in America.—The most comprehensive study of eminent women was made by Castle at Columbia in 1913.[12] Following the method used by Cattell in his earlier study of eminent men, Castle scanned the lists of women in six of the leading dictionaries of biography, selecting the name of every woman who was mentioned in at least three of the six sources. The study was originally designed for 1,000 names, but only 868 were available on this basis. Rank order was established upon the number of lines accorded each woman listed. The analysis showed that 16.3 per cent, or 142 of the 868 women, had not married. This number takes on meaning as one observes that 49.2 per cent of the unmarried group belonged to the nineteenth century, and 72.5 per cent were born in the last two centuries. While nineteen nations were represented in the unmarried group, more than half the women were English and American. In summary, the author states:

The number of cases born in earlier centuries is too few to give definite results, but the data tend to show an increasing incompatibility through the last two hundred years between eminence and marriage, until in the Nineteenth Century one distinguished woman in every five has chosen to work and live alone.[13]

An earlier study of eminence, dealing with American women exclusively, was made by Northrop [14] in 1904. This investigator, like Castle, also made a statistical analysis but on a considerably smaller scale. Northrop analyzed the list of women appearing in the 1902 edition of *Who's Who*, and discovered that of the 977 women appearing among the 11,000 names listed, only 54 per cent had married.

In an investigation made in 1924, Kitson and Kirtley [15] were chiefly concerned with the vocational changes of women listed in *Who's Who* but noted incidentally that only about half the group had married. It is interesting that although more than a score of years elapsed between Northrop's investigation and this one, the proportion of single women in the two groups remained approximately the same.

Two important studies were published in 1928 and 1929, respectively. In the earlier of the two, Hutchinson [16] analyzed the list of women who were awarded the degree of Doctor of Philosophy by American colleges and universities from 1877 through 1924. Thirty-nine different institutions, forty-eight subject-matter fields, and 1,025 of the 1,600 women solicited by questionnaire were represented. Hutchinson reported that three fourths of her group were single, although in the last ten years covered by the study, the period from 1914 to 1924, the data showed an increased tendency for the women to combine marriage and a career. The study published in 1929 by Pressey [17] made a similar analysis of 687 women who had won eminence in scientific endeavor. This investigator, unlike most of the others, made a point of age and records that the youngest woman represented was twenty-seven, the oldest eighty-four, and that sixty-six women refused to divulge their age.[18]

Pressey's investigation, like that of Hutchinson, dealt with an intellectually superior group of women, composed chiefly of college graduates, with well over half the number holding the degree of Doctor of Philosophy. Although an overwhelming majority of these women were working in the field of biological sciences, only seventy-two of the entire number, or approximately 10 per cent, were married.

An analysis of the women appearing in *Who's Who* furnished the data for a thesis by Pletsch [19] which showed that of the 1,857 women listed, 43.5 per cent were single. Six hundred and twenty-two of the number were authors, while educators ranked second but with barely half the number.

The most recent study of eminent women was made about a decade after that of Pletsch, when Hergt and Shannon [20] analyzed the life-sketches of all women listed in *Who's Who in America* for 1936. This list included 1,967 women "presumably old enough to be married," the authors fractionating the list into fifteen occupational groups as well as into age ranges, the latter also classified with respect to marriage. The data showed that in the group of age 70 and older, 56 per cent had married; of age 60–69, 52 per cent; of age 50–59, 59 per cent; of age 40–49, 63 per cent; and under the age of 40, 70 per cent.[21] Of the total number of women this study included, approximately 40 per cent were single.

Comparisons of the several investigations cited above, unfortunately, cannot yield decisive conclusions. There is no uniformity in method or treatment of data. One list overlaps another at some points. Some women in each "contemporary" group may since have married. In some instances, one cannot know whether the married or the single group includes the widows and women divorced or separated from husbands.

The combined results of these investigations, however, cannot fail to convey some meaning to the present study of single women. Within the limitations noted, and in so far as their data are representative of that to be found in other annals of eminence, one fact must be observed. In the investigation in which the group had the highest marriage rate, that of Hergt and Shannon, 40 per cent were single; and in the group representing the other extreme, Pressey's analysis of women in science, as many as 90 per cent were single.[22] In the face of such statistics it seems hardly necessary to reemphasize the enormous contribution single women have made to the welfare of society in America.

Single women and economic dependency.—An investigation made by Hewes [23] in 1919 is not only one of the earliest studies of women and economic dependency, but of the group to be reviewed briefly here it is also the first which deals with members of the teaching profession. Hewes collected her data from the teaching staffs of four of the large colleges for women: Smith, Vassar, Wellesley, and Mount Holyoke. And since only seven of the 239 women (out of 289 teachers reporting) had married, her investigation may be said to have dealt chiefly with single women. Results of the Hewes study showed that 41.2 per cent of the unmarried teachers were contributing to the support of dependents and that in four fifths of the cases the dependents were either aging parents or younger brothers and sisters.

Exactly twenty years later, in 1939, a doctoral study was made by Pyle [24] based upon 775 questionnaires obtained from elementary and secondary schoolteachers in different localities in the United States. Single women made up 500 of the entire number; 52.1 per cent of them had someone dependent upon them for support. It is interesting to observe that essentially the same pattern of dependency was reported by both Hewes and Pyle, although they dealt with widely different groups of teachers and twenty years elapsed between the two studies.

Other investigations made between 1919 and 1939 also reveal a similar situation. Hutchinson,[25] in her investigation of women who had earned the degree of Doctor of Philosophy, also collected data on dependents. She found that of the 485 who reported on this item, 69 per cent were providing partial or total maintenance for one or more dependents. Hutchinson's data also showed that most of the dependents were adults. Mead's [26] investigation did not differentiate between men and women, but showed that more than half of the 2,064 teachers in twenty-four Florida counties were single. Among the latter group, total dependents averaged

1.97 per teacher and partial dependents, 3 per teacher. The National Education Association [27] reported a study made in 1935 to determine how teachers used their incomes during a twelve-month period. It included 2,358 teachers, of whom 1,955 were single women. Using the "dependency unit" which gave the teacher one unit for her own support, one unit for two partial dependents, and one unit for each total dependent, it was found that single women had 1.9 dependency units.

A doctoral study made by Peters [28] in 1934, though dealing ostensibly with the married woman teacher in the public schools of the state of Virginia, matched 921 pairs of single and married women teachers with respect to certain factors, including their dependents. His data showed that single women teachers had approximately three fourths as many individuals wholly dependent upon them for economic needs as did the married women teachers, and that the same ratio also existed for those having partial dependents.

These investigations indicate that among teachers, whether in private or public schools; whether at the elementary, secondary school, or college level; whether in 1919 or 1939, essentially the same dependency pattern emerges. A large majority have someone dependent upon them economically, and in the main, these are aging parents, whose dependency increases rather than decreases.

One cannot conclude, however, that this picture of dependency is unique among teachers. If one consults the numerous bulletins of the Women's Bureau, the dependency picture among women workers in many different occupations is shown to be similar to that among teachers.

Three of these bulletins,[29] particularly those published in 1923, 1929, and 1937 respectively, give summaries of numerous investigations in which the economic burden of single women can be observed. The earliest of these bulletins reports in much detail an investigation of wage earners in the shoe industry of Manchester, New Hampshire, where 70 per cent of the women workers were single. Almost three fourths of this number, 68.7 per cent, were daughters living with parents, and of these daughters, 59.9 per cent contributed all their earnings to their families, 30 per cent of them for a period of five years or more. Bulletin No. 75 reports an investigation of 1,987 single women employed in the men's ready-made clothing industry in five cities. Of this group 87.7 per cent contributed all their earnings to dependents; not one of them contributed nothing at all. In Bulletin No. 155 some seventy-two earlier reports are summarized, among them, an investigation of business and professional women made in 1930. Here, of the 9,096 women who reported dependents, 60 per cent were single.

Material of this kind is abundant if the research worker has the patience to winnow out of the numerous investigations which have been made and reported by the Women's Bureau those isolated bits which deal with the single woman specifically.[30] Other sources, such as the statistical bulletins of the actuarial divisions of insurance companies,[31] offer similar material on many of the more general aspects of dependency. Or one may go directly to the reports and releases of the United States Bureau of the Census and find there the raw material which can be fashioned into a meaningful mosaic revealing the burden of economic dependency being carried by single women.

This brief survey is included in this study for two reasons. First, it illustrates the potentialities in an almost inexhaustible field for future research, an area which must be carefully examined in order to gain a complete picture of the status of the single woman in contemporary America. Frequent comment in the sources mentioned above, as well as general observation, would indicate that "the public" still believes that single women "have only themselves to support" and should, therefore, receive less than married persons in wages and pensions. Secondly, and chiefly, this sociological sur-

vey is included to furnish a backdrop of social fact against
which the fiction of the past century can be more clearly
seen, understood, and interpreted. In its dramatic implications, the problem of economic dependency is an appropriate
theme for fiction. It is related to a study of single women because a woman's dependents, more often than not, stand as
deterrents to marriage and prevent her achieving a natural
and normal life of her own. A man's dependents furnish the
greatest and richest experience of his life, whereas the dependents of the single woman often deny the fulfillment of
her natural destiny. A man feels joy and pride and achieves
a kind of immortality in his family. The single woman has
less pleasure in the present and little or no expectation in the
future. She may be genuinely devoted to her dependents and
derive satisfaction in knowing that she has performed a duty
toward them, but she has seldom undertaken this support
voluntarily and her attitudes in the matter are seldom wholly
constructive. Not infrequently, her economic dependents
place her in a kind of emotional bondage that may add to her
sense of futility and frustration.

These psychological aspects of economic dependency
suggest a rich mine of material for the writer of fiction.
Novelists for decades have been writing about the maiden
aunt who was herself the dependent member of the family.
Are the novelists aware of the fact that Aunt Millie's economic role in society has been almost completely reversed
—that her struggle to renounce the passive role has often
forced her into an active role in which the burden of the
family dependents is placed upon her shoulders—that her
new freedom, ironically enough, has brought with it a new
kind of responsibility?

SOCIOLOGY OF THE AMERICAN NOVEL

Among doctoral dissertations which deal with fiction in
relation to some phase of social or literary history, only one
touches upon the status of the single woman. This is Need-

ham's [32] literary study, completed at the University of California in 1938. While this study deals with English fiction, one can trace through its pages certain attitudes toward single women which later were transplanted and took deep root in American thought and custom.

Since single women first emerged as a societal group in urban centers, their new status is revealed in a number of studies which deal with fictional portraits of urban life. The earliest of these is Dunlap's [33] analysis of three eastern cities, New York, Philadelphia, and Boston, which is a doctoral dissertation, also in the English Department, written at the University of Pennsylvania and published in 1934. While the author of this study looks at more than a century of fiction, he chooses comparatively few novels to illustrate social, political, and religious life.

In 1935 two important studies were completed under the auspices of the Department of English Language and Literature at the University of Chicago. Grey's [34] study on the "Chicago novel" is notable for its scope and its painstaking detail. The study by Rose [35] gives an almost microscopic treatment of less than a decade. Both studies are, to date, unpublished.

In his "critical approach" Grey explores at length "the novelists' history" of Chicago from its beginnings to the middle 1930's, emphasizing its symbols or "epic" events. Though incidental to his larger theme, he touches briefly upon the subject of women in industry and observes the "new woman" as an emerging heroine of fiction. Rose's investigation deals with the urban scene indirectly but not exclusively. It covers only the seven years of the Theodore Roosevelt administration and merely catalogues its material, but it brings to light much of the ephemeral and minor fiction of the period. Rose's work is valuable to the bibliographer, but from the standpoint of sociology it offers no broad generalizations.

Four other investigations, somewhat related to each other,

also deal with the novel of economic criticism. Regier's [36] dissertation, published at the University of North Carolina in 1932, places more emphasis upon the era than the fiction, but the author comments upon a few important novels and novelists in his broader consideration of the periodical literature of the decade. In the same year appeared Chamberlain's [37] widely known investigation of what he calls "The Rise, Life, and Decay of the Progressive Mind in America." Chamberlain, like Regier, is only incidentally concerned with fiction and only with such fiction as supports his thesis; but he gives a lucid discussion of David Graham Phillips, Robert Herrick, and certain other novelists whose fiction is chiefly a social criticism of their times.

As Regier's work may, in a sense, be linked with that of Chamberlain, so Flory's [38] study completed in 1936 at the University of Pennsylvania paved the way for Taylor's [39] more extensive work on essentially the same subject. The latter was begun at the University of North Carolina in 1928 but was not published until 1942. Whereas Flory gives a general treatment of his subject and in the literary manner, Taylor concentrates upon five novels which he considers the most significant of their kind.

In contrast to the several investigations dealing chiefly with urban life are the work of Herron,[40] which considers the small-town community, and in a lesser way, and Hazard's [41] earlier study in English at Mills College, completed in 1927. Published at Duke University in 1939, Herron's study etches a composite portrait of the small-town spinster: a figure in contrast to the more energetic young woman referred to in the urban studies, who migrated to the city to make her own way and quite possibly to avoid the lethargy and loneliness of village spinsterhood.

Another group of doctoral studies dealing with early American fiction gives a passing glimpse of the single woman as the novelists portrayed her. The first of these was done by Loshe [42] at Columbia in 1907. Although brief, it offers pertinent criticism of the novels of Cooper and Charles Brockden Brown. Loshe's work also marks the beginning of research in an area later to be developed by Brown [43] in a work done at Duke University and published in 1940. Brown's investigation shows more pointedly than any other the prevailing attitude of the time: that woman's place is in the home. Remotely related to the work of Loshe and Brown is Benson's [44] study carried on in the Department of Political Science at Columbia and published in 1935, which also gives passing attention to women in early American literature.

Though not linked with any of the studies previously mentioned, Barnett's [45] study on divorce, a doctoral dissertation in sociology completed at the University of Pennsylvania in 1939, has been especially useful. In tracing "literary reflections of social influences," Barnett observes in the novel social attitudes toward a problem as the present investigation observes social attitudes toward a personality. Similarly, he uses a sampling rather than the whole of American fiction. His study covers approximately the same period in time. He uses an objective classification in analyzing his problem. Certain of his conclusions, furthermore, have served as points of reference and have lent emphasis to the findings of this study. Within the limits of its subject, Barnett's investigation has been more useful than any other in pointing the way in an unexplored sociological area.

2

THE METHOD OF THE
INVESTIGATION

*A survey of the Best Books . . . made by A. D. Dickinson
. . . disclosed the intellectual and moral evaluations of the
reading public. . . . It would be said, of course, that the expert opinion so registered was principally middle class in
source; even so, the appraisals expressed the concerns and
dominant ideas of the largest reading and writing class amid
the upswing and crash of American economy, revolutions
and wars abroad, and overturns in domestic politics. Who-
ever sought to meditate upon American culture thus pos-
sessed a group of impressive materials in books widely distributed and elaborately praised . . .*

CHARLES and MARY BEARD, America in Midpassage

To ARRIVE at a satisfactory definition of "the single woman"
was far more difficult than it would first appear. In a general
sense, every woman character in any novel who has not
married is a single woman, yet the problems of singleness are
very different for a girl of twenty and for an older woman.
For purposes of research, one must establish some basis to
distinguish the mature single woman from the younger single
woman.

DEFINITION AND DELIMITATION

The present study, therefore, borrows verbatim the definition used by Young in which he applies the term "single
woman" to "women thirty years of age or older . . . the
woman whose probability of marriage is so slight that she
has had to adjust herself consciously, if not unconsciously,
to the idea of remaining unwed." [1] This seemed an especially
appropriate definition since it was the older woman and her

adjustment which motivated the original interest in this problem. One might reasonably assume that society will also have adjusted its attitudes toward the woman who has not married by the age of thirty.

Consequently, the investigation limited itself to a consideration of the woman-in-fiction who is still single at thirty years of age, who remains single throughout the novel, and who expresses no plan or intention to marry. In instances where the novel does not mention age specifically, the study retained those characters, and only those, concerning whom there could be no reasonable doubt in the reader's mind. Women were assumed to be single only if they were referred to as such. Furthermore, only those characters who had a given name by which they could be identified and classified were retained in the analysis.

Certain other working definitions had to be constructed. A major character, for example, was defined as one of three main characters in the novel. This is more rigid than the usual literary definition, but it has the advantage of precision, and seems especially appropriate when one considers that the plot of many novels rests upon a triangle. The adjective "admirable" as applied to a single-woman character was reduced from the general to the specific by defining it to mean "worthy of emulation." It appeared more meaningful to view the character from the viewpoint of a young girl since the implications of the study as a whole were to be given an educational emphasis.

Even more difficult than definition was bringing the many-faceted "problem of the single woman" into focus. To do this the fiction material had to be delimited, and this was not easily achieved. In fact, arriving at a body of material which would provide an adequate representation of the American novel, together with a sufficient number of single-woman characters for detailed analysis, and at the same time eliminate the element of personal bias in the selection, constituted one of the greatest difficulties the study had to meet. Earlier investigations which had used fiction as a social document had not solved the problem of selection in such a way as to offer a satisfactory precedent.

DESCRIPTION AND EVALUATION OF THE SAMPLING

The present investigation solved the problem of selection by using a previously compiled list of American fiction. The Dickinson list of so-called "best novels," known to librarians and historians alike, appears in three published volumes.[2] The books listed therein are not the personal selection of Dickinson himself, but a compilation "selected by a consensus of expert opinion as most worthy the attention of intelligent American readers." The author, who was formerly librarian at the University of Pennsylvania, devoted many years to this work, and notes in the Preface to one of the volumes the quotation from Samuel Johnson, "A man will turn over half a library to make one book." This is, literally, what Dickinson has done.

The selection in each volume was based upon numerous sources of information, including library book lists, review digests, anthologies, critics' appraisals, booksellers' selections, best-seller lists, prize awards, and many other similar citations. For the earliest volumes, 59 criteria of this kind were used; for the second, 62; and for the latest volume, 102. In one volume the actual citations were mentioned, but in the later work, a point-score for each book was substituted. The exact criteria of selection appear in each volume, and therefore are not reproduced in this study.[3]

In his first volume, Dickinson lists 104 titles of American fiction; in the second, 265 titles; and in the third, 52 titles, making a total of 421 titles altogether. Between the first and second lists, however, 27 titles appear in duplicate, so that the total may be more accurately stated as 394 titles. This duplication is accounted for by the fact that when Dickinson made his first selection of the best books of all time (in 1924) he included some, naturally enough, which were published after 1900. Similarly, in the next volume, which was published four years later, and considered the best books of the period from 1901 to 1925, he again included some of the same books.

The three lists, thus adjusted, were combined into one, placing all the works of one author together; then the comprehensive list was arranged alphabetically under authors' names. This complete list of the 394 titles will be found in the Appendix, together with other data pertaining to each title, indicated there by legend, but fully explained in the following paragraphs.

After the Dickinson list of novels had been adopted as the fictional sources for the investigation, it appeared desirable to prune the several hundred works of fiction into a main stem which would be more sturdy than tall. The investigation might legitimately have used only one of the Dickinson lists, even the shortest of the three, but it seemed more profitable to use all three and achieve a longer time-span in which a more marked change in the status of the single woman might be observed.

The comprehensive list of 394 works of fiction, therefore, was further delimited and adapted to the present investigation in two ways: first, on the basis of structure; and second, with regard to content. As for structure, it seemed advisable to use only fiction of novel-length. Earlier studies resembling this one had made a similar decision. Grey [4] soundly supports his decision, and Needham,[5] after grappling with the same problem, also found it advisable to limit her material to the novel form rather than to include shorter fiction. Examination showed that almost one hundred of the titles of American fiction on the comprehensive Dickinson list were volumes of short fiction, each containing from three to more than a dozen short pieces. Several notable examples of the single woman appear in short fiction—and in a few instances, the line of demarcation between a long short story and a short novel is admittedly faint. Whatever the sacrifice, short fiction would have cluttered up the study far more than it would have contributed to it. Moreover, the loss in different authors was not great, for all but eight of the authors of short pieces were represented elsewhere in the study by longer works.

The next step in the pruning process, also with regard to structure, was to eliminate those novels which were found to be sequels, trilogies, or single novels thus related to other novels not included by Dickinson. The decision to use only novels complete in one volume seemed particularly justified inasmuch as a recent study by Kerr [6] defines the sequence novel as differing in certain respects from the ordinary novel form. Only a comparatively few of the Dickinson books fell into this category, and of those few, most would have been eliminated for other reasons about to be explained.

On the basis of content, the investigation limited itself to novels in which the setting, action, and characters are all wholly within the boundaries of the United States and are contemporary with the author's lifetime. Preliminary reading disclosed that a considerable number of the novels on the Dickinson list, although written by American novelists, had their setting, wholly or in part, somewhere other than in the United States. Some were stories of the sea. Some were Canadian, some South American, a few Alaskan in their setting. Others took place on American soil but dealt chiefly with Indian, Negro, or Oriental characters. Excluding novels of this kind did not assume that they were less worthy or had no contribution to make—only that they were too few in number to support a comparison or to represent their respective groups or races fairly. They deserve more important consideration than this study could give them.

If the setting were to be limited in place, it seemed necessary to limit it also in time, and to retain for the detailed analysis only those novels in which the action was wholly contemporary with the author's lifetime. The investigation would use the novels as primary source material; hence it seemed wise to consider only those which presumably utilize the author's personal experience or direct observation. Historical novels must be assumed to have been written at least partially from secondary sources. The majority of historical novels written by American writers or, at least, those Dickinson included, center in the Revolutionary or the Civil War. Some depict episodes of pioneering days. One novel on the list strikes back to the Middle Ages and another to the Trojan War. Several deal with ancient Rome and Greece. Some of these are more substantial novels than others which are contemporary, but since the span of the Dickinson list reaches from early America to 1935, historical perspective is maintained for the study as a whole.

Also eliminated on a corollary basis was the fiction of fantasy. This small group of novels may be true to life in the sense that they delineate certain truths about life, as in allegory, but they do not lend themselves to objective analysis. Either they are not fixed in time or place, or they deal with personifications rather than flesh-and-blood persons, or they are so intangible as to defy classification altogether.

This pruning process, which constituted a preliminary but considerable portion of the work of the study, reduced the comprehensive Dickinson list to less than one third its original size. The investigation proceeds with 125 novels especially well adapted to the subject. All of the action of every novel takes place in the United States and is contemporary with the author's life. All novels deal chiefly with persons of the white race and are sufficiently realistic to allow the classification of characters. All of the fiction used is of novel-length to permit full development of theme and character on the part of the novelist. Thus critically arrived at, the sampling the study uses is assumed to be adequate and appropriate and may be expected to reveal a composite portrait of the single woman, "the woman thirty years of age or older," in American novels.[7]

CLASSIFICATION OF THE SINGLE-WOMAN CHARACTERS

In order to arrange the single-woman characters in most significant progression, the 125 novels were classified once again, this time according to the earliest date of copyright or publication. This arrangement again separated different works of different authors, but the chronological development was considered more important in the analysis of characters than the entity of an author's total work. Some variation was found among sources in the matter of exact dates, but it is believed the errors are neither numerous nor significant.

Each title was followed by the name of each single-woman character appearing in the novel, provided she had a name by which she could be identified and otherwise fit the definition of the study, that is, that she had not married by the age of thirty and made no plans for marriage throughout the course of the novel. A character was considered to be single only if some statement or other direct evidence was given to that effect. In other words, all characters had to be considered in terms of the information given by the novelist, and this varied a great deal from one book to another. If a novel contained no single-woman character, this fact was also recorded, since many instances of this kind might have a certain significance.

For each of the identifiable single-woman characters, an extensive classification was made. Her prominence in the plot was first indicated: whether she was major or minor in relation to the other characters; whether she had little or much influence upon them. The age-span of each character was also recorded, showing whether she appeared in the novel from childhood or adolescence through maturity; from early maturity (the age of twenty-five) into middle age; or whether she was beyond thirty when she first entered the story. Actually, two kinds of classification were desirable: the first, a developmental or genetic approach to the character herself; and second, a cross section analysis of certain elements common to all characters. The developmental approach was an effort to capture some of the subtle quality of personality and social attitude, while the cross section analysis, achieved by assigning letter-symbols, was a means toward isolating specific elements, not with relation to the individual, but to the status of the group as a whole.

Since the investigation considered these woman characters as real persons, the purpose was to glean from a meticulous reading of the novel such information about each character as would constitute a kind of case study. Since the amount of material furnished by different authors varied greatly, not all facts generally included in a case study were available about some; but, in general, the larger cross section classification established five different categories: Childhood and Adolescence; Ambition and Achievement; Human Relationships; Attitudes; and Factors in Nonmarriage and Adjustment.

Each of these categories, in turn, was extended into its further constituents. *Childhood and Adolescence* included family pattern, socioeconomic background, kind of education received, choice of vocation, and early heterosexual relationships.

Ambition and Achievement considered central ambition, nature of frustrating circumstances, nature of her success, nature of her failure, her interest in her community, and adult vocation.

Human Relationships noted the quality of relationships in general, specific sources of tension, with special emphasis upon the nature of adult heterosexual relationships.

Under *Attitudes* were recorded the characteristics for which the single woman was admired, those for which she was not admired, her attitude toward her vocation, her attitude toward marriage in general, her attitude toward her own life, and the attitude of other characters or the author toward her.

Factors in Nonmarriage and Adjustment observed and recorded the woman's own reasons for not marrying, the reader's judgment as to why she did not marry, and finally, the nature of the adjustment she effected by the time she left the story or as the story closed.

Each of the subcategories under the five general headings was extended into a kind of scale, ranging in most instances from positive to negative. Each individual statement within the scale was assigned a letter, and the letters were subsequently recorded in the classification as indicated above. The final score was arrived at by a simple tallying of the letter-symbols. Items in the scale were derived from, and built upon, an earlier test-reading of a number of novels which were known to contain the kind of character the study wished to analyze, novels in which a single-woman character held an important place.

Because of the variable amounts of detail furnished by different novelists, difficulty in classification arose at two points. The major characters were so complex and the reader learned so much about them, it was often necessary to check more than one response within a given category. For example, a woman may have been admirable in not one, but several ways, so that to get anything like an accurate analysis, several items had to be checked, each independently of the other. The result is that the number of letter-symbols sometimes exceeds the number of characters analyzed.

With the exceedingly minor characters, the classification was even more difficult. With them the difficulty was that so little information was given about them. It could hardly have been anticipated that great numbers of single women in fiction are such very minor characters, appearing only on a few pages of a long novel. The reader learns almost nothing about them, neither what they look like nor how they think or feel. This discovery was, of course, an important finding of the study, and the structure of the analysis could hardly be altered after this discovery became evident. In the case of the very minor characters, therefore, the items of the classification were less applicable than the original intention had been.

When very little is known about a character, one has a tendency to read into the character more than the novelist has actually stated or implied. It would have been easy to assume, for example, that most of the single women had ambitions to marry, but with many of them there was no foundation for such an assumption. Furthermore, the fact that so many of the single women were such minor characters and were not described in detail by the novelist caused the investigator to want to assume that if a characteristic was not mentioned of a certain individual, this element did not exist in the personality: whereas all one can actually say is that the novelist did not see fit to include or emphasize this element. The reader does not need to decide, actually, for the very fact that certain details are omitted, is, in itself, a reflection of the culture.

To guard against the tendency to force a character to fit the classification, the scale in each category was extended to include a "no comment," to be used when no mention was made of a given characteristic, and also an "unclassified" item in each category which permitted wide variation. In the instances in which the unclassified item comprises a large response, one of two situations is reflected: either that the response could not reasonably have been anticipated and provided for, or that the actual facts concerning a given character did not quite fit the statement as expressed. What could not be classified in one category, however, would often fit precisely into another, so that most of the elements which characterize a personality are retained at some point.

The variables thus were provided for in what seemed to be the best possible way. A whole chapter will be devoted to a detailed developmental synthesis of each of the major characters, and the chapter on findings will cite many specific illustrations of the kinds of response which were too miscellaneous, individual, or elusive to classify objectively.

It must be admitted that any objective classification of a subjective material such as fiction must in itself remain somewhat subjective. The ideal way to get at such subtleties as attitude, for example, is by means of direct quotation. In some instances an attitude must be gained from the whole context of the novel rather than from any one or more statements which can be directly quoted. The important factor to consider, therefore, in proceeding to the discussion of the findings which follows, is not that all the single-woman characters do not lend themselves equally well to the objective classification, but that the classification reveals as much as it does.[8]

The analytical classification described above was made first, but in proceeding to show what the investigation has found, it seems more meaningful to present first the synthesis—the "portraits in miniature"—of the seven major single-woman characters as they were determined by the classification. To present the narrative sketches first will give the reader, especially the reader less familiar with the novels, specific portraits to keep in mind as he proceeds to the socio-psychological analysis. These portraits, individually and collectively, illustrate the stereotype of the older single woman.

When the study was originally charted, it appeared desirable to include a few interpretive sketches in order to emphasize the psychological and social forces influencing the lives of the single women portrayed in fiction. But it was impossible to determine at the beginning which characters or how many should be thus considered. The act of selection, in itself, could reflect a bias and throw the whole study out of focus. If one were to choose a group of the "best" characters, best in the sense of possessing the more favorable aspects of personality, the study could be weighted in that direction. If, on the other hand, one chose the worst or most unpleasant characters, they would appear to be representative of the entire group.

It seemed advisable, therefore, to proceed with the cross section or objective classification of characters, and discover in the process which were major characters and which were minor according to the definition formulated for the study. One of the impressive findings which grew out of this classification was the fact that of the 150 single-woman characters which appeared in the 125 novels, only seven conformed to the definition of "major." All the rest were minor, most of them exceedingly minor, characters. After this discovery, it seemed appropriate that whatever interpretive sketches were included should deal with major rather than minor characters, partly because of their importance in the novels and partly because major characters were fully enough described by their authors to permit detailed analysis.

Since the emphasis was upon a certain kind of character rather than the novel itself or the novelist, it is to be expected that the novels thus chosen are a somewhat uneven representation of American novels as a whole, but they probably comprise as worthy a group of novels as any seven which might be chosen upon any other controlled basis. Here is one, at least, of the enduring classics: Hawthorne's *The House of the Seven Gables*, which contains the excellent portrayal of Hepzibah Pyncheon. Here is Jennie Gerhardt, title character of Theodore Dreiser's memorable novel. *Ethan Frome*, an atypical but superior work by Edith Wharton, should be considered in any extensive appraisal of the

American novel. Mattie Silver, it is true, won her place among the seven major characters merely upon a "technicality," since only three characters appear prominently in this short novel, and Mattie is "past thirty" only in the brief epilogue. But she is unquestionably major, and her invalidism presents a critical point.

The remaining four novels are of no small significance. Ruth Suckow's *The Folks* presents not only a finely drawn major character in Margaret (Margot) Ferguson, but a gallery of small-town single-woman characters of every kind. *Mountain Blood* by Joseph Hergesheimer is perhaps not a major American novel, but the character Meta Beggs, being so unlike other schoolteachers of the group, is worthy of special notice.

Two of the seven novels are of the more popular variety and were widely read during the early 1900's. They bring to attention two pairs of single-woman characters (one major and one minor) which are not only drawn in interesting detail, but are illustrative of groups which deserve more than passing mention. In Kate Douglas Wiggin's *Rebecca of Sunnybrook Farm* are the maiden sisters, "the Sawyer girls," presented deftly in contrast; in *The Circular Staircase* by Mary Roberts Rinehart, the wealthy mistress, Rachel Innes, and her servant-companion, Liddy Allen. Both pairs present a spinster-to-spinster relationship familiar to readers of American fiction. Rachel Innes is further representative of a group of spinster detectives who find themselves involved in murder mysteries, of which this novel is still an interesting example.

The choice of the seven single-woman characters whose personalities are synthesized in the following chapter, therefore, was arrived at critically and without bias. They are the major characters of representative American novels, and are presented in the order, and for the reasons, mentioned above.

3

WHAT DOES THE READER FIND?

*Old maidhood is a wretched, pitiable condition, to which the
most unhappy marriage would be vastly preferable, as life,
though wretched, is better than annihilation.*

C. BURDETT, Blonde and Brunette

THE seven sketches which follow present the seven single
women who are major characters in the novels used in this
study. Though arrived at by objective classification and
analysis, the characters represent a wide variety in time,
style, and authorship. They represent both the classics and
the popular novel, and each character is an excellent example
of its kind. In order to give a full-length synthesis as briefly
as possible, the character has been drawn from the novel
piecemeal and reassembled, like a miniature mosaic, against
a background of the plot. Thus the essential characterization
is presented in a mere fraction of the long novel in which it
appears.

THE SYNTHESIS: PORTRAITS IN MINIATURE

HEPZIBAH PYNCHEON

It is both significant and appropriate that the series of
single women in the American novel to be presented in this
chapter should begin with Hepzibah Pyncheon. The novel
in which she appears, Nathaniel Hawthorne's *The House
of the Seven Gables,* is the first notable American novel in
which a single woman is a major character.

The novel ranks among the best works of a master writer.
For several decades it has been consistently listed as required
reading for high school and college students, which is another way of saying that few novels in America have been so

widely read by an above-the-average reading public. The fact that it was published in 1851, at a time when the Feminist Movement was gathering momentum under the leadership of Susan B. Anthony, is also worthy of note.

According to the author's declaration, this novel is intended to be a "history of retribution for the sin of long ago." [1] For the reader of the present day, however, the characters furnish a greater interest than the ecclesiastical idea. Though Hepzibah is incidental to the *raison d'être* of the novel, the diligent reader can piece together a complete mosaic of this unfortunate woman, a portrait which not only reaches the heights of literary and artistic creation, but in the process also reflects many of the social ideas concerning women in nineteenth-century America.

Hepzibah is one of a family which lives chiefly on its past glory—a family that for more than two centuries maintained large holdings of land in New England and resided for many generations in the gloomy old House of the Seven Gables, presumably situated in Salem, Massachusetts. This once-prominent family is dying out, and the Pyncheon descendants are only five in number: Hepzibah and her half-imbecile, half-insane brother, Clifford; their cousin, Jaffrey, known as Judge Pyncheon; his single surviving son, then traveling in Europe; and the last and youngest, a little country girl of seventeen, Phoebe Pyncheon, the daughter of a remote cousin. As the story opens, Hepzibah lives a recluse in the ghostly old house, Clifford is about to come home from a long and mysterious absence, the prosperous Judge resides on his country estate near by, and since little Phoebe's father has died, and her mother, a woman "of no family or property" [2] had recently married again, Phoebe arrives, uninvited, to make her home with Hepzibah.

The House of the Seven Gables, like all novels which survive the test of time, tells an absorbing story. In the course of the tale, the prosperous and successful Judge Jaffrey

Pyncheon, so highly respected among his contemporaries, is gradually revealed as an archvillain. His mysterious death, which is finally attributed to natural causes, marks the fulfillment of the curse which had hung like a pall over the family—a curse imposed by one of witchlike power who had been "sinned against" by a Pyncheon, generations before.

Not until after the Judge's death does his earlier dealing with the members of his family become known or his early perfidy become revealed. Then, in the manner of unrelenting justice, it is his cruel "fate" to be remembered, not for his worldly achievement or his princely deeds, but as the one who cheated the imbecile Clifford and his sister out of their rightful inheritance and who turned the finger of suspicion upon Clifford in the strange death of an uncle.

The denouement of the story hangs upon the discovery of a map of certain land, once belonging to the family, to which the title has been lost. The Judge goes unhappily to his death, erroneously believing Clifford to be in possession of the coveted document; when it does come to light, in an unexpected manner, the family fortunes are restored, and the fact that the Judge's son dies of cholera on the eve of his return to America leaves the three surviving Pyncheons to fall heir to vast wealth.

In this final turn of events the reader comes to understand the threat Judge Jaffrey has held over his unfortunate relatives, and why Hepzibah in her poverty repeatedly refused his offers of financial aid. The reader understands that it was the Judge's false accusation which had aggravated Clifford's mental affliction and that it was "the bitter sense of wrong" which had made old Hepzibah into a "kind of lunatic." [3]

Hepzibah is an individual and also a symbol. In her attitude toward having to earn her own living, in her lack of training in practical matters, and in the limited means of livelihood open to her, she is a symbol of the "old gentility" brought face to face with the hard necessities of living. As such, she marks an important transition among women— from a state of utter economic dependency to one of economic self-sufficiency—which was beginning to be apparent even in Hawthorne's day.

However unfortunate Hepzibah's need may have been, it was good fortune that there was in the old House of the Seven Gables the remains of a cent-shop, once operated by a disreputable ancestor in financial straits, but long since boarded up and left to gather dust. After considering all other possibilities futile, as "the final throe," Hepzibah,

who had fed herself from childhood with the shadowy food of aristocratic reminiscences, and whose religion it was that a lady's hand soils itself irremediably by doing aught for bread—this born lady, after sixty years of narrowing means, is fain to step down from her pedestal of imaginary rank. Poverty, treading close upon her heels for a lifetime, has come up with her at last. She must earn her own food, or starve! And we have stolen upon Miss Hepzibah Pyncheon, too irreverently, at the instant of time when the patrician lady is to be transformed into the plebeian woman . . .

Let us behold, in poor old Hepzibah, the immemorial lady,— two hundred years old, this side of the water, and thrice as many on the other,—with her antique portraits, pedigrees, coats of arms, records and traditions, and her claim, as joint heiress, to that princely territory at the eastward, . . . born, too, in Pyncheon street, under the Pyncheon Elm, and in the Pyncheon House, where she has spent all her days,—reduced now, in that very house, to be the hucksteress of a cent-shop.[4]

Following this characteristic nineteenth-century introduction to Hepzibah, Hawthorne explains that the business of setting up a petty shop is almost the only resource of women in circumstances at all similar to those of "our unfortunate recluse." Later, one of his minor characters remarks that "this business of cent-shops is overdone among the womenfolks." [5] Several such shops then existed in Salem, shops in which "a decayed gentlewoman stands behind the counter." [6] Apparently, these ventures were seldom successful. The two laboring men who chance to pass by on the day Hepzibah opens her shop prophesy "poor business!" They comment that there is another shop just around the corner, and one of them remarks that his wife "kept a cent-shop three months, and lost five dollars on her outlay!" [7] Also, at the end of the narrative, when the same two workmen discover that Hepzibah has fled from the old house, they at once conclude that she "has run in debt, and gone off from her creditors." [8]

Like other gentlewomen of her time, Hepzibah was not equipped to earn her living. "With her near-sightedness, and those tremulous fingers of hers, at once inflexible and delicate, she could not be a seamstress." [9] She had considered opening a school for little children, and at one time had begun to review the New England Primer with such a plan in mind, "but the love of little children had never been quickened in Hepzibah's heart, and was now torpid, if not extinct." [10] As she watches the neighborhood children from her window, "she doubted whether she could tolerate a more intimate acquaintance with them." [11] Besides, "a modern child could teach old Hepzibah more than old Hepzibah could teach the child." [12]

By the time she was sixty—when the story opens—Hepzibah's accomplishments could be summarized merely as "recollections" of having "thrummed on a harpsichord, walked a minuet, and worked an antique tapestry-stitch on her sampler." [13] She had no practical ability. She was "not quick at figures" and would give herself a head-ache over the day's accounts at the cent-shop.[14] She had "no natural turn for cookery." [15] She "had no taste nor spirits for the lady-like employment of cultivating flowers, and . . . would hardly have come forth under the speck of open sky to weed and hoe among the fraternity of beans and squashes." [16]

Hawthorne points up his delineation of Hepzibah by presenting gay little Phoebe in contrast, or, as he says, he offers "a fair parallel between the new Plebeianism and the old Gentility." Hepzibah is the "born and educated lady," while Phoebe has "the gift of practical arrangement." [17] Phoebe is young and pretty, wholesome and vivacious, and as yet untainted by the Pyncheon curse. Though Hepzibah could not at first accept the idea of Phoebe's coming to the old house, she later relies more and more upon her young relative. Phoebe proves herself indispensable in the management of the cent-shop, but it is when the afflicted brother Clifford returns home that Hepzibah most appreciates her help. When Clifford appears at the breakfast table for the first time, Hepzibah is in "an ecstasy of delight and happiness." She

would fling out her arms, and infold Phoebe in them, and kiss her cheek as tenderly as ever her mother had . . . as if her bosom were oppressed with tenderness, of which she must needs pour out a little, in order to gain breathing-room. The next moment, without any visible cause for the change, her unwonted joy sprang back, appalled, as it were, and clothed itself in mourning; or it ran and hid itself, so to speak, in the dungeon of her heart, where it had long been chained, while an old, spectral sorrow took the place of the imprisoned joy, that was afraid to be enfranchised,—a sorrow as black as that was bright. She often broke into a little nervous, hysterical laugh, more touching than any tears could be; and forthwith, as if to try which was the most touching, a gush of tears would follow; or perhaps the laughter and tears came both at once, and surrounded poor old Hepzibah, in a moral sense, with a kind of pale, dim rainbow.[18]

While this novel is essentially serious in tone as well as in theme, and all the other characters are presented in straight-

forward manner, Hawthorne seems to be somewhat amused
by Hepzibah. In the beginning he offers his apologies to the
reader for being "compelled to introduce" as one of the
prominent characters, "not a young and lovely woman, nor
even the stately remains of beauty, storm-shattered by affliction—but a gaunt, sallow, rusty-jointed maiden, in a
long-waisted silk gown, and with the strange horror of a
turban on her head!" "Her visage," he goes on to say, "is not
even ugly. It is redeemed from insignificance only by the
contraction of her eyebrows into a near-sighted scowl." [19]
This scowl, he explains, had done old Hepzibah a "very ill
office" by establishing her character as "an ill-tempered old
maid." He has one of the neighbors declare that her face
"would frighten the old Nick himself." [20] He endows her
with only one attractive feature, but even that carries an
undertone of the ridiculous. Referring to her reputation for
ill temper, Hawthorne explains that "her heart never
frowned." "It was naturally tender, sensitive, and full of
little tremors and palpitations." [21] Indeed, he describes her
in a rich variety of amusing phrases. She is a "far-descended
and time-stricken virgin," [22] and again "a mildewed piece of
aristocracy." [23]

"She had never had a lover—poor thing, how could she?—
nor never knew, by her own experience, what love tech-
nically means." [24] All her warmth and affection had been
turned toward her brother, who was, in his unfortunate affliction, dependent upon her. It is in her relationship to this
brother that she is most clearly revealed as an individual;
but here again, what might have been portrayed as a noble
spirit of sacrifice or generosity is described in a fashion bor-
dering on caricature. The novelist's own words must be observed in large measure in order to preserve the tone of his
portrayal: "How patiently did she endeavor to wrap Clifford up in her great, warm love, and make it all the world
to him, so that he could retain no torturing sense of the

coldness and dreariness without! Her little efforts to amuse
him! How pitiful, yet magnanimous, they were!" [25]

Remembering her brother's love of poetry and fiction,
Hepzibah tried to read to him, but both her choice and her
reading were unfortunate. She tried Pope's *Rape of the
Lock*, then the *Tatler*, then Dryden's *Miscellanies*, but with
no success. She then took up *Rasselas* and began to read of
the Happy Valley, but, says Hawthorne, "the Happy Valley
had a cloud over it."

Hepzibah troubled her auditor, moreover, by innumerable sins
of emphasis, which he seemed to detect, without any reference
to the meaning; nor, in fact, did he appear to take note of the
sense of what she read, but evidently felt the tedium of the lec-
ture, without harvesting its profit. His sister's voice, too, naturally harsh, had, in the course of her sorrowful lifetime, con-
tracted a kind of croak, which, when it once gets into the human
throat, is as ineradicable as sin. [26]

Her reading a failure, Hepzibah searched for some other
more exhilarating diversion. Her gaze finally rested upon
the long-neglected harpsichord, and she considered playing
it for Clifford's benefit and singing to her own accompani-
ment. To this the novelist adds his amusing comment: "Poor
Clifford! Poor Hepzibah! Poor Harpsichord! All three
would have been miserable together!" [27]

But worst of all . . . was his invincible distaste for her appearance. Her features, never the most agreeable, and now harsh with
age and grief, and resentment against the world for his sake;
her dress, and especially her turban; the queer and quaint manners, which had unconsciously grown upon her in solitude,—
such being the poor gentlewoman's outward characteristics, it
is no great marvel, although the mournfullest of pities, that the
instinctive lover of the Beautiful was fain to turn away his eyes.
There was no help for it. It would be the latest impulse to die
within him. In his last extremity, . . . he would doubtless press
Hepzibah's hand, in fervent recognition of all her lavished love,

and close his eyes,—but not so much to die, as to be constrained to look no longer on her face! [28]

To make the situation more pitiful than it might otherwise have been, Hepzibah herself realized her own shortcomings. The novelist continues:

> She took counsel with herself what might be done, and thought of putting ribbons on her turban; but by the instant rush of several guardian angels, was withheld from an experiment that could hardly have proved less than fatal to the beloved object of her anxiety.

> To be brief, besides Hepzibah's disadvantages of person, there was an uncouthness pervading all her deeds; a clumsy something, that could but ill adapt itself for use at all for ornament. She was a grief to poor Clifford, and she knew it.[29]

As if to redeem her—or himself—a little, at the end of the narrative, Hawthorne leaves his "forlorn old maid" presumably looking ahead to better days, and in a somewhat happier frame of mind. She will share with the others in the restored family fortunes and will quit the gloomy old house to reside in the elegant country home of her cousin, the late Judge Jaffrey. As she is about to ride away in her handsome carriage, she spies Ned Higgins among the children assembled. Remembering little Ned as her earliest and stanchest customer at the cent-shop, she presents him "with silver enough to people the Domdaniel cavern of his interior with as various a procession of quadrupeds as passed into the Ark." [30] So the story ends on the economic note which resounds throughout the novel. Yet even with this one redeeming gesture of generosity, one can hardly imagine a more pitiful and pathetic creature than Hepzibah. As the reader looks back from the vantage point of time, she appears a caricature, yet undoubtedly she exemplifies many of the social ideas held by, and expressed toward, women in America a century ago. She approaches, more nearly than any other single woman the study considers, the prototype of the "old maid" of the eighteenth-century English novel.

JENNIE GERHARDT

Exactly sixty years elapse following the publication of *The House of the Seven Gables* before another American novel of the first magnitude presents a single woman as a major character. This is Theodore Dreiser's *Jennie Gerhardt*, which appeared in 1911. Jennie's story—the woman taken in adultery—is a familiar theme of fiction; it is Dreiser's attitude toward his heroine and toward the world which condemns her that makes this novel distinguished. Jennie Gerhardt stands—magnificently or ignominiously—as one of the great women of American fiction.

At first thought, Hepzibah Pyncheon and Jennie Gerhardt are so dissimilar as to seem to evade comparison. Yet they are alike in certain respects. Both spring from a background of orthodoxy. The theme of both books is fundamentally religious. Both women grapple with family problems and find within their respective families great affectional loyalties as well as bitter enmities. Both women struggle with poverty. Both must make their way in the world alone, and without any training which would enable them to earn their living.

But their differences are much greater than their similarity. Jennie is young when her story begins; Hepzibah faces old age. Jennie is attractive in person and personality; Hepzibah is ugly and uncouth. Hepzibah is a gentlewoman of a prominent New England family; Jennie is of the great Midwestern middle class. Hepzibah felt disgraced to have to earn even an "honest" living; Jennie worked willingly and felt no disgrace about anything, even her unconventional life.

Jennie is unusual in her combination of qualities; as her author sees her she is the personification of goodness:

From her earliest youth goodness and mercy had molded her
every impulse. . . . Many were the hours in which she had
rocked her younger brothers and sisters to sleep, singing wholeheartedly betimes and dreaming far dreams. Since her earliest
walking period she had been the right hand of her mother. What
scrubbing, baking, errand-running, and nursing there had been
to do she did. No one had ever heard her rudely complain,
though she often thought of the hardness of her lot. She knew
there were other girls whose lives were infinitely freer and fuller,
but it never occurred to her to be meanly envious; her heart
might be lonely, but her lips continued to sing.[31]

She is the oldest of six children in a German-American
family living in Columbus, Ohio. The family is always in
some kind of difficulty: her father is in debt, some one of
the children is sick, injured, or in the clutches of the law.
The mother works wherever she can to supplement the
family income. The reader first meets Jennie when she comes
with her mother to do the cleaning at the largest hotel in
the city. The girl is then (1880) eighteen years of age, and
it is at Columbus House that she first sees persons and things
of substance. Among those for whom she and her mother
worked was the junior senator from Ohio, who at once was
attracted by Jennie's warmth and wholesome nature. At
that time Jennie had achieved

that perfection of womanhood, the full mold of form, which
could not help but attract any man. Already she was well built,
and tall for a girl. . . . Her eyes were wondrously clear and
bright, her skin fair, and her teeth white and even. She was
clever, too, in a sensible way, and by no means deficient in observation. All that she lacked was training and the assurance of
which the knowledge of utter dependency despoils one.[32]

There was a wide gulf between Senator Brander and Jennie, but he was a man of integrity, and his intentions toward
the girl were probably honorable. He courteously called at
her home, provided a merry Christmas for all the children,

and made generous gifts not only to Jennie but also to her mother. Though he was approaching middle age, the senator had never married; now he was well established in his political career, but was lonely for companionship. Whatever he thought Jennie lacked in education, he felt sure she could acquire. But the vigilant neighbors, observing Jennie's better clothes and their frequent walks together, are sure that a man like the senator—"old enough to be her father"—cannot possibly want anything good of a girl so far beneath him. When the gossip reaches her father, he reprimands his daughter severely and forbids the man to come to the house. A glass blower by trade, her father

had inherited the feeling that the Lutheran Church was a perfect institution, and that its teachings were of all-importance when it came to the issue of the future life. His wife, nominally of the Mennonite faith, was quite willing to accept her husband's creed. And so his household became a God-fearing one . . .[33]

Naturally, such a deep religious feeling made him stern with his children. He was prone to scan with a narrow eye the pleasures and foibles of youthful desire. Jennie was never to have a lover if her father had any voice in the matter.[34]

Thus Dreiser sets his stage for the events which follow in quick succession. The senator dies suddenly, Jennie is "in trouble," and the irate father relentlessly drives her out to seek whatever shelter she can find.

This bitter experience, plus the need to provide for her illegitimate child (whom she names Vesta), prepares the way for Jennie's second liaison, with a man not quite of the caliber of Senator Brander, but a person of wealth and position. What began as a casual flirtation, when Lester Kane was a guest in the household where Jennie was a maid, develops into a relationship which was to last for many years. Kane is loyal and devoted to Jennie, and gives her reason to believe that he will marry her. Yet, as time goes on, Kane's family—a wealthy Cincinnati family which had made its fortune in the manufacture of carriages—threatens to disinherit him if he does not marry within his social milieu and assume his share of responsibility in the management of the family fortune. Once again, gossip is Jennie's undoing. When the neighbors and the newspapers, relatives and friends, finally reveal that Kane and Jennie are not "Mr. and Mrs. Lester Kane," as they have appeared to be for almost twenty-five years, Kane's business ventures are undermined, and he is forced to give Jennie up in order to "keep" her. When the whole truth of the situation filters through to Jennie, it is she who insists that Kane marry the young widow—his family's choice—who is better fitted socially to be his wife.

In every respect, however, except her social position and bearing, Jennie is superior to the woman Kane marries. Jennie is not vulgar or licentious; neither is she a coquette. She is loyal and devoted to the man who loves her. She is quiet and dignified rather than gaudy, and when dressed in the modish clothes Kane provides for her, she makes such a "stunning" appearance that people turn to gaze at her.[35] The novelist explains her attraction from a masculine point of view. He says, "Around a soft, yielding disposition men swarm naturally. They sense this generosity, the non-protective attitude from afar. A girl like Jennie is like a comfortable fire to the average masculine mind; they gravitate to it, seek its sympathy, yearn to possess it."[36] He comments upon her "pre-eminent femininity," and that something about her "which suggested the luxury of love."[37] And again, "her warm womanhood, a guileless expression of countenance—intimated a sympathy toward sex relationship which had nothing to do with hard, brutal immorality. She was the kind of woman who was made for a man—one man. All her attitude toward sex was bound up with love, tenderness, service."[38]

As Dreiser sees her, Jennie has no serious faults. Though

she lies to her father about her relations with Kane and deceives Kane for many years about her child, Dreiser never censures her. Her motives are always reasonable, never questioned. The end always justifies the means. Jennie is utterly unselfish. She helps all her family; even the father who cruelly thrust her out, she cares for tenderly in his old age. But in return for her sacrifice, perpetual suffering is her lot. She loses everything that is dear to her; even her daughter dies of typhoid. She openly meets the censure of his family to come to Kane on his deathbed, and attends his funeral, alone and unrecognized. Though he leaves her with meager means—a modest home and enough to provide simply for herself and two orphan girls she had befriended—"before her was stretching a vista of lonely years . . . days and days in endless reiteration." [39]

Dreiser not only defends Jennie by making her noble and good and "irresistible," but he also departs from the usual fiction pattern by likewise defending her lover. Kane, too, is a creature of circumstance, "weighed upon by too many things." The novelist steps out of his role as storyteller to plead with his reader:

Let us be just to Lester Kane; let us try to understand him and his position. Not every mind is to be estimated by the weight of a single folly; not every personality is to be judged by the drag of a single passion . . .

His was a naturally observing mind, Rabelaisian in its strength and tendencies, but confused by the multiplicity of things, the vastness of the panorama of life, the glitter of its details, the insubstantial nature of its forms, the uncertainty of its justification. Born a Catholic, he was no longer a believer in the divine inspiration of Catholicism; raised a member of the social elect, he had ceased to accept the fetish that birth and station presuppose any innate superiority; brought up as the heir to a comfortable fortune and expected to marry in his own sphere, he was by no means sure that he wanted marriage on any terms. [40]

The "villain," consequently, is not the man who draws freely upon Jennie's generous spirit. The villain is society and its false attitudes. Dreiser's exposition on virtue, for example, is basic to his theme. Thus he defends his heroine when she meets her first disgrace:

The world into which Jennie was thus unduly thrust forth was that in which virtue has always vainly struggled since time immemorial; for virtue is the wishing well and the doing well unto others. Virtue is that quality of generosity which offers itself willingly for another's service, and, being this, it is held by society to be nearly worthless. Sell yourself cheaply and you shall be used lightly and trampled under foot. Hold yourself dearly, however unworthily, and you will be respected. Society, in the mass, lacks woefully in the matter of discrimination. Its one criterion is the opinion of others. Its one test that of self-preservation. Has he preserved his fortune? Has she preserved her purity? Only in rare instances and with rare individuals does there seem to be any guiding light from within.[41]

More striking, perhaps, than Dreiser's unorthodox views on virtue is his revival of the medieval theory of "fate in love," which, curiously enough, still persists as an ingredient of the romanticism of present-day marriage, and which, undoubtedly is a considerable factor in singleness among women.

Dreiser makes the conduct of his characters not only plausible but inevitable. Kane, he says, "was instinctively, magnetically, and chemically drawn to this poor serving-maid. She was his natural affinity—though he did not know it—the one woman who answered somehow the biggest need of his nature." [42] Jennie, too, was helpless. Her lover "had only to say 'Come' and she must obey; it was her destiny." [43]

Upon Jennie's misdemeanor, the novelist sermonizes at length. His ideas on this subject are especially interesting in the light of current Freudian ideas and the various manifestations of science, sociology, and psychology which have become accepted thinking since the appearance of this book, a little more than three decades ago:

Certain processes of the all-mother, the great artificing wisdom of the power that works and weaves in silence and in darkness, when viewed in the light of the established opinion of some of the little individuals created by it, are considered very vile. We turn our faces away from the creation of life as if that were the last thing that man should dare to interest himself in, openly.

It is curious that a feeling of this sort should spring up in a world whose very essence is generative, the vast process dual, and where wind, water, soil, and light alike minister to the fruition of that which is all that we are. Although the whole earth, not we alone, is moved by passions hymeneal, and everything terrestial has come into being by the one common road, yet there is that ridiculous tendency to close the eyes and turn away the head as if there were something unclean in nature itself. "Conceived in iniquity and born in sin" is the unnatural interpretation put upon the process by the extreme religionist, and the world, by its silence, gives assent to a judgment so marvelously warped.

Surely there is something radically wrong in this attitude. The teachings of philosophy and the deductions of biology should find more practical application in the daily reasoning of man. No process is vile, no condition is unnatural. The accidental variation from a given social practice does not necessarily entail sin. No poor little earthling, caught in the enormous grip of chance, and so swerved from the established customs of men, could possibly be guilty of that depth of vileness which the attitude of the world would seem to predicate so inevitably.[44]

For its basic philosophy, *Jennie Gerhardt* is unusual in American fiction, as its heroine is unusual among the single women of the study. Dreiser's writing, by belles-lettres standards, is often clumsy, the plot is trite, his heroine is sentimentalized, and he is unrestrained in his pity. But the novel has an emotional power which cannot be denied. The philosophical argument may or may not be convincing, but its narrative implementation is unforgettable.

Though more than half a century intervenes between Hepzibah Pyncheon and Jennie Gerhardt, the theme of economic necessity among women still persists. Jennie, like Hepzibah, was driven by poverty, and having been scarcely more trained to earn her living than the older woman, seized upon what seemed the most expedient means to that end. Hepzibah, it is true, would have been horrified at Jennie's solution of her problem; but Jennie would likewise have looked with disapproval upon Hepzibah's gross inefficiency in the kitchen and her bigoted sense of her own importance. Jennie never considered herself "too good to work." Vocationally, both women were domestics; both lives were hemmed in by the daily round of living, but Jennie, through a combination of personal endowment and circumstance— "fate," Dreiser would call it—was able to use her domestic ability as an asset in her extralegal relationships. Jennie's warmth and beauty, surpassing anything Hepzibah had known even in her youth, were both her advantage and her undoing. The economic need and Jennie's solution of it were by no means a new idea; even in Hepzibah's day, if not from the beginning of time, there have been women who earned their livelihood as Jennie earned hers.

This novel, however, does introduce an idea that is "new" —the idea that Sin is not Absolute, and men and women are not altogether responsible for their deeds. It marks a milestone in the redefinition of feminine virtue, and carries a social significance far beyond the mere story it tells.

MATTIE SILVER

No brief interpretation can possibly convey the tragedy of Mattie Silver. *Ethan Frome*, in which she appears as one of the three major characters, was published in 1911, the same year as *Jennie Gerhardt*. It is a little book, barely half the length of an average novel, but it suggests by innuendo far more than it says. Employing a device used with great effectiveness by such masters as Balzac and Poe, Edith Wharton tells the story piecemeal and entirely in retrospect, years after the major incident has occurred. The fact that the book is short enough to be read at a single sitting may contribute somewhat to its intense dramatic power.

The story of Ethan Frome, told as the central narrator, an engineer, imagines it to have been, is as bleak as the Massachusetts hills in which he lived; there is symbolistic significance even in the name of his village: Starkfield. When the story opens, Ethan appears to be an old man, so bent and broken in body and dejected in spirit that it is difficult to imagine him as he once was—tall and straight and rugged —when little Mattie Silver, gay and lighthearted, first came to make her home with him and his ailing wife, Zenobia.

Ethan felt sorry for Mattie, because of her previous misfortune which had, in a sense, indentured her to them. Mattie was the daughter of a cousin of Zenobia, who at his untimely death was remembered chiefly for his poor reputation and his bad debts. The wife, Mattie's mother, died "of the disclosure," and Mattie, at twenty, was left alone to make her way on the fifty dollars obtained from the sale of her piano.

For this purpose her equipment, though varied, was inadequate. She could trim a hat, make molasses candy, recite "The Curfew Shall Not Ring Tonight," and play "The Lost Chord" and a pot-pourri from "Carmen." When she tried to extend the field of her activities in the direction of stenography and bookkeeping, her health broke down, and six months on her feet behind the counter of a department store did not tend to restore it. Her nearest relations had been induced to place their savings in her father's hands, and though, after his death they grudgingly acquitted themselves of the Christian duty of returning good for evil by giving his daughter all the advice at their disposal, they could hardly be expected to supplement it by material aid. But when Zenobia's doctor recommended her looking about for someone to help her with the housework the clan instantly saw the chance of exacting a compensation from Mattie. Zenobia, though doubtful of the girl's efficiency, was tempted by the freedom to find fault without much risk of losing her; and so Mattie came to Starkfield.[45]

The reader first sees Mattie at a village dance where Ethan has gone to bring her home. It had been agreed when she came to work without pay that she was to have an occasional evening out. At first Ethan had objected to walking the two miles to the village after his day's work to see that she got home safely, but later it gave him pleasure. As he caught sight of "her light figure swinging from hand to hand in circles of increasing swiftness," of "her dark head wound in a cherry-coloured fascinator," [46] he could not resist feeling jealous of the village swain who seemed to have caught her favor. On this occasion, Mattie and Ethan walk home across the snowy fields, gazing playfully at the stars. Ethan had studied astronomy and was both flattered and amused by Mattie's childlike questions. Though no endearments are spoken or expressed, the reader realizes that Ethan's sympathy for Mattie has grown into warm affection. They plan to go sled-riding some night when the stars are bright in the heavens.

Mattie had then been in the Frome household about a year. By that time, Zenobia, becoming more and more disturbed by Mattie's inefficiency and her husband's thoughtful attentions to the younger girl, contrives a scheme to get rid of Mattie. Zenobia insists that she needs to see a new doctor, but her plan, actually, is to arrange for another hired girl. Zenobia is to be gone two days. Relieved of her scowling presence, Ethan and Mattie are free to express their fondness for each other. Mattie wants to use the pretty china and make things comfortable for Ethan, and he laughs aloud at her happy little girlish ways. For the first time in their lives, each finds warmth and understanding in another human being.

When Zenobia returns, she discovers the broken pickle dish which Mattie and Ethan have carefully replaced high on the cupboard shelf, and with mingled rage and smug satisfaction she tells them that another hired girl is coming. Mattie will have to go at once, though she has no place even to find a shelter. Ethan, too, is helpless, for he has no money to help either Mattie or himself. He sets out to take her and her trunk to the village—but on their way they stop for the sled-ride they had planned. Once again there are no words, but a kind of transcendent understanding passes between them; Ethan guides the sled, and it crashes into the great elm which stands half way down the long hill. The reader is not told, and therefore must decide for himself, whether it was an "accident," as the villagers call it ever after, or a deliberate attempt at suicide. In either case, the intolerable circumstance is the predisposing factor. It is the aftermath of the incident rather than the incident itself which contributes to the sense of tragedy. In fact, the reader does not discover immediately what the outcome was.

Twenty-four years have passed since the accident, when the main narrator of the story, the engineer stationed for the long winter near Starkfield, is being driven by Ethan on a two-day journey and stops to spend the night at the weather-beaten Frome farmhouse.[47]

There the visitor sees the two women: Zenobia, a "tall, bony figure," moving listlessly about preparing the sparse supper, and Mattie Silver "huddled in an arm-chair near the stove," whining in a thin shrill voice about the cold house.

Her hair was as gray as her companion's, her face bloodless and shriveled, but amber-tinted, with swarthy shadows sharpening the nose and hollow temples. Under her shapeless dress her body kept its limp immobility, and her dark eyes had the bright witch-like stare that disease of the spine sometimes gives.[48]

It is Mrs. Hale, with whom the engineer boards in the village, who tells him how Zenobia took Mattie back to the farm after the accident, though everybody thought Mattie would have been "better off dead," and how Ethan was so badly injured that he was never able to farm again, and in the score of years has rarely spoken to anyone. Gradually the three have been reduced to grim poverty until now they do not have "a dime to spare." " 'It's a pity,' Mrs. Hale ended, sighing, 'that they're all shut up there'n that one kitchen. In the summer time on pleasant days they move Mattie into the parlour, or out in the door-yard, and that makes it easier . . .' " [49]

As with Hepzibah Pyncheon and Jennie Gerhardt, here again is a single-woman character who is brought to an unfortunate position largely because of her lack of fitness to make her way with economic independence. Mattie was indentured into the Frome family after she had been orphaned, because she had no training of any kind at which she could earn her living elsewhere. Mattie was not an efficient worker, however, even at the domestic tasks at which Jennie excelled. In every way she was less stable than Jennie, and could hardly have succeeded at any kind of exacting work, some of which she had previously tried, but at which she had failed. When faced with an emotional problem which offered no ready solution, Mattie could only rely upon someone else.

Mattie and Jennie were alike in that they both had youth and warmth and a naïve spirit which endeared them to others, but otherwise their relationships were very different. Jennie's life with Kane lasted many years and was public knowledge; Mattie's and Ethan's love for each other was tacit and inarticulate, apparently not recognized even at the time by anyone except the jealous-hearted Zenobia who drove them to their tragic fate. There is also a vast difference in the attitude of their respective authors toward them.

Dreiser condones Jennie's unconventional behavior; Edith Wharton condemns Mattie, though the latter's transgression seems far less flagrant. Mattie's is silent suffering, but few heroines in American fiction have been called upon to suffer so long or so poignantly.

META BEGGS

I loathe children—the muddy little beasts—do you suppose I'd stay in this damn hole if I could get anywhere else? . . . I'll grow old and die in pokey little schools, and wear prim calico dresses, with a remade white mull for commencements. . . . I want to live. . . . I want to see things, things different, not these dumb, depressing mountains. I want to see life! [50]

In these words Meta Beggs of Joseph Hergesheimer's *Mountain Blood* introduces herself. She is the village schoolteacher, but by no means a familiar figure in that role. She hates her position, resents all that it implies, and longs to escape from the destitute life she leads. The reader learns nothing of her early life or how she came to the Virginia mountain village. She appears in only a small portion of the book, yet is a pivotal character in that her relationship to the hero marks an important step in his gradual degeneration.

The novel is primarily concerned with Gordon Makimmon. He is the third generation of a violent-tempered, improvident mountain family and rises from his modest position as driver of the local stagecoach to a place of social and financial importance by marrying the dull daughter of the richest man in the county. Meta Beggs had met him first several years before when she was boarding at the home of the Universalist minister; Makimmon, penniless and in debt, had been hired to do some carpenter work around the parsonage. They remember each other, but it is not until he becomes a rich man that the schoolteacher takes an interest in him. Then she sees the possibility of his helping her to escape the life she detests.

She dreams of Paris with its gaiety and romance, and envisions herself as much sought after in that society. But to get to Paris she must have money. Makimmon also has dreamed of something beyond the mountains, but Richmond is as far away as his imagination can comprehend. He suggests to her that they run off to Richmond—but Richmond is not Paris, and Meta Beggs will not agree to anything less than her dream. She tells him, "Any man I go with has got to go far: I don't intend to be left at some little way station with everything gone and nothing accomplished." [51]

"The Beggs woman," as she is called, is not unattractive. Her skin has a luminous quality, and her pointed hands are like folded buds of the mountain magnolia. She herself places a high value upon her body. She says, "You see, my body is all I have to take me out of this, and I can't afford to have it spoiled. The religious squashes can say all they like about the soul, but a woman's body is the only really important thing to her. No one bothers about your soul, but they judge your figure across the street." [52]

Her virtue, also, she guards only because of what it can ultimately provide for her: [53]

I know what I want, and I'm not afraid to pay for it. Almost everybody wants the same thing—plenty and pleasure—but they're afraid of the price—they are afraid of it alive and when they will be dead. Women set such store on what they call their virtue. . . . I'll make it serve me; I wouldn't be a silly slave to it all my life.[54]

Using her "slim, provocative body" to her advantage, the teacher encourages Makimmon to buy her expensive feminine gifts, once a necklace of pearls finer than anything the local jeweler had ever seen. In exchange, she promises herself, but she is worse than wanton, for even that primitive game she will not play fairly. Her promises remain only promises; she is actually "untouched" and "impersonal."

"You wouldn't take fire from a pine knot," Makimmon tells her. On one occasion she reminds him of "a venomous snake; he had never seen such a lithe, wicked hatred in any other human being." [55]

Luring him by her promises and her dream of Paris, she arranges a secret meeting and gives him "two hours to decide" whether he will go with her or not. He wants to go, but there is something honorable in him which makes him realize that if he goes he can never come back, and his "mountain blood" will never let him rest "out yonder." His decision is to be final. She tells him: "No more penny kisses. No more meetings like this; it must be all or nothing. Some man will take me to Paris, have me." [56]

The reader does not know how Makimmon might have decided the issue, for his decision is, in effect, made for him. By means of the jeweler's box in which the expensive strand of pearls has been encased, his young wife discovers his apparent disloyalty. In dramatic fashion, Lettice, his wife, appears at the place of the secret meeting, having made the rough journey in a light carriage. For all her callousness, Meta Beggs is moved to pity at the sight of the young girl, clumsy and heavy with child. When the wife censures the schoolteacher, "caught like this trying to steal somebody's husband—and you set over a school of children," Meta Beggs flings back, "I don't choose to be. I hate it but I had to live. If you hadn't all that money to keep you soft, yes, and get you a husband, you would have had to fight and do, too. You might have been teaching a roomful of little sneaks, and sick to death of it before you ever began . . . or you might be on the street—better girls have than you." [57] When the husband helps his wife back to the carriage, the teacher's "red-clad arm" supports her on the other side.

At this point, Meta Beggs becomes the symbol of something stronger than herself—the counterpart of the many women, in fiction and in life, who defy convention rather than accept the traditional role of marriage. It is the familiar theme of the "eternal triangle," but Hergesheimer lifts the familiar above the commonplace when he reflects:

The two women standing in the foreground of Gordon Makimmon's vision, of his existence, summed up all the eternal contrast, the struggle, in the feminine heart. And they summed up the duplicity, the weakness, the sensual and egotistical desires, the power and vanity and vain-longing for men.

Meta Beggs was the mask, smooth and sterile, of the hunger for adornment, for gold bands and jewels and perfume, for goffered linen and draperies of silk and scarlet. She was the naked idler stained with antimony in the clay courts of Sumeria; the Paphian with painted feet loitering on the roofs of Memphis while the blocks of red sandstone floated sluggishly down the Nile for the pyramid of Khufu the King; she was the flushed voluptuousness relaxed in the scented spray of pagan baths; the woman with piled and white-powdered hair in a gold shift of Louis XIV; the prostitute with a pinched waist and great flowered sleeves of the Maison Dorée. She was as old as the first vice, as the first lust budding like a black blossom in the morbidity of men successful, satiated.

She was old, but Lettice was older.

Lettice was more ancient than men walking cunning and erect, than the lithe life of sun-heated tangles, than the vital principle of flowering plants fertilized by the unerring chance of vagrant insects and airs.

Standing in the flooding blue flame of day they opposed to each other the forces fatally locked in the body of humanity. Lettice, with her unborn child, her youth haggard with apprehension and pain, the prefigurement of the agony of birth, gazed, dumb and bitter in her sacrifice, at the graceful, cold figure, that, as irrevocably as herself, denied all that Lettice affirmed, desired all that she feared and hated.[58]

When the shock of this discovery and the grueling experience subsequently causes the death of his wife and the child, born prematurely, it brings Makimmon to his senses, but he is already well on his way to his ultimate undoing. He never sees the schoolteacher again. Even though through his wife's death he falls heir to her fortune and is later given to much generosity, he shows no inclination to help the teacher achieve her dream.

Nor does the reader hear of Meta Beggs again. One can only suppose that she may have carried out her plan which she revealed to Makimmon while awaiting his decision. If he decides not to go with her—and of course he did not go —she tells him she will take the money she has earned from teaching and go to New York. She will have just enough, she says, to get herself there and to buy a pretty hat. She will go into a café and get a bottle of champagne, and pick out the man with the best clothes. "I'll tell him I'm a poor school teacher from the south who came to New York to meet a man who promised to marry me, but who had not kept his word. I'll tell him that I'm good—I can, you know; no man has ever fooled anything out of me—and that I bought the wine to get the courage to kill myself." Makimmon admits "it sounds right smart," and believes she can do it, too, for "you can lie like hell." [59] Possibly her own words were prophetic: "Some day a man will murder me . . . perhaps I'll get a thrill out of that."

While "the other woman" is a familiar figure in fiction— both Mattie Silver and Jennie Gerhardt answering that general description—it is rarely that a novelist thinks of her as a schoolteacher. Spinster schoolteachers, likewise, are familiar in the novel—as has been pointedly shown—but they are not often involved in unconventional conduct. Teachers are generally portrayed as unsophisticated and with a high sense of propriety. As a matter of fact, the schoolteachers in this study are seldom involved in affairs of the heart at all; a situation which probably reflects the fact that their profession offers them small opportunity for meeting eligible men. "The Beggs woman" is unusual among school-

teachers of fiction as well as among the single women of the
study, because of her highly colored vocabulary, her physical attractiveness, and her lack of morals; also for one other
highly important element, her spirit of rebellion. In all these
respects, as well as in many smaller details, her story offers
an interesting comparison with that of Margaret (Margot)
Ferguson, the next single-woman character to be considered.

MARGARET (MARGOT) FERGUSON

Margaret Ferguson is one—the major one—of an as-
semblage of single-woman characters who emerge from the
pages of Ruth Suckow's novel *The Folks*. Published in 1934,
it is among the most recent novels the study includes.

In numerous ways, Margaret Ferguson resembles Meta
Beggs. Both women possess a stark kind of physical beauty.
Both are somewhat above their associates in level of intelligence, both have some formal education, both strongly
resist accepted and respected feminine vocations. They both
cling to an adolescent dream of romance, both long to lose
(or find) themselves in great cities, both consider marriage
as incidental or unimportant. Both have an overpowering
sense of frustration which brings them into conflict with the
prevailing mores; both rebel vigorously, not only against
"convention," but also against the drabness, the pettiness,
the unvarying round of life in their small towns.

Margaret is one of the four Ferguson children, two boys
and two girls, whose lives are described in painstaking, if not
painful, detail in this long novel of "life among the American
middle-class." Through the developing lives of the four Fergusons, the reader meets all the family, as well as many of
the other inhabitants of the Iowa town. Some are likable,
some admirable, but in the main they are simply "the folks";
the ordinary, the conventional, the mediocre.

Margaret has always been a misfit. She first appears as
a child, intensely jealous of her younger sister. Dorothy is

the one everybody likes; she is fair and pretty and has long golden curls, while Margaret is thin and dark and sallow. "Margaret was always hoping that some wonderful stranger would notice her dark eyes and her long braids and say 'Who is that child?' " [60] Her family could not understand her; it seemed to them that her whole idea was "to get out of doing everything she possibly could." [61] She was "dark and different," "sullen and defiant," "always at odds, and incalculable." She always chose the peculiar rather than the popular children for her friends, if she made friends at all. She "felt all the time as if she were just on the verge of some dark knowledge"; [62] she "knew that somewhere there would be a wonderful, shining, special fate for her." [63]

The Fergusons are leading citizens of Belmond. The father has worked himself up to a respected position in the local bank, and ever so gradually Mrs. Ferguson has climbed the social ladder until she can afford to have "help" and belong to the most exclusive women's club. They are Scotch and Presbyterian, faithful members of the church, and much of their lives is taken up with gossip and refreshments—getting out and putting away the good silver and the china plates. Annie has done right well to marry Fred Ferguson. If he can never fully comprehend nor appreciate his wife—which at times hurts her deeply—still, she tells herself, Fred is a good provider and as fine a husband as any woman could hope to have.

Though Margaret does not want to teach, she seizes the opportunity to attend the normal school near by because it offers her some means of escape. Once there, however, she is bitter and lonely, and again chooses the wrong friends. When she tells a lie to help a girl elope, Margaret is suspended by the dean of women and sent home with "failure" added to her already keen frustration.

Her father reprimands her severely for this "disgrace," and as her relations with her family become more and more strained, she is more unhappy than ever. She finds some solace in books: she has always been "such a reader." [64] "The discovery of the 'dark lady' was the one thing she had got out of that dreadful old Shakespeare class where all they ever did was read the different speeches and then 'tell the meaning in their own words.' " [65] Now she reads more than ever: "her own personal, intimate favorites—Marie Bashkirtseff, and *Wuthering Heights*, and Mrs. Gaskell's *Charlotte Brontë*, because in the seclusion and stormy emotions of the Yorkshire sisters she felt some of her own loneliness and rebellion." She also likes some of the *Sonnets from the Portuguese*, excepting "those that talked about God and the angels." [66]

To make things appear a little more settled, she takes a small job in the library. It "was tedious . . . but it was a refuge": [67]

She couldn't actually make herself intend to be a librarian. But after the things Sibyl had said about the girls who wanted to be teachers, she couldn't bear to think of teaching. Besides, being a teacher, always made Margaret afraid that she would get to be like Fannie Allison, who had taught the third grade ever since anyone in Belmond could remember, who stuck little net yokes into her collarless dresses, and who lived with her brother and his wife and took care of the children when they went to card parties.[68]

She is unhappy in the library after a time also, but it is her sister's wedding which makes her existence in Belmond intolerable. Margaret can see herself "getting older and older, a spinster daughter and a fixture in the house!" [69] "Somehow she had to escape from that humiliating superiority of married women"; [70] she "could not stand the humiliation of her innocence any longer." [71] "She wanted to get away from the places that kept the sense of failure alive in her—that made her as she had always been, and yet knew she wasn't." [72] "She had had her little triumphs, but they had all been the wrong ones." [73]

Her consolation, however, is her dream of romance: her dream "of herself in marvelous clothes and long earrings, coming back to Belmond (from say, New York)—not to stay, of course!—but interesting and a little weary, after a life of passionate, tragic and glorious experience." [74] She fancies herself attracted by, and attractive to, several of the more glamorous and successful men in Belmond and weaves fantasies out of wondering what it would be like "if they knew she loved them." This was reasonably satisfying, for, she tells herself, she is not interested in marriage.

Regular marriage meant being like the folks, presenting a united front to the world, neither one doing as he or she wanted to do. Or like Aunt Ella and Uncle Ben, stuck together and forever bickering. Or like Grandma and Grandpa, who had always seemed to think that young people when they reached a certain age must just naturally get married unless there was 'something the matter with them,' and then the next step was to begin raising a family. . . . Marriage, Margaret had always thought of as just the end.[75]

After a time, she conceives the plausible idea of going to New York to take a library course at Columbia, where she can stay with some people who used to live in Belmond. The plan meets with the approval of her family. Once in New York, she carries on her library work "with meticulous competence" for a little while, but as she becomes more and more restless, her friends begin "to be a little doubtful." [76]

Greenwich Village attracts her, and in a tearoom she meets a girl whom she used to know back home, an odd girl she had called "Squirrel Eyes," who came "from the wrong part of town." The two remember each other in New York, and presently Margaret begins to be included in the "aristocracy of exile." [77] She bobs her hair, moves into a cellar apartment with a green door, and at a gay party she is re-christened "with a few drops of gin on her head." Hence-forth, she is to be called "Margot."

After a few casual experiments with men, she meets Bruce Williams, older and handsome and sophisticated, who fulfills her romantic dream. When Margot finds him, he is in "the dry rut of existence," and the two establish a liaison upon congenial terms. The fact that Bruce already has a wife and two children does not deter them because Margot has always maintained that marriage is no part of her plan. Here she feels more at home than she had ever been. Now, "when she was thirty," and for the first time, her stark dark beauty is admired. "She was coming into her blooming." [78]

Partly at her wish, partly to shield themselves from dis-covery, Bruce takes Margot on a vacation to the Southwest. For a time, she believes herself to be happy: then they meet a mutual friend from New York and Bruce gradually regains his sense of duty to return to his family. As Margot con-templates his leaving her, she realizes that her emotions are more deeply involved than she had thought. For the first time in her life she longs for the permanence and security of marriage. She could even see "why women want children—of someone they really love." [79]

Bruce offers to keep Margot where she is, but she is un-willing to accept more of his favors, and when he returns to the East, she goes back to Belmond—back home again worse than lonely; "thin, bitter, proud." Now "she was re-turning home after what she used to think of as a great, tragic experience . . . but this was how it really felt. She had taken her love for what it was—anyway, for a time—now it left her to this blackness." [80] And "she was still the spinster daughter." [81]

Obviously, she cannot stay in Belmond. She is uneasy with her family, and they, then more than ever, eye her with bewilderment and suspicion. She goes back to New

York, uses all her wiles to win her lover back, and the reader assumes, as the story ends, that their unconventional alliance will continue on the same basis as before.

Margaret "loved him unwillingly for his conscientiousness, aware of her own ruthless lack of scruples." [82] She had neither the strength nor the will to resist what she knew to be a far from satisfactory way of life. She is drawn irresistibly, she can no longer dream of happiness to come; rather she knows that the pattern of life she has chosen will yield diminishing returns as times goes on. Her life in bondage to this man who can offer her nothing more than he had given, she cannot choose but to go on as she had been, continuing to be his mistress, "recovering life on what terms they could." [83]

Margaret Ferguson has several points in common with Jennie Gerhardt, Mattie Silver, and Meta Beggs, who precede her. Like them, she becomes involved in an emotional relationship of an unconventional pattern. Like them, she is faced with the necessity of earning her own living, though not quite such grim necessity as the others experienced. To have remained with her family, who were well-enough established financially to provide for her, would mean either conforming to the mores of the small town, which is intolerable to her, or bringing "disgrace" upon her folks, which would have been intolerable to them. Like Jennie, and all the other single-woman characters previously analyzed, she has a strongly fundamentalist religious background which apparently offers her no positive values.

Like Jennie Gerhardt (and presumably Meta Beggs, also), Margaret goes to New York where she can live in a manner not acceptable to the smaller community. Her spirit of rebellion—in this, like Meta Beggs—turns against a genteel profession at which she is equipped to earn an honest living; not that she does not enjoy being a librarian, but rather that it places limitations upon her social life. Her personal alliance, which resembles that of Jennie Gerhardt in certain respects, differs markedly, however, in that Jennie is drawn into the relationship under the promise of marriage and the need and wish to provide for her child and her destitute family, while Margaret Ferguson realizes from the beginning that the man to whom she has given herself is already married and can offer her nothing except himself and his affection. Jennie yearns for the security and respectability of marriage; Margaret has no desire for what she calls the mediocrity of marriage, and only later realizes that it might offer certain advantages even to her. For her, as for Jennie, there seems no bright future ahead, just as there can be nothing but more suffering and eventual death for Mattie Silver, and quite possibly for Meta Beggs also.

Margaret Ferguson's story parallels that of Meta Beggs particularly in the force and nature of her rebellion, and in this they are nearly unique among all the single women of the study. Both rebel against the small town, against middle-class morality, against their respectable professions, against the limitations of every sort which their communities place upon them. Both have a deep yearning for an indefinable something they call "life," both flee to the large city to seek for it, but being women conspicuously lacking in talent and stamina, find neither success nor satisfaction there.

RACHEL INNES

The Circular Staircase is a worthy representative of the work of a popular novelist, Mary Roberts Rinehart. This novel is of interest in this investigation in that it presents a single woman in a role which has become familiar to millions of readers who find recreation in this kind of tale: the woman who becomes involved in an intricate series of events and emerges as the unwitting heroine who solves the mystery.

Why a spinster should be the "last person" the reader would suspect of having committed the crime or of possessing strategic information leading to its solution may be worthy of brief consideration. The situation probably implies either a supposed innocence of mind verging upon stupidity or a vein of cleverness for which she has not previously been given due credit. If she is flighty or jittery or swoons at the sight of the corpse or asks inane and apparently meaningless questions, she lends herself all the better as a device for heightening the mystery. Rachel Innes is perhaps a little more intelligent, more stable, and more astute than many of her descendants in mystery fiction, but, in general, she is the prototype of what has become a familiar pattern.

This novel is of interest also in presenting a secondary character which is representative of a group. Here she is Liddy Allen, a spinster of approximately the same age as Rachel, who occupies the dependent position of housekeeper but is also Rachel's constant and loyal companion. In this instance, Liddy is foil to Rachel; it is Liddy who shrieks and faints, and Rachel who loses patience with her. As housekeeper, Liddy is far from efficient, but in her inability to get along with the cook and the butler she contributes to the series of new servants who subsequently become suspect in the mystery. Although a good deal of banter and gentle sarcasm passes between them, Rachel and Liddy are warmly devoted to each other. Theirs is a spinster-to-spinster relationship which is likewise a familiar pattern in American fiction.

So far as the story is concerned, this mystery tale is hardly unlike hundreds of others, except that it is among the originals instead of the imitators. Here is the baffling murder, the missing cufflink, the strange woman, the stolen money, the broken mirror, the faithful clock which stops mysteriously, the architectural peculiarities of the hidden room, and here, the circular staircase. The author makes all the familiar uses of coincidence, but what the tale may lack in conviction it supplies in dynamic action and a pleasing, humorous style.

In an early paragraph, Rachel Innes, the central character

and narrator, not only introduces herself but also sets the pace for the rapid complications which are to follow:

This is the story of how a middle-aged spinster lost her mind, deserted her domestic gods in the city, took a furnished house for the summer out of town, and found herself involved in one of those mysterious crimes that keep our newspapers and detective agencies happy and prosperous. For twenty years I have been perfectly comfortable; for twenty years I had had the window-boxes filled in the spring, the carpets lifted, the awnings put up and the furniture covered with brown linen; for as many summers I had said good-by to my friends, and, after watching their perspiring hegira, had settled down to a delicious quiet in town, where the mail comes three times a day, and the water supply does not depend on a tank on the roof.[84]

The Innes family is well-to-do. "Sunnyside," the summer place where the strange events occur, is a house of "twenty-two rooms and five baths," [85] and usually carries a staff of several servants.[86] When the plot quickens, Rachel wishes someone could tell her where she can find her "four-thousand-dollar motor-car." [87] As guardian of her brother's two children, she "sent them to good schools, managed their finances, and brought Gertrude out!" The winter of the latter event, Rachel recalls, was "nothing but a succession of sitting up late at night to bring her home from things, taking her to the dressmakers between naps the next day, and discouraging ineligible youths with either more money than brains, or more brains than money." [88] At one time during the unraveling of the mystery, the Innes family fortune is in jeopardy.

Rachel says little about her early life but establishes her social position by declaring herself as a "granddaughter of old John Innes of Revolutionary days, a D.A.R., a Colonial Dame." [89] Rather wistfully she recalls that thirty years before she had known a young fellow "straightforward, honest, and willing to sacrifice everything for the one woman, but he died a long time ago." Rachel seems reconciled enough, however, to life as she has found it, for she adds, "And sometimes I take out his picture, with its cane and its queer silk hat, and look at it. But of late years it has grown too painful: he is always a boy—and I am an old woman. But I would not bring him back if I could." [90]

In her wide range of interests, Rachel Innes is rather a remarkable woman. A detective credits her with having "too much intelligence." [91] She reads herself to sleep (on one occasion, at least) with Drummond's *Spiritual Life*.[92] In quieter moments she turns to her knitting, revealing that she had brought along to the country house "two dozen pairs of slipper soles in assorted sizes" and remarking that she always sends knitted slippers to the Old Ladies' Home at Christmas.[93] She observes that the detective with whom she spends a good deal of time while they work together toward solving the mystery "played a fair game of cribbage, but he cheated at solitaire," [94] implying that she was familiar with the rules of both games. She has her frailer moments, however, for while she repeatedly prides herself upon not being nervous, she admits that she is afraid of revolvers.[95]

Certain other details in the description of Rachel Innes are of interest in connection with the composite portrait of the spinster in fiction. For example, she owns a black cat named Beulah.[96] Rachel is an aunt, having reared the niece and nephew who figure prominently in the plot. She credits her foster-motherhood with having done much to bring her a sophistication and modern point of view previously lacking. Among other things, she says, she learned "to say *lingerie* for undergarments, 'frocks' and 'gowns' instead of dresses, and that beardless sophomores are not college boys, but college men." [97] She still believes, however, that "smoking is a filthy and injurious habit," [98] cannot understand why "certain men cling to a messy upper lip that must get into things," or why "women build up their hair on wire atrocities." [99]

Rachel, characteristically, has a quick wit and a sense of humor, qualities which rarely appear in the analysis of the single women studied. On one occasion she comments, "Strange it must have seemed to Halsey [her nephew] to come across me in the middle of the night, with the skirt of my gray gown over my shoulders to keep off the dew, holding a red and green basket under one arm and a black cat under the other." [100] And again, she realizes she has neglected to remove her wrinkle eradicators, "and I presume my appearance was very odd. I believe it is a woman's duty to care for her looks, but it is much like telling a necessary falsehood—one must not be found out." [101]

It is in the relationship between Rachel and Liddy Allen that the personalities of the two women are more clearly delineated, for they are shown in sharp contrast to each other. Rachel is a large woman; Liddy is small.[102] Rachel is wealthy; Liddy is economically dependent upon her mistress. Rachel is the gentlewoman; Liddy is less cultured. Liddy is superstitious, but Rachel merely laughs at Liddy's concern over such things as broken mirrors.[103] Rachel shows herself to be remarkably shrewd and adroit; Liddy is altogether inefficient. Rachel says of her, "She is a very unreliable person: always awake and ready to talk when she isn't wanted and dozing off to sleep when she is." [104] Rachel often prods Liddy by referring to the latter's age. At one time Rachel says of her companion, "she owns to forty—which is absurd . . . [she] must be at least as old as I." [105] At another time, "A woman of your age ought to have better sense," says Rachel.[106] And again, "Go right in and change your clothes," Rachel says to Liddy, sharply. "You're a sight, and at your age!" [107] The reader does not know exactly how old either of the women is, though Rachel at the end of the summer remarks that she is "an elderly woman with an increasing tendency to live in the past." [108]

The relationship between Rachel and Liddy has existed over many years. Liddy's mother cooked for Rachel's grandfather,[109] and there is every reason to believe that the two women will spend the rest of their days together. Liddy calls her mistress "Miss Rachel," [110] and in spite of Liddy's inefficiency and her trouble-making proclivities among the servants, Rachel is patient and forbearing. Rachel says, "sometimes Liddy threatens to leave, and often I discharge her, but we stay together somehow." [111] In fact, at the end of the novel, when the last detail of the mystery has been cleared up, and the weddings of the young lovers are being planned, Rachel anticipates that Liddy will ask her for her heliotrope poplin to wear to the church.[112]

"When I am bored," says Rachel, "I ring for Liddy, and we talk things over." At other times, "We are very quiet, just the two of us." [113]

MIRANDA SAWYER

During the decade following its publication in 1903, *Rebecca of Sunnybrook Farm* by Kate Douglas Wiggin was widely and enthusiastically received. In 1909 the stage version met with instantaneous success, and according to the publisher's note appearing in the 1910 edition, within seven years after publication the book had sold 337,000 copies, without the aid of either illustrations or sensational advertising. The publisher ranks it along with Louisa May Alcott's *Little Women*, notes that it has been translated into several languages, and comments on a point that takes on special interest at the end of a second World War with Germany: the fact that this novel "is used for English reading in the public schools of Berlin." While its literary merit may be questioned, this novel may be observed as an outstanding example of the popular fiction of its time, and presents several points of interest in the delineation of its single-woman characters.

Miranda and Jane Sawyer are the two maiden aunts with whom the little heroine, Rebecca Randall, aged ten, comes to make her home. Although the sisters are approaching sixty when the story opens, the New England village of Riverboro still calls them "the Sawyer girls." Rebecca's mother, their sister Aurelia, had made what she called "a romantic marriage," but what her sisters would have called "a mighty poor speculation." "There's worse things than being old maids," they say, reflecting upon poor Aurelia's sad fate, but the author adds, "whether they thought so or not is quite another matter." [114]

Miranda is the more aggressive of the two sisters, and therefore the major character. In the words of the novelist,

She was just, conscientious, economical, industrious; a regular attendant at church and Sunday-school, and a member of the State Missionary and Bible societies, but in the presence of all these chilly virtues you longed for one warm little fault, or lacking that, one likeable failing, something to make sure she was thoroughly alive.[115]

The child Rebecca has a difficult time at the hands of the unyielding Aunt Miranda. How can she succeed, Rebecca wonders, when she can never be herself in her Aunt Miranda's presence? It is chiefly through the little girl's eyes that the reader sees the older woman:

The searching look of the eyes, the sharp voice, the hard knotty fingers, the thin straight lips, the long silences, the "front-piece" that didn't match her hair, the very obvious "parting" that seemed sewed in with linen thread on black net,—there was not a single item that appealed to Rebecca.[116]

In a more general appraisal, the author classifies Aunt Miranda as one of those "narrow, unimaginative, and autocratic old people who seem to call out the most mischievous, and sometimes the worst traits in children. Miss Miranda, had she lived in a populous neighborhood, would have had her doorbell pulled, her gate tied up, and 'dirt traps' set in her garden paths." [117]

Miranda not only has little patience with the child, but has even less with her sister Jane. "You're soft, Jane," Miranda tells her on one occasion, "You allers was soft, and you allers will be. If it wa'n't for me keepin' you stiffened up, I b'lieve you'd leak out o' the house into the dooryard." [118] The reader soon concludes, however, in spite of Miranda's harsh judgment, that Jane is by far the more lovable of the sisters. Jane has had the advantage of a better education. She has gone to an academy, and also to a boarding school for young ladies, which may have given her her "soft," gracious manner of gentility. But this, in itself, according to the author, is not the only reason. For Jane has had "the inestimable advantage of a sorrow." [119]

Jane's "lost love" is not only representative of a number of similar episodes found in the fiction studied, but also, in this instance, points up a certain note of contrast between the Sawyer sisters. As the story goes, Jane was engaged to marry young Tom Carter. Then came the Civil War. When word was received that Tom was wounded, Jane packed her trunk, and "without so much as asking Miranda's leave," [120] she started for the South. After Tom died, Jane stayed on and nursed other soldiers, "for Tom's dear sake," and "it sent her home a better woman." [121]

The novelist's comment upon the social as well as the psychological effect of Jane's experience is noteworthy. The social advantage of her sorrow is thus made more clear:

Though she had never left Riverboro in all the years that lay between, and grown in to the counterfeit presentment of her sister and of all other thin, spare, New England spinsters, it was something of a counterfeit, and underneath was still the faint echo of that wild heartbeat of her girlhood. Having learned the trick of beating and loving and suffering, the poor faithful heart persisted, although it lived on memories and carried on its sentimental operations mostly in secret.[122]

Miranda, thus inadvertently characterized with "all other thin, spare, New England spinsters," had not had the educational advantages of her sister Jane. Miranda attended only the neighborhood district school, and she seemed to have no desire or ambition beyond the management of the house, the farm, and the dairy. Miranda's rustic manner is constantly in contrast with Jane's gracious manner, and is emphasized especially by her careless errors of speech. The two sisters had taken care of their parents as long as they had lived, then had inherited the farm and continued to live on in the big old house. In spite of her severity and impatience with her sister and little Rebecca, Aunt Miranda, as the story ends and she approaches her death, is shown to have a heart of gold; she wants to be sure that the family property will become Rebecca's after Jane is gone.

This novel, for all its sentimentalism, brings to attention several points worthy of mention in connection with the analysis of the lives of single women in fiction. First is the fact that Miranda and Jane Sawyer are representative of a considerable group of maiden sisters. They are typical in that they are strongly contrasted in personality, as well as in education and experience. It is Jane, the "softer" one, who has had the advantage of a tragic love affair, while Miranda, who has never known romantic love, is portrayed as possessing the shrewish disposition. Second, the sisters are typical in that they continue to live in the old family home and on a meager income inherited from their parents.

Their contrasting personalities are also typical of the group of unmarried sisters. Miranda is tall; Jane is slighter of build. Miranda's voice is sharp and shrill; Jane is soft-spoken. Miranda is the good manager; Jane is less efficient. Miranda has many good qualities, but they are "chilly virtues." Jane,

in Miranda's eyes, at least, is full of faults, but she is portrayed by the novelist as the more appealing of the two women.

Miranda offers also, in a few details, at least, an interesting contrast with Rachel Innes of Mary Roberts Rinehart's *The Circular Staircase*. Both Miranda and Rachel are tall, strong, capable women. Both are shrewd and calculating and meet the tasks that face them with remarkable efficiency. Both have a certain missionary conscience. It is in their sense of humor—a quality noticeably lacking among the single women as a group—that they differ markedly. Rachel is amused at how she must have appeared when discovered with her wrinkle eradicators on her face, while Miranda, apparently, sees nothing humorous in her false hair arrangement and in her efforts thus to be more personable.

Here, in summary, are the seven major characters of the 150 single women appearing in 125 representative American novels. Two of the women, Hepzibah Pyncheon and Mattie Silver, are financially, and therefore emotionally, dependent; the former ends her days happier and more secure, while the latter can see only more unhappiness ahead. Meta Beggs and Margaret Ferguson are women in whom rebellion is strongest. Both try to make their way in respectable professions, but are not well adapted to conventional life. The other four know how to do nothing except domestic tasks, and two, Hepzibah Pyncheon and Mattie Silver, are notably inefficient at those. Miranda Sawyer, being more resourceful, manages to make a comfortable living for herself, her sister Jane, and her niece Rebecca. Six of the seven women are first met in small towns or cities, though three of the six, Jennie Gerhardt, Meta Beggs, and Margaret Ferguson, eventually migrate to larger, metropolitan centers. All are distinctly middle-class, though one, Rachel Innes, possesses some degree of wealth and luxury, and Hepzibah Pyncheon regains the family fortune in her old age. Mattie Silver, as a

girl, is described as small of stature, but all the others are tall, sturdy women, most of them also thin and gaunt. Not one of the seven women is successful in an endeavor of her own; not one is widely and wholesomely influential. All are regarded as amusing, queer, or grimly tragic figures.

The Analysis

In 85 of the 125 novels which are the central data of this investigation, 150 single-woman characters appear—women who have not married by the age of thirty and who do not marry or plan to marry during the course of the novel.

At first glance, it may seem significant that 40 of the 125 novels contain no identifiable character of this kind, but on further analysis it was found that only 12 of the 64 individual authors represented had not somewhere portrayed such a character. Most of the authors (four fifths of the authors as compared with two thirds of the novels) include one or more single women in some of their works of fiction. In his *Elsie Venner*, Oliver Wendell Holmes presents no single woman whom he clearly indicates as past thirty and unmarried, but in *The Guardian Angel* there are two such characters. Willa Cather omits single women in *A Lost Lady*, but her other novels contain a generous number. Edward Eggleston's *Hoosier School Boy* contains none, but *The Hoosier Schoolmaster* presents the well-drawn character of Miss Nancy Sawyer. This seems to indicate that the large majority of novelists were aware of the single woman in the society of their day and saw fit to include her in some part of their writing.

On the basis of either the novels or the novelists, therefore, one must reach the same conclusion—and this may be stated as the first conclusion of the study: single women have appeared in considerable numbers in American fiction.

Names of the single-woman characters.—Names of the single-woman characters, in the light of the study as a whole,

may be said to carry some significance. It would be out of place to assume that one name is superior to another, but it is undoubtedly a fact that most novelists give some thought to the name of a character, being sensitive, as they must be, to the connotation it may have with their readers. Names, for example, like Hepzibah Pyncheon, of Hawthorne's *The House of the Seven Gables,* or the three sisters, Seena, Texanna, and Tabitha Sneed, who appear in Ellen Glasgow's *Barren Ground,* could hardly have been chosen without some conscious thought or purpose. Selina Tibbs, Melissa Busteed, Euphrasia Cotton, Zillah Saunders, Kesiah Blount, Anastasia O'Hern, Olinda Pepper, and Octavia Hiatt likewise may be said to be strange and unfamiliar names.

Some of the names have a quality of quaintness about them. Among them are old names which have never gone out of fashion and others which have taken on a new vogue. Names such as Mary, Ann, Sally, Martha, Sarah, Jane, and Nancy, all of which appear in the list, may be considered of the former variety. One might expect a certain quaintness in the names of characters appearing in novels published many decades ago, but one might venture that Abigail, Miranda, Saidie, Temperance, Eliza, Jemima, Hortense, Liddy, Beckie, Amanda, Essie, Etta, and Mattie, though once perhaps common and acceptable, would hardly be considered particularly desirable names to modern readers or parents.

Certain names which occur more than once suggest certain interesting similarities which may further indicate their connotative quality. Two single-woman characters named Tillie occupy subservient positions. Two named Priscilla are schoolteachers. Two named Rachel are rich. Both women named Marietta are amusing individuals. Two of three women named Althea are given to malicious gossiping. Two named Amelia are exceedingly proud.

Scanning the whole roster of 150 names, one finds few

which could be said to be either attractive or desirable. Few convey anything of a "romantic" quality. The preponderance of quaint, odd-sounding, if not to say peculiar, names is impressive, and one seems justified in concluding that they may reveal some bias on the part of novelists which they, in turn, have wished to convey to their readers.

Age.—By far the majority of the single-woman characters are thirty years of age or older when they first appear in the novel. Some are very old, but most are middle-aged. To be more specific, 133 of the 150 are beyond thirty when the story opens. Ten appear from early maturity (defined for the present purpose as twenty-five years of age) but are past thirty by the end of the novel. Only six appear in adolescence, and only one is introduced as a child and grows to maturity as the novel proceeds.

Prominence in the plot.—Of the 150 single women the study considers, a total of 143 are minor characters in the novels in which they appear. About one third of these exert some influence upon the main characters, but most of them have little or no influence upon anyone. A number seem to have been included by the novelists merely to furnish local color or comic relief. A few others act as a pivot in the plot but are not otherwise important. A device of the novelist, used often enough to be noticeable, is to have the town gossip, often a single woman, prattle information necessary to the denouement of the plot. These are sometimes post office clerks who read mail intended for others; sometimes dressmakers who go from family to family carrying the common talk of the community. Most of these, however, are minor characters.

Only six of the 150 characters are major characters in the novel. One is not only major, but her name is also the title of the book. This is Theodore Dreiser's *Jennie Gerhardt.* A few others of the fictional single women would perhaps be considered major under a more general definition, but cannot be considered so under the present definition. The seven major characters which emerge in the analytical classification have already been considered in much detail.

The first steps of the analytical classification yield the following generalizations:

1. Single women appear frequently in the American novels under consideration.

2. The names of these women have, in many instances, a quality of quaintness, suggesting that the women themselves are quaint or peculiar individuals.

3. Most of the women are middle-aged or older when they appear in the novel.

4. All except seven are minor characters.

CHILDHOOD AND ADOLESCENCE

Since most of the single-woman characters are past thirty years of age when they enter the story, the analysis of factors under *Childhood and Adolescence* revealed little. As has been stated previously, this category, as planned, included five factors: family pattern, socioeconomic background, kind of education received, factors in choice of vocation, and the nature of early heterosexual relationships. But since so few of the characters appear as children or adolescents, and the information in these five categories is so scant, several of these factors were almost lost sight of as the classification proceeded.

In some instances, although the woman does not appear except as middle-aged, the reader is given an occasional glimpse of her early life. A few who are rich remember the day when they were poor, and vice versa. One or two teachers declare that they chose their vocation because it seemed the most genteel profession for young ladies, or because it was the easiest way to earn a living. Some of the novelists explain that the single woman they present had lost a lover in her youth; others, that the woman had never had a lover;

but such comment cited briefly, and only in retrospect, could hardly be tabulated.

Some information concerning the youth of the single woman could occasionally be inferred, but again, this could hardly be regarded as explicit fact. If a woman in adult life has brothers and sisters, it is a fairly safe conjecture that she grew up with them. If she becomes a teacher, one might infer that she is at least literate. If she is a seamstress, she may have acquired her skill through some kind of apprenticeship. On the whole, however, the kind of information one would hope to find about the childhood or the adolescent years of these fictive women is conspicuously lacking. It seemed better, therefore, to consider the exceptions as such than to carry into tabular form an almost empty classification.

Of the seven single-woman characters whom the reader sees in childhood or adolescence, three are major characters and have been discussed in detail. These are Theodore Dreiser's Jennie Gerhardt; Margaret (Margot) Ferguson of Ruth Suckow's novel, *The Folks;* and Mattie Silver, one of the three main characters of Edith Wharton's *Ethan Frome.*

Two appear in some detail, but are minor characters. In Willa Cather's *My Ántonia*, Lena Lingard and Tiny Soderball are Scandinavian farm girls who come to the Nebraska village as domestic workers and there become friends of Antonia and the narrator, Jim Burden. Lena shuns marriage because, as she says, she has "seen too much of it" as one of a large, hard-working, impoverished family. In the village and later in the city, she lives loosely though she is successful as a dress designer for a wealthy clientele. Tiny begins as a waitress in the village boardinghouse, has a dramatic experience in the Klondike, and in a somewhat devious way, accumulates a fortune. The reader last hears of the two women living together in San Francisco.

The remaining two are promiscuous in their relationships with men. Judith Feldt of Joseph Hergesheimer's *Linda*

Condon is one of a wealthy family devoted to the arts. Her silly emotionalism is revealed in vulgar contrast to the exquisite restraint of the heroine. Dixie Lee, first seen as a young girl who beats the hero to a claim in the exciting landrace in Edna Ferber's *Cimarron*, later becomes a prostitute in the Oklahoma frontier town. She is said to have come from "decayed Southern aristocracy," but becomes financially successful in her notorious profession.

AMBITION AND ACHIEVEMENT

Many of the single women in the novels are characterized by lack of expressed ambition. In 64 characters there is no evidence of any ambition to change or improve their status. They merely enter the story, appear briefly, and remain as they were.

Central ambition.—The most frequently recurring ambition, when ambition is evident, is altruistic. Twenty-two want to help some friend achieve his or her goal, and 14 want to help some one of their immediate family or a more distant relative. Two are zealously bent upon improving their community according to their own ideas, one upon becoming socially important. Not one is concerned with being merely accepted.

Fourteen, a considerably smaller number than one might have expected, express a desire for a husband, children, or a home. This may be partly attributed to the fact that so many of the women are past the age when this ambition is likely to be fulfilled; also that such desires are not freely expressed.

Twelve wish to become financially secure, and five others are struggling to extricate themselves from emotional and economic dependency. Considering the fact that many single women in the past were economically dependent, one may venture that this is a significantly small number to be expressly concerned with improving their financial status.

A very small number show any evidence of vocational

ambition. Career, in its present-day interpretation, is not a matter of concern to the fiction women, but here the picture is quite in accord with the vocational pattern of the times in which they lived. Only four are obviously struggling to get ahead in their respective careers.

In 19 instances, a distinguishable ambition can be detected, but of an individual kind which could hardly have been anticipated. Selina Tibbs of Booth Tarkington's *The Gentleman from Indiana* has a consuming desire to have her romantic verses printed in her local weekly newspaper, and in Willa Cather's *Lucy Gayheart*, the older, practical-minded Pauline wants her more attractive sister Lucy to marry the banker's son and thus bring the improvident, music-loving Gayheart family greater financial security.[123]

Nature of frustrating circumstances.—Since ambition is not strong among the single women studied, circumstances are not greatly frustrating. Unless one actually struggles to achieve some goal, he is not likely to be aware of the obstacles which stand in his way.

In the large majority, no evidence of frustration is revealed. When frustration is expressed, the lack of money is most often indicated. Nineteen feel handicapped in achieving their ambition for that reason, though as the earlier analysis of ambition showed, most of them wish for more money, not for themselves, but to give to someone else to enable him to achieve some ambition of his own.

Significantly small numbers feel other kinds of frustration. In three instances, adult domination prevents achievement. Five feel thwarted by tradition, family or otherwise. Four feel that their social position is a deterring factor. Six have one or more dependents, needing either actual care or economic support. Six are themselves wholly dependent, victims of partial or complete invalidism. No one believes herself to be handicapped because of the lack of training to realize a vocational goal, this being consistently in line with the lack of vocational ambition.

In 24 cases, frustration of some kind is present but could not be classified. Hepzibah Pyncheon's whole life, as told in Hawthorne's *The House of the Seven Gables,* seems overshadowed by the curse she believes had been placed upon her ancestor. Anneke DeVoe of Paul Leicester Ford's *The Honourable Peter Stirling* thinks her parents restricted her social life too severely when she was young. Miss Thomasia Gray, the genteel aunt in Thomas Nelson Page's *Red Rock,* cannot bring herself to marry her aging but persistent suitor because of her loyalty to a lover of her younger days.

Nature of success and failure.—The nature of success and the nature of failure among the single women, though analyzed separately, seem more revealing if summarized together, one as the antithesis of the other. In the portrayal of the lives of the majority, neither success nor failure is dominant. As has been shown, most of the women have no ambition to attain a specific goal; therefore one can hardly say that they succeeded or that they failed. Consequently, in 76 instances in the analysis of success and 119 in the analysis of failure, neither one nor the other can be recognized.

The vocational situation continues to be consistent with that previously noted. Twelve meet some degree of success by advancing in their careers, while five others, either through their own devices or otherwise, become financially independent. None of those engaged in a gainful occupation can be said to have failed utterly, but one becomes financially dependent and three others become ill, desperately lonely, or otherwise distressed.

Twenty-two, the greatest number in the analysis of success, derive their happiness—which is to say, their success—from seeing someone else succeed. Similarly 15, the greatest number in the analysis of failure, definitely express a wish to marry, but fail to achieve marriage.

Smaller groups of responses account for the others. Nine succeed in relieving themselves of frustrating circumstances. Five achieve a place in the community to which they aspire. Only one fails noticeably to get along with those with whom she lives.

A similar number in the analysis of success as in that of failure, 25 in each instance, meet success or failure in ways which the classification did not predict. Two characters, appearing in two of Ellen Glasgow's novels, aptly illustrate. Angela Wilde in *The Wheel of Life* succeeds in her strange desire to remain a recluse for forty years to atone for her early disgrace. At the other extreme, Kesiah Blount of *The Miller of Old Church* fails to become an artist because she was never allowed to begin her career.

Interest in her community.—Analysis of the concern that single women of fiction take in their community reveals an interesting situation. The investigator hoped to discover whether the single women were portrayed as wielding an influence in their communities or whether they lived narrow, self-centered lives. What comes to light, however, is that many of these women do take an active interest in the affairs of their neighbors, but it is by no means a constructive interest. They are the purveyors of gossip, ferreting out and spreading scandal. These women generally live alone but work at some humble task which places them in an advantageous position to hear of *sub rosa* activities. This unpredicted situation—in itself a major discovery—made it difficult to classify the factor of "interest in community" in the lives of the fictional women. Many of those who were judged to be active are of this unwholesome variety, being both sought after and feared.

Those who are inactive could be more easily classified. Thirty-seven limit their interests to one individual, their home, or their immediate family group. Two others live alone and are completely self-centered. Three express some wish to take part in neighborhood affairs, but are held down by frustrating circumstances. Three long to leave where they are and go elsewhere to a place where they believe they might be more influential. These, in the aggregate, account for approximately one third of the women studied.

Within the larger group who in some way reach out into the lives of others beyond their own family, several lesser groups emerge, though for reasons explained above, they were not numerically classified. By far the largest of the subgroups are the town gossips who hold an active interest but of a destructive kind. Frequently they are dressmakers, though sometimes, domestics or charwomen. A few work in the village post office, also a point of vantage for keeping informed of scandalous activities.

Another small group is made up of women who are active in the suffrage movement, but whose activities are regarded with ridicule. These women distribute pamphlets and sometimes march in parades, but invariably they are looked upon with ridicule. Whether their interest is constructive or otherwise may be a matter of opinion, but in their own time and place they are considered as queer individuals and a general nuisance. Some are even judged to be dangerous in their evil influence, and a few actually fall martyrs to the Cause.

The schoolteachers, one might assume, by the very nature of their position, to be actively interested in the families of the children they teach, and that they would comprise a wholesome, active group. While this, in general, is found to be true, such a sweeping assumption is not justified. In a few instances, the influence of a teacher is definitely destructive.

Another small group is composed of the well-born women of means who devote themselves in an amateur fashion to some local charitable enterprise. These women are respected and their philanthropy is appreciated by the unfortunates who benefit by it, but they generally go about their duties in the dignified, quiet, and aloof manner befitting their station, and are seldom persons who otherwise exert what could be called an influence.

Seventeen of the single women show a miscellany of interests in their communities which could not be classified. Aunt Meggie Fincastle of Ellen Glasgow's *Vein of Iron* is a homebody, but she unfailingly carries a bowl of broth to the sick and lends her capable hand in any emergency. The rich and cultured Miss Norton in Louisa May Alcott's *Little Women* attends uplifting lectures and concerts but takes no active part in them.

The most significant finding which comes to light in this classification is the small number of single women who occupy a position of wide importance or constructive influence. Not one holds a public office and not more than five or six could be said to be important persons in their communities.

Adult vocation.—The analysis of vocation proved to be one of the most interesting categories of the classification. Slightly more than half the women studied have no vocation in the present-day sense of the word. Fifty-two live upon what might be called "invisible means," which is to say that the novelist gives no explanation as to how they manage to exist. In some cases, the author states that the woman lives on a small income, but does not explain how it had been established. Many of these women continue to live in the family home after the parents die, so one might reasonably assume they have inherited some money along with their place of residence. Generally, the women manage and keep their own houses, though a few have one or more servants.[124] In the South, particularly, there is evidence that relatives provide for indigent members of the family, but it seems to have been not quite respectable to let such private matters be divulged.

Fifteen of the women are more obviously dependent. These, for the most part, live in the household of a relative as a kind of indentured servant and work to pay for their maintenance. A few are respected, but most of them are merely tolerated. Concerning eight others, the novelist gives no clue as to how they manage to live, so they also had to be classified along with the other two groups as having no vocation.

The fact that so many of these women have no vocation may be said to be in keeping with the times in which they lived—a time when in real life few women had a vocation beyond the home. This is not so surprising, therefore, nor so significant, as the vocational picture of the women who did work for their living.

It had been anticipated that a rather fine distinction among vocations would be possible. While this did not prove to be so, the over-all picture is clear enough. A total of 47 are unquestionably modest and humble, as compared with 24 whose work could be called ordinary or, perhaps, important. The former group is largely composed of seamstresses, domestics, child-nurses and governesses, charwomen and other odd-job workers, while the schoolteachers comprise the largest unit among the 24. The numerical picture, however, is somewhat more favorable than is actually justified. The teachers were all presumed to be important, yet some of them are really extremely humble persons, possessing neither superior ability nor importance of any kind. This situation is partly balanced by the fact that a few women show superior skill in modest occupations. Two who illustrate this point aptly were mentioned previously in another connection: Tiny Soderball makes a fortune out of running a boardinghouse, and her friend Lena Lingard is unusually successful at dressmaking. Both these women appear in Willa Cather's *My Ántonia*. Only ten of the 150 single-woman

characters follow occupations so miscellaneous or individual
that they could not be classified. Most of these characters are
major and have already been discussed.

In its bold outline, the vocational pattern which emerges
is significant. The majority of the single women in the fiction studied have no vocation or are wholly dependent; the
next largest group occupy humble or modest positions;
while an extremely small group, even on the basis of a very
favorable estimate, are portrayed as occupying positions of
importance.

Superimposing the vocational pattern, by way of summary, upon the results of the other categories, previously
considered, one cannot escape certain salient factors in the
lives of the single women of fiction. Either ambition is lacking or the novelists do not consider it a sufficiently important element to portray in detail. Since ambition is not
strong, neither success nor failure is dominant, and circumstances do not seem greatly frustrating. A considerable
number are interested in their communities, some carrying
gossip, some engaging in more commendable charitable activities, but only a few occupy places of unquestioned respect or wide constructive influence.

RELATIONSHIPS

The analysis of *Human Relationships* was an effort to discover the relationship of the single woman to her family and
neighbors, her friends and her enemies. It sought to determine the objects of her animosity, and especially how she
regarded and was regarded by men among her contemporaries.

Quality of adult human relationships.—The general quality of human relationships among the single women is high.
Most of them are either well liked or get along reasonably
well with most people. A total of 89 were classified in one or
the other of these two categories. Thirty-two, the third

largest number, are such minor characters that their relationship to others could hardly be judged. Thirteen others are so highly individualized or so miscellaneous that they, likewise, did not lend themselves easily to classification.

A relationship of a negative or unfavorable kind appears in surprisingly few instances. Five are well enough liked by most of their associates but cannot get along with one or two persons. Seven have trouble with those nearest them. Three are definitely quarrelsome, and five live entirely to themselves and have no commerce with anyone.

Specific sources of tension.—In this category an attempt was made to analyze more specifically just who it was or what kind of person it was with whom the single woman in question could not get along. It was believed this item of analysis might emphasize more pointedly the personality of the woman herself. But since such unfavorable relationships existed in so few cases, this category reflected only a small proportion of the women studied.

In more specific terms, but with considerable overlapping, this classification substantiates what was stated above. In exactly two thirds of the cases, 100 out of the 150, the novelist indicates no such source of tension whatever. These are, for the most part, quietly amiable women who get along well enough with those with whom they live and venture no marked difference of opinion. This is highly characteristic of the women as a whole: they are not dynamic enough to clash with anyone.

Of those who are involved in some overtly expressed personal strife, nine direct their resentment toward men and boys, seven cannot get along with girls or women, and seven have trouble with their brothers and sisters. Five quarrel openly with one or both parents. In the less differentiated categories, six differ strongly with their contemporaries, one with her elders, one with her superiors, and one with her inferiors. Twenty-one others have sharp differences of opinion with someone but in a manner too individual to classify.

Nature of heterosexual relationships.—Investigating more pointedly the nature of adult heterosexual relationships among the single women of fiction, one finds once again that the greatest number, here a total of 66, are such minor characters that the novelist gives no clue concerning their personal relationships. Thirty-eight of the women whom the novelists portray in greater detail can be said to have no affectional relationships with the opposite sex. Eight had formed some such relationship but of a sort too miscellaneous to be classified.

Only twelve of the entire number have what might be called a natural and wholesome heterosexual relationship. Seven others who have none live under such circumstances that they have no opportunity to form such a relationship. Four are devoted to men who return their affection but cannot marry, while three spend their affection upon men who show no affection for them.

A detailed analysis of the cases which were too miscellaneous to classify reveal several who remain true to the memory of a lover of their younger days, the implication being that they could never thereafter consider marriage to another.[125]

Most significant of all, perhaps, is the small number of the single women of fiction who engage in some unconventional sex relationship. Only two, the heroine of Theodore Dreiser's novel, *Jennie Gerhardt*, and Margaret (Margot) Ferguson of Ruth Suckow's *The Folks*, form a lasting liaison without marriage, the former being the only one to bear a child out of wedlock. Only two, Flossie of *Vandover and the Brute* by Frank Norris and Dixie Lee of Edna Ferber's *Cimarron*, are prostitutes, while two others, Judith Feldt of Joseph Hergesheimer's *Linda Condon* and, probably, Lena Lingard of Willa Cather's *My Ántonia* are described as being promiscuous. Two others, appearing in novels by Ellen Glasgow, Aunt Agatha Littlepage in *They Stooped to Folly* and Angela Wilde in *The Wheel of Life*, have had unfortunate experiences in their youth from which they are never able to recover and spent their later lives in seclusion. One, Kate Chancellor of Sherwood Anderson's *Poor White*, might be called a homosexual.

In summary, therefore, the single women of the fiction studied are well liked by their friends, relatives, and neighbors, but apparently are not expected to have suitors. Only a few are shown as having a natural relationship of this kind. Some are said to have had offers of marriage when they were younger, but equally as many are said explicitly never to have had a lover. In a few instances, the poignant memory of a lost love presumably prevents any subsequent emotional attachment. In others, the novelist seems to "defend" the woman's singleness by declaring that she had in some earlier day been desirable as a wife. Yet in spite of being denied natural relationships with men, these women are a highly conventional group. Only a few—hardly ten in all—are shown as having engaged in some unconventional sex relationship.

ATTITUDES

It has become almost a commonplace assumption that a personality is largely molded by the attitude of the individual toward himself and the attitude of others toward him. If this is true, one should be able to learn much about a person if one can determine what the person thinks of himself and how other people regard him. This analysis was an effort to isolate these factors in the lives of the single women of fiction.

Attitude toward her vocation.—Since a majority of the single women of fiction have no vocation at which they earn a living, it is not surprising to discover that a similar number, 106 to be exact, make no comment or give no clue as to their attitudes toward such work.

Of those who do follow a vocation of some kind, 28 seem to find extreme pleasure in their work. Seven others find their work pleasant, but not absorbing. Four enjoy their work, but hope life may hold something more for them.

The unpleasant side of work among these women shows up only briefly. Two dislike their work intensely, and one has definitely unpleasant relations in connection with her work. Two others, notably Hepzibah Pyncheon of Hawthorne's *The House of the Seven Gables*, express ideas too difficult to classify, such as that it is a disgrace for a woman to have to work for her living.

Attitude toward marriage.—Exactly two thirds of the women express no attitude whatever toward marriage or the fact that they have not married. Added to this number are five who more properly may be said to be indifferent. This situation is partly explained, as in several previous instances, by the fact that these women are glimpsed so briefly and that they are so minor among the characters of the novel that the novelist provides no opportunity for them to express themselves. But this very fact, that the novelist has so often relegated these women to such a minor role, must in itself carry some cultural significance.

The few women who express themselves with regard to marriage show, in the main, a wholesome point of view. Twenty believe a woman should marry and ten others, that marriage is desirable, but it is not everything in life. Four believe some women should not marry, and the investigator assumed that they consider themselves in this group. Six take a stronger stand and express the idea that no woman's life can be complete without marriage, but four believe no marriage preferable to an unhappy marriage. A similarly small number are more impressed by the social than the personal aspects of marriage. Four state that they believe marriage to be a social badge of success, while six do not see why a woman should feel a sense of failure if she does not marry. Only six express some attitude which could not be classified. The selfish Meta Beggs, for example, of Joseph Hergesheimer's *Mountain Blood*, believed no marriage could bring her happiness unless it also brought her money.

It is interesting to observe that what has been variously said to have been a prevailing attitude of an earlier day does not apply to this group of women. Not one woman says she thinks *any* marriage is preferable to *no* marriage.

Attitude toward her own life.—Concerning their attitude toward life in general, the women of the study are somewhat more expressive, yet even in this realm in which everyone may be assumed to have *some* point of view, 78, or slightly more than one third of all the characters, make no comment.

Only a few, hardly more than one sixth if one were to consider every constructive element which is expressed, feel that some part of life has been good. Twelve take this wholly positive stand, while nine others feel life has been good but marriage would have enriched it. Four think their lives have been successful but sense that society does not regard them so. Three express the opposite point of view: they believe they have failed because they have not married, but that their lives are otherwise regarded as successful. A still smaller number express a more negative opinion. Two believe life would not have been good even with marriage, and two others that their lives are an utter failure. Six are best described as indifferent.

Thirty-four of the women express distinguishable attitudes, some of them vigorous enough, but of a kind too individual to classify. Rachel Arrowsmith, appearing in Zona Gale's novel entitled *Birth*, who is denied what she wants most—a baby to care for—declares she is a good deal of a failure. Kesiah Blount, of Ellen Glasgow's *The Miller of*

Old Church, who wanted to be an artist but was never allowed to develop her talent, says poignantly that she has never lived. There are other occasional hints of regret among the women; either they feel that they have been cheated of life or that life has nothing more to give.

Hardly one shows any enthusiasm for life. All things considered, Louisa Goddard of Ellen Glasgow's *They Stooped to Folly* is perhaps the outstanding example of a woman who lives a full life apart from marriage. She is a woman of inherited wealth and social position in the Virginia town who gives freely of her money and lectures in the interest of social uplift. She seldom dwells upon what life has denied her, but devotes herself wholeheartedly (however pathetically) to the wife and children of the man she loves but cannot marry.

The women whose chief concern in life is to gossip often show some enthusiasm to seek or to carry the latest scandal. Like old Miss Beal of Robert Nathan's *Autumn*, they want "to live a while longer, just looking around." The two who appear to be most nearly happy live in humble places. They are the poor dressmakers, Augusta of Willa Cather's *The Professor's House* and Miss Willy Whitlow of Ellen Glasgow's novel *Virginia*. Both are deeply religious, both live alone, both devotedly serve their employers, and both baffle their friends as to how they can be so happy on so little.

Even the negative attitudes, however, are not so impressive as the fact that the greatest number of the women in each of the three categories—attitude toward vocation, toward marriage, and toward life itself—reveal nothing at all of their attitude. Either they are presented so briefly by the novelist that they have no opportunity to speak their minds, or they are placed in such a position of emotional dependency that they dare not speak, or nobody would care what they would say even if they did speak. This spirit of resignation, of emotional stagnation, and of inarticulateness is the dominant pattern among them.

Characteristics for which others admire her.—Up to this

point the matter of *Attitudes* has been devoted to three aspects of the attitude of the woman toward herself and her own life; from this point the discussion will deal with three aspects of the attitude of others toward her. The first of these is concerned with those characteristics for which she is admired.

More of the single women are admired for their goodness of character than for any other one quality, this in line with the earlier finding that they are a highly conventional group. Thirty-nine call forth such admiration, while 31, the next highest number, are admired more specifically for their unselfishness, devotion, loyalty, or sacrifice. The latter aspect again reflects the spirit of altruism previously commented upon, and includes those women whose primary ambition is to help someone else succeed, as well as those who are devoting themselves and their resources to some work of charity.

Admiration of appearance and achievement ranks second, but in a considerably lesser number of cases. Twenty-three are classified in each of these two categories. Those who are admired for their appearance are rarely described as beautiful, but rather are admired for some one feature: their hair or eyes or hands. Achievement is interpreted here to mean either vocational or social, and as has already been shown, it is so rare a quality as to call forth admiration wherever it is found.

Seventeen, the next largest number, are admired for their pleasant disposition, thus supporting the earlier statement that many of these women are amiable and well liked. Sixteen others draw forth admiration for their courage, endurance, or patience in a difficult situation, and 12 for some kind of efficiency. The latter figure might also have included six others, listed separately, who were admired for a specific skill or handiwork. Most often this was in connection with their housekeeping.

Concerning 38 of the women no comment could be made.

One might assume they had no admirable qualities, but it is fairer, perhaps, to say that most of these are the minor characters who appear so briefly in their respective novels that the reader cannot discover whether they have admirable qualities or not.

Some, though a comparatively small number, are shown as admirable, but for characteristics too miscellaneous to classify. Illustrative of these thirteen women are Miss Grayson of the novel *Peter* by F. Hopkinson Smith, who has a quality rare among these women, a sense of humor; and Miss Graham of Margaret Deland's *The Rising Tide*, who is admired for her dignity.

Characteristics for which others do not admire her.—Approaching the matter of personal qualities from the opposite angle—characteristics for which the single women were not admired—the investigator found that in a large number of cases, no specific comment was made. The 67 which were listed in this category probably reflect two earlier findings: first, that many of the characters were too minor and too briefly portrayed to classify; and second, that these women were, in the main, more worthy of admiration than otherwise.

Specifically, 21 of the women are not admired because of their unpleasant disposition; 16 are women who have some fault of character; 14 are called peculiar; and six are grossly inefficient. Thirteen are thought to be unusually homely or unattractive in appearance, and seven are criticized for their selfishness.

In 31 cases, undesirable characteristics were noted but are different from those which the classification had listed. This group includes several who are not admired because of their malicious gossiping, some who are snobbish, and a few who are considered too domineering. Octavia Hiatt of *The Interpreter's House* by Struthers Burt and Miss Knapp of Edward Noyes Westcott's *David Harum* are lacking in courage; Miss Villets of Sinclair Lewis's *Main Street* is too narrow-minded. The Allen sisters are portrayed by Joseph C. Lincoln in *Partners of the Tide* as being much too "fussy." Among the nonadmirable characteristics which appear more than once but hardly often enough to classify are prudishness, tactlessness, indecisiveness, and jealousy.

Attitude of others toward her.—Determining the attitude of other characters (or the author) toward the single women proved to be much easier than analyzing the attitude of the single woman toward herself. The attitude of others toward her is, in fact, the most revealing of all the categories of the analysis, with the possible exception of *Vocation*. Only 11 had to be classified under "no comment."

It is consistent with earlier findings to discover that in 49 cases, admiration of some kind is expressed toward the single woman. In seven more, sympathetic appreciation is shown of the real circumstances which had prevented her marriage and makes her life what it is. Also, some of the 29 who could not be classified could be said to call forth some element of admiration or appreciation in the general attitude expressed toward them.

From this point, however, the attitudes change noticeably. Seventeen characters are best described as indifferent to the attitudes expressed toward them, while 37 are definitely objects of pity and 33 are ridiculed for being queer personalities. Two are scorned for having shunned the responsibilities of marriage, and not one among them is envied for her freedom from responsibility.

The picture of pity and ridicule is more striking even than the above numbers reveal for the reason that some kind of admiration is often mingled with adverse attitudes. The citizens of Belmond in Ruth Suckow's *The Folks* recognize Vanchie Darlington as the town's most distinguished spinster, but they wonder where she gets those queer-looking hats. The family horse is named for one of the Miller twins in *Man of the Hour* by Octave Thanet, and the confusion over the name is the source of much humor, yet the neighbors have much regard for the cheerful, hard-working, but frivolous Miss Ally.

Certain other complexities occur in connection with this category of the analysis. Occasionally, the attitude of other characters toward the single woman is not the author's own attitude toward her. This is especially well illustrated in certain novels of Ellen Glasgow. Miss Priscilla Batte in the novel *Virginia*, for example, is wholly admired and respected in the Virginia town where she conducts her select seminary for young ladies, but the author does not admire Miss Priscilla's Victorian ideas. In fact, the whole theme of the novel is condemnation of the tradition which stifled the life of the main character. Sometimes, as in this instance, the reader must deduce, not from any specific statement, but from the entire context of the novel, what the author's attitude is.

In general, however, the nuances of attitude can be best detected in the explicit phrase. This seems especially true of the condemnatory point of view which lends itself readily to satire or the pointed quip. Short phrases descriptive of attitudes are represented by the characterization of Cynthia Badlam, who is called an unfortunate maiden lady in *The Guardian Angel,* by Oliver Wendell Holmes. Abigail Nutter in *The Story of a Bad Boy* by Thomas Bailey Aldrich is referred to as "that pink of maidenly propriety." Marie Spencer in Margaret Deland's *The Rising Tide* is severely censured for her gossiping and is dubbed the town scavenger. People say that Emily Saunders in *Saturday's Child* by Kathleen Norris is hopelessly shelved. Miriam Finch of Theodore Dreiser's novel *The "Genius"* is described as a woman who had never had a real youth or a real love affair, but who clings to her ideal of both.

Concerning the more derogatory attitudes, several characteristics of the single woman noticeably recur. One is an unflattering reference to age. The commonly used terms "old maid" and even "spinster" carry with them an implication of age, but one also finds more specific phrases. Hawthorne calls Hepzibah Pyncheon in *The House of the Seven Gables* an antiquated virgin. Marie Spencer, referred to in the above paragraph, is also called an old hag and a silly old ass. Several, like Aunt Tillie Kronborg in Willa Cather's *The Song of the Lark*, are referred to as silly old girls, or foolish old girls, or poor old things. Althea Bemis in Joseph C. Lincoln's *Doctor Nye* is called an old cat.

A number of references are also made to mouselike qualities of personality, this illustrating specifically the general passivity and apathy of the women as a whole. Tessie Kearns in Harry Leon Wilson's *Merton of the Movies* is described as sedate and mouselike, and Miss Hendricks in *A Certain Rich Man* by William Allen White is called a faded, mousy little woman in her despairing thirties.

The most marked characteristic, however, is the repeated reference to unattractive physical qualities, more often than not to ugliness of face or angularity of form. A neighbor calls Susan Hood a homely old spinster in S. Weir Mitchell's *Constance Trescot*, but homeliness probably reaches its crux in Beckie Meriweather of the novel *Brass* by Charles Norris, whose ugly, mannish face is said to be as pretty as an old roan mare.

Apparently, angularity and spareness are thought to be a characteristic attribute of the single woman. Louisa May Alcott calls Miss Crocker in *Little Women* a thin, yellow spinster with a sharp nose and inquisitive eyes. Thomas Bailey Aldrich in *The Story of a Bad Boy* describes Abigail Nutter as tall and angular. Miss Esther Kingsley of Gladys Hasty Carroll's *As the Earth Turns* is very tall and thin. Miss Ann Teetum in *The Fortunes of Oliver Horn* by F. Hopkinson Smith is thin, severe, and precise. Aunt Etta Archibald in Ellen Glasgow's *The Sheltered Life* is frail, plain, and sickly, with a bleak face like an insect. Miss Smith of Ellen Glasgow's *Life and Gabriella* is a thin, soured, ugly little woman. Only a few of the women are described in opposite terms. Miss Sarah Teetum, younger sister of Miss Ann mentioned above, is stout, coy, and kittenish. In Joseph Hergesheimer's *Linda Condon*, the author describes Miss Skillern as short and broad, reminding one of a wadded chair. But such instances are very rare.

In summarizing the various aspects of attitudes expressed by and toward the single women of fiction, two factors are especially impressive. First is the lack of expression among the women themselves concerning the work they do, the lives they lead, or the fact that they have not married. For most of them, life is monotonous and without hope of adventure, but they seldom complain. Apparently they are resigned to what life had brought or denied, and whatever they may think they do not reveal.

The second impressive factor is the inconsistency between the detailed description of these women and the attitude of others toward them. They are described, generally, as having some admirable quality of personality or character, but, more often than not, are regarded by others with pity or ridicule.

FACTORS IN NONMARRIAGE AND ADJUSTMENT

One might expect that the women would offer some explanation as to why they were single, even if it were only a rationalization, and this would form the basis for an interesting comparison with what appeared to the reader to be the probable reasons for their singleness. Such a comparison could not be made, but perhaps something equally significant comes to light.

Further analysis reveals still more strikingly the pattern of apathy, of resignation and reticence, among the women studied. With respect to the women's own reasons for not marrying, 117 out of the 150 characters make no comment whatever as to why they have not married. Or, approaching the matter more positively, a very small number, only 33, offer any reason for their being single, and 19 of these are not of a sort that can be satisfactorily classified. Three of Ellen Glasgow's novels yield individual examples of the latter: Angela Wilde of *The Wheel of Life* believes that her early "disgrace" prevented her from marrying. Miss Matoaca Bland of *The Romance of a Plain Man* thinks she had held too steadfastly to her principles. Aunt Meggie Fincastle of *Vein of Iron*, devout believer in Calvinism, had left marriage, like everything else in her life, to the Lord.

Other responses included in the 33, though small in the aggregate, are more interesting for what they do not state than for what they say. Five of the women declare that the "right man" could not marry them. Three cherish an ideal rather than a real person, while three others, whose lovers had died, declare they could never marry another. One cannot leave her parents or family; one needs her job and what she earns. One believes it a mistake to marry late in life; and one thinks herself too ill for marriage.

Three of the anticipated responses did not apply in even one instance. No character said that she feared marriage and childbearing, no one believed her own standards of living too high to permit her to marry below her social level, and not one thought herself unable to adjust to the different social level of a prospective husband.

In the main, whatever reasons most of these women may have for not marrying they keep to themselves. Singleness is not a topic either they or the novelist discusses. This finding, added to the previously expressed pattern of inarticulateness, takes on a growing significance.[126]

Reader's judgment as to why the women did not marry.— The reader's judgment of these women, particularly as to reasons why they had not married, shows a more evenly distributed classification, but once again, the largest number, 45 in all, were those concerning whom no comment could be made. These were, for the most part, the very minor characters whom the novelist did not delineate sufficiently for the reader to judge.

When reasons could be determined, they included some of the same factors which have already been emphasized. Some corresponded with the qualities for which the woman was not admired, some with the attitude of others toward the woman. Of those about whom more was known, the reader judged that 29 were prevented from marrying by factors outside their own lives, a combination of circumstances over which they presumably had no control. Twenty-eight others were judged to be too unattractive physically to have appealed to a partner in marriage, and 13 to have been too unpleasant in disposition. Nine were judged to be not at all adapted to marriage, eight to be wholly unromantic persons, and eight to be definitely queer or peculiar.

Concerning 38 of the women, the reader was not able to classify the reasons why they had not married. Liddy Allen, for example, the faithful servant and companion to Rachel Innes in *The Circular Staircase* by Mary Roberts Rinehart, exclaimed with fervor that no man ever made a fool out of her—a remark which undoubtedly carries with it at least one reason why she did not marry, but which would be difficult to classify. Sometimes reasons were obvious but were involved in a complex circumstance. Two examples will aptly illustrate. In Ellen Glasgow's *The Romantic Comedians* Amanda Lightfoot did not marry because the lover to whom she was engaged suddenly jilted her and married another; and thirty years later, after his first wife had died and he was free to marry again, he preferred to marry a woman younger than Amanda. The more subtle reasons, however, which the author means to emphasize, is that Amanda was too narrow in her principles to reconcile herself to the quarrel which drove her lover to marry another, and through all the years which had intervened she had clung so rigidly to her standards that she had become more of a symbol than a woman. Her unyielding code of perfection would not permit her to reveal the warmth which might have made her desirable as a wife. Flora Burgess in Dorothy Canfield Fisher's *The Squirrel Cage* was undoubtedly kept from marriage by the social caste ideas instilled in her by her mother. The daughter became the snobbish society editor on a suburban paper where she could cultivate the "right" people and move in what she and her mother considered "select circles." Within such rigid restrictions there must have been very limited opportunity for her to marry.

Adjustment she effects as she leaves the story.—In the last category of the objective classification which deals with the kind of adjustment the single woman effects as she leaves the story, it was assumed that she would occupy a fairly important role and show some change in character or personality as the plot evolved. Since most of the single women proved to be minor characters, however, they appeared in only a small portion of the book and left the story just as they had entered it, unchanged in every particular. The analysis here, therefore, did not attempt to indicate change of status but merely to record what was happening to the single woman at the time she left the story. This may be at the end of the novel or it may not; the analysis records merely the last glimpse the reader catches of her.

Even though so many of these women are minor in relation to the novel as a whole and appear only briefly in its plot, some of them are highly individualistic. A total of 47 are, in fact, too individual to classify. Hepzibah Pyncheon, as the reader leaves her at the end of Hawthorne's *The House of the Seven Gables,* has inherited wealth and regained her family pride. Fanny Minafer of Booth Tarkington's *The Magnificent Ambersons,* after losing her fam-

ily fortune, comes to an unhappy end: living in a shabby
boardinghouse where her only recreation is playing bridge
with the remaining few of her old cronies who knew "who
she was." Aunt Agatha Littlepage in Ellen Glasgow's *They
Stooped to Folly*, after her long years of disgrace and seclusion, has finally mustered enough courage to take an interest in such simple pleasure as the movies, banana sun-
daes, and sewing for the Red Cross.

On the side of the least favorable, tragedy is reflected in
only a comparatively small number of the lives of the single
women. Thirteen, for a variety of reasons, are at the end
miserable, wretched, or desperately unhappy. Eight die with
a sense of unfulfillment, while a few others approach death
but with no expression of futility. Twenty-six give little
evidence of satisfaction, but are apparently adjusted philosophically to things as they are. The 20 more, concerning whom no comment could be made, probably fit this category, since nothing either positive or negative can be said
about them. A considerable number of the 47 thought to be
too individual to classify also have this passive quality about
them.

A somewhat larger number, a total of 74, manage to live
tolerable lives. Thirty-three of these are seemingly contented
in whatever work or endeavor occupies their days. This
number includes many, though not all, of those who follow a vocation, together with a few others who gain satisfaction from their extremely humble tasks. Eleven are devoting themselves to children: nieces, nephews, or children
they have adopted. Four find solace in religion.

Concerning the great majority, however, the reader can
only say that he leaves them going on just as they first appear—making the best of a situation in which they have little
hope of change, but saying and doing almost nothing about it.

To summarize, the objective classification shows that
single women thirty years of age or older appear in con-

siderable numbers in the 125 American novels analyzed. While 40 of the novels which form the central data of the investigation contain no character which fits the definition, in the remaining 85 novels, 150 such characters appear. Considering the novelists rather than the novels, only 12 of the 64 authors represented in the central data do not include a character of this kind. This number, by almost any criterion, is a goodly representation.

The place, however, to which these novelists assign the single woman in relation to the other characters they have created, is impressive. Only seven of the 150 single-woman characters are major. Of the seven who are major, only one is so dominant as to lend her name to the title of the novel in which she appears. All the rest are minor, varying from the extremely few who are important and influential figures, though less than major, to the many who are so minor as to have little or no influence. A few act as pivots in the plot, supplying the bit of strategic information which contributes to the denouement, but are inconsequential characters. Many are included, apparently, merely to furnish local color or comic relief.

The large majority of the single women are well past thirty years of age when they enter the story. Some are elderly; most are middle-aged. Only three of the major characters and three of lesser importance appear in early life. Since most of the women are minor characters and over thirty years of age when they enter the story, the analysis of factors in *Childhood and Adolescence* did not yield sufficient information to be carried into tabular form.

The remaining four divisions in the cross section analysis —*Ambition and Achievement, Human Relationships, Attitudes*, and *Factors in Nonmarriage and Adjustment*—suggest two significant generalizations.

The first generalization calls attention to an inconsistency in the attitude of society toward single women: while they are portrayed in fiction as being an admirable group of in-

dividuals, they are more often pitied or ridiculed than admired by their associates. With notably few exceptions, they
are respected for their goodness of character; in a petty sort
of way they take an interest in their neighbors; they are altruistic in wanting to help others achieve their goals. They
are personable, well liked, and get along well enough with
most people. They are decorous in behavior and rarely indulge in unconventional activities. But this is by no means
unqualified praise. Even when admirable qualities are ob-
servable, the total portrait of the individual or of the group
is often less than favorable. Their interest in their communities is chiefly motivated by the desire to gossip. There are
repeated references to mouselike qualities, homeliness of
face, and unpleasing angularity of figure. Only a few have
suitors, and where such a heterosexual relationship does exist,
it is looked upon as being ridiculous. Many of the women
are pitied or ridiculed, even extending into such details as
their names. Many are thought of as being peculiar or queer
individuals. Of those who work for their living, by far the
majority follow modest or humble vocations, and a very
few could be said to occupy places of genuine respect or
wholesome influence in their communities. Even those who
follow worthy professions are by no means worthy examples of those professions.

The second generalization is the striking pattern of apathy
and resignation among these single women. The first hint of
this becomes evident in the fact that either ambition among
the women studied was lacking or else the novelist did not
consider it an important element to include, either of which
has cultural significance. Furthermore, while attitudes toward the single women are freely expressed by friends, family, and neighbors, the feelings of the women about themselves and their lives are rarely spoken. They do not discuss
their singleness. Only a few show any zest for living. Life
is not good and they are not happy, but they patiently ac-

cept their lot. Their lives flow along in even tenor, with not much worth struggling for and not much success. Apparently, they feel they are at the mercy of circumstances beyond their control, and the spirit of rebellion, or even of protest, is strangely lacking.

Hence, no matter how one approaches the fictional data, one must reach the same result. Whether one breaks down analytically the sociopsychological components as here shown, or builds them up into a synthesis, as in the earlier chapter, the stereotype of the single woman becomes increasingly evident. This will be more fully discussed in the chapter which follows.

The Emerging Pattern

While analyzing the classification of personnel factors in the lives of the single women of fiction, one finds a recurring pattern, a pattern in which the stereotype is even more forcibly brought to light. This emerging pattern consists of a number of generalizations derived from the detailed analysis of each single-woman character. The major generalizations fall under either one of two main headings: the positive generalizations based on what the data show and negative generalizations growing out of what the data fail to show.

POSITIVE CONCLUSION: THE TENDENCY TO STEREOTYPE

The more impressive element—the positive element—may best be described as the tendency to stereotype. Even more than has already been shown, certain characteristics occur again and again, some with startling frequency and among novelists widely differentiated in time, locality, and style of writing. These recurring elements are most clearly evident with respect to vocation. The preceding chapter emphasized that considerably more than half of the women studied had no vocation at which they earned a living. This included those who made their homes with parents or other relatives, those not physically able to work, and those who were the recipients of local charity. It must also include those about whom the novelist made no comment as to vocation. This lack of vocation is, in one sense, a recurring pattern, and might be emphasized as one element in the stereotype. But as has been stated, though less than half the women had a vocation, the kinds of vocations at which they were employed are particularly impressive. The majority of the women who worked for a living were engaged in one of three occupations: schoolteaching, dressmaking, and domestic work.

The schoolteachers.—Twenty of the single women are teachers, and almost without exception they are poor representatives of their profession. The positions they hold are relatively unimportant, and the women resemble each other in that they are not particularly attractive in person or personality, are not efficient or constructively devoted to their work, and are strict, prudish, and ultradignified.

Those who teach and are also petty administrators in boarding schools for young ladies are especially prim and precise. The Misses Cabot of Massachusetts are described by Joseph C. Lincoln in *Mary 'Gusta* as being all that the name might imply, and Miss Priscilla Batte of Ellen Glasgow's *Virginia* did her utmost to implant Victorian ideas in the minds of the young ladies entrusted to her care. The girls under her tutelage thought Miss Waring was much too severe, in Meredith Nicholson's *A Hoosier Chronicle.* The chief concern of Miss Dorothy Gibbs in *The Story of a Bad Boy* by Thomas Bailey Aldrich was to keep her girls away from men. Miss Tapley of the Petersport Academy took her powers of chaperonage very seriously; the author, Mary Ellen Chase, has the heroine's lover in *Mary Peters* tell her that he is glad her years of teaching have not made "a Miss Tapley" out of her.

Others teach in a variety of schools in a variety of places,

but there is little variation from the stereotype. Rose Mc-
Coy of Sherwood Anderson's *Poor White* is described as
being repressed. She turns to teaching after she had been
jilted, and when she subsequently falls in love with the hero
she makes herself undesirable by dwelling upon her in-
feriority. Ida Chisholm, after thirty-five years, still teaches
Latin in the high school at Belmond, Iowa, where she taught
the Ferguson children in Ruth Suckow's novel *The Folks*.
She is described as a "cross" to the other teachers. Meta
Beggs, heroine of Joseph Hergesheimer's *Mountain Blood*,
described in detail in an earlier chapter, struggles to escape
what she believes to be the tyranny of her profession. Several of the teachers are elderly and have retired from teaching. One of these, Miss Simmons in Thornton Wilder's
Heaven's My Destination, is so emotionally unstable that
she goes into hysterics when rough boys call her obscene
names.

The few teachers who show a religious devotion to their
profession are somewhat more admirable but are described
as strict disciplinarians. St. Theresa of William Allen White's
In the Heart of a Fool is called a Protestant nun, while Mother
Bridget of Edna Ferber's *Cimarron* rules her Catholic school
with a firm hand. With the exception of these, hardly one
of all the teachers could be said to be a credit to her profession.

The dressmakers.—The second vocational group which
runs to stereotype is approximately the same size as the first.
These are the women who earn their living as dressmakers.
Almost without variation they live in small towns, are
middle-aged or older, poor but honest, respectable and respected—but much given to gossip. They move around
from one family to another, carrying with them the petty
scandal of the various households, and thus are instrumental
in spreading the news of the neighborhood. Though minor
and humble, their knowledge of intimate affairs occasionally

makes them pivotal characters in the development of the plot. As has been pointed out, a common device of the novelist is to use such a humble person to make known to the reader what he needs to know about more important characters and events.

The dressmakers are most aptly illustrated, perhaps, by two characters appearing in novels of Willa Cather and Ellen Glasgow. Though minor in relation to the plot, the sewing woman Augusta in *The Professor's House* and Miss Willy Whitlow in *Virginia* resemble each other in several ways. They both live alone and both have a simple but devout religious faith which makes it possible for them to bear the weary round of pettiness in their lives. Both are admirable and respected, but pitied by the families which know them best.

The domestics.—A third vocational group composed of women who work for their living is that of the household domestics. These women are the maids-of-all-work, the general houseworkers, often skilled in their humble tasks but seldom calling forth commendation from the families for whom they work. Most of them are illiterate or unlearned, and the reader knows nothing of their lives other than in their current connection. Loyalty to their employers is their most admirable characteristic.

These women divide themselves into two fairly distinct subgroups: the "poor relations" who are dependent upon, and subservient to, some more substantial member of the family in whose home they live and move and have whatever being they possess; and the second group who are not related to the families for whom they work. In neither instance can one say how much they earn or whether they earn anything beyond their maintenance. Among the domestics who are not related to the families they work for are several immigrant women who contribute humor by their lack of understanding of American ways. Such a character is Anastasia

O'Hern ('Tashie) in Dorothy Canfield Fisher's *The Squirrel Cage*.

The indentured poor relations may further be divided
into two subgroups: the lamentable household drudges, completely dominated and subservient, and those who are more
respected by those they serve. The latter is by far the smaller
group, and may be illustrated by Aunt Meggie Fincastle in
Ellen Glasgow's *Vein of Iron*. Aunt Meggie is utterly dependent upon her brother's family, with whom she makes
her home, but all of the family is much devoted to her. Most
of the poor relations, however, though indispensable in their
households, are not held in respect.

The poor-relation variety of domestic worker is here emphasized to contrast with another group which does not
emerge under the vocational approach, but is definitely related to it. These are also dependent female relatives, but
they are gentlewomen who do not actually work for their
living. They are not domestics in the usual sense, for some
of them have their own servants, but their lives are generally
circumscribed by the domestic round of duties. Some, however, devote their time along with their financial means to
charity or social service.

Characteristically, these gentlewomen are middle-aged or
elderly. They have no vocation, but either they have some
small means the source of which is not explained, or they
occupy places of respect in the homes of relatives who can
also afford to hire servants. They are most frequently found
in novels of the South, are much impressed by the importance of their families, and are chiefly concerned with "keeping up appearances." Numerous examples appear in the
novels of George Washington Cable, notably Miss Martha
Harper in *The Cavalier* and "Sister Jane" in *Dr. Sevier*.
Another is Miss Thomasia Gray in Thomas Nelson Page's
Red Rock. Miss Lavinia Clendenning in F. Hopkinson
Smith's *The Fortunes of Oliver Horn* is such a woman. Not

all of them, however, live in the South. Louisa May Alcott
in *Little Women* describes the New Englander, Miss Norton, as very cultured, and Miss Anneke DeVoe of Paul
Leicester Ford's *The Honourable Peter Stirling* and Miss
Kingsbury of *The Rise of Silas Lapham* by William Dean
Howells are gentlewomen *and* Northerners. This group
could be enlarged by including several who were characterized as being rich rather than genteel, and still a few
others who lived, more or less parasitically, with relatives.
Miss Fanny Minafer of Booth Tarkington's *The Magnificent Ambersons* (a Hoosier family) is an outstanding example of the latter variant.[127]

If one disregards vocational boundaries and approaches
the matter of stereotype from a different angle, two other
distinct patterns emerge. The first is the gossipmongers and
the second, the pairs of maiden sisters, both comprising
groups considerably larger than any one vocation.

The gossipmongers.—As noted, the dressmakers were
often purveyors of neighborhood gossip, but they were by
no means the only ones whose interest in community affairs
was motivated by the desire to keep thus informed. Many
of the domestics had more than a reasonable curiosity about
the families who employed them. The relations, poor or
otherwise, generally guarded the secrets of their own families, but were often absorbed in the questionable activities
of their neighbors. Several of the women, like the Sneed sisters in Ellen Glasgow's *Barren Ground,* worked in the village postoffice and thereby came upon most of the current
news. Some, like Miss Crocker in Louisa May Alcott's *Little Women* (the March girls called her "Croaker"), made it
their business just to snoop around in the guise of friendly
callers.

If one were to include the gossipmonger wherever she is
found, it would make a long list, for she is a familiar figure
and her gossiping a significant element in the stereotype of

the single woman in fiction: the woman whose own life is empty of normal discourse, but who makes it her business to keep herself informed about her fellow men. All these women are overly curious, all both sought after and shunned, all more or less malicious in their troublemaking proclivities.

The maiden sisters.—Seventeen pairs of maiden sisters are represented in the data of the investigation, comprising a group considerably larger than any one vocation, with the possible exception of the domestics. These sisters invariably live together, generally in the old house after the parents have died, and are emotionally dependent upon each other. Some live on a small income, presumably inherited, though several earn their living by dressmaking. Many of them are of the gentlewoman variety, much given to family pride.

Typically, the pairs of sisters are either so much alike that they completely share each other's destiny and are never differentiated, or they are so unlike that one acts as a foil for the other. Anna and Louisa Halleck in *A Modern Instance* by William Dean Howells are illustrative of those who are alike, while the "Sawyer girls" in Kate Douglas Wiggin's *Rebecca of Sunnybrook Farm* are very unlike.[128]

It will be evident at this point that a great deal of overlapping occurs between the groupings here delineated, but it should also be obvious that regardless of specific occupation, the similarities among these single women are more striking than their individual differences. Almost without exception these women are old and drab and unattractive. Theirs are humble skills, if indeed they have any skills at all. Their occupations seem merely expedient, not work which has been planned for or in which they have exercised any choice or for which they have made any preparation. Even the teachers are less than worthy representatives of what is generally conceded to be a worthy profession. Their lives are closely circumscribed within a small orbit, and most of the women have no interest beyond the domestic routine or the latest gossip. A few of the women find solace in religion, but for most of them there is little or no adventure in their lives. They have achieved nothing beyond their mere existence and show no ambition to improve or escape their lot in life. Though the gentlewomen are personable and their surroundings tolerable, nothing colorful or animated touches their lives. Regardless of the occupation they follow, the most excitement they ever know is something which happens to other people. They are wooden women. Even where there is loyalty and devotion, there is also pity or ridicule.[129]

NEGATIVE CONCLUSION: THE DISCREPANCY BETWEEN FICTION AND FACT

In order to show more clearly what the fiction portrait of the single woman lacks, it is revealing to compare what the fiction shows with the factual data concerning single women, reviewed in the discussion of previous research. Since the data in that chapter were presented under four different headings, the comparison here will be made on the same basis. The discrepancy thus shown between the fiction and the facts constitutes the negative conclusion of the study.

Fiction and the psychosexual studies.—First, in contrast to the psychosexual studies in which the single woman appears as a recognizable entity—the medical study by Dickinson and Beam; the Davis study of factors in the sex life of a large group of women; and the Strakosch and Landis studies exploring factors in normal and abnormal sex development—it must be observed that the "abnormal" has not been explored deeply by many of the American novelists represented in this study. There are numerous instances of fiction women whose personalities might be described as "neurotic" by a psychologist, but few novelists have probed the inner reaches of personality on a psychosexual level.

As has been noted earlier, Oliver Wendell Holmes concerned himself with patterns of deviational behavior in his self-termed "medicated novels," such as *The Guardian Angel* and *Elsie Venner*. S. Weir Mitchell, also a physician as well as a novelist, was much concerned with various manifestations of the neurotic personality, but though his *Constance Trescot* deals with a fiendish woman, sex is not an obvious factor in her villainy. Ellen Glasgow, in *They Stooped to Folly*, deals with the theme of frustration and the conflict in the sex mores, but these antagonistic forces are first sociological and only secondly psychological; her "fallen women" live only in the shadows of their "disgrace." Theodore Dreiser pleads for a reevaluation of the sex code in *Jennie Gerhardt*, but his quarrel is with society, not with the individual in her transgression. Sherwood Anderson, perhaps more than any other novelist represented in the study, deals with the theme of deviant sex behavior in terms of the individual. In his *Poor White* is the only example found in this investigation of a single woman who outwardly shows homosexual tendencies, homosexuality being one of the concerns of the Davis, Strakosch, and Landis studies.

It should be reemphasized that the single women of the study are, on the whole, a highly decorous group, and that sex, in and of itself, comprises only a small part of the total picture. There are remarkably few instances in which a single woman has entered deliberately into a liaison without the sanction of marriage. A few others are living in disgrace "with their memories and their shame," but the reader hears of those early events only in retrospect. Only one, Jennie Gerhardt, has borne a child out of wedlock. This situation undoubtedly reflects the social structure of American society in its traditional emphasis and its enduring assumption in the social mind that virginity must be a corollary to spinsterhood. Masturbation, although a factor in scientific psychosexual research, is nowhere stated or even implied with regard to fiction characters.

The resemblance, therefore, between the psychosexual research which deals with single women and the fiction portrait is slight. Only a few novelists in America, apparently, have been concerned with the theme of sex deviation as it pertains to the individual; those who have dealt with deviational patterns of sex behavior have presented it chiefly in its social aspects, and are concerned only secondarily with adjustment of the individual to the social reaction.

Fiction and the "new dependency."—The previous psychosexual research seems only remotely related to the study of single women in fiction, but to a far greater degree the changed pattern of socioeconomic dependency is absent from the fiction. There are numerous examples, to be sure, in which the single woman herself is the dependent: the poor relations, the gentlewomen, the pairs of maiden sisters, are almost all dependent upon more affluent members of their families, but the "new dependency" wherein the single woman herself is economically independent but must contribute to the care and maintenance of others is almost entirely lacking from the novelists' picture. As the factual data so impressively show, this situation is an unforeseen concomitant of woman's "new freedom," one which carries with it a new kind of emotional bondage and becomes a new deterrent to marriage. It is difficult to say exactly when this change began to be evident, but the studies of the Women's Bureau as well as the studies of professional groups of women show that it began to be statistically measurable as early as the 1920's, about the close of the First World War. Since that time, and especially since the Great Depression of the 1930's, the economic burden upon women has been greater than ever before. The emotional stresses and strains which always accompany economic dependency are just as great now as they ever were. The woman who does not marry is still a major victim.

Surely this new kind of dependency is an equally appro-

priate theme of fiction, but where is the novelist who is sufficiently attuned to this situation to incorporate it into his
writing?

It is certainly one of the climactic conclusions of the present study that in all the novels it analyzed, only one catches
the implications of this new dependency; only one portrays
a major episode in which a single woman contributes to the
care of a dependent. This one instance is the work of Kathleen Norris in one of her early novels, *Saturday's Child*,
which preceded even the earliest factual studies by several
years.[130] In this novel, dealing, as the title suggests, with
women who must work for their living (Saturday's children), there are three pairs of sisters, more or less emotionally and economically dependent upon each other. The most
significant instance, however, is that of the Lord sisters,
Lydia and Mary, one of whom is utterly dependent upon
the other. Even the stronger is herself a pitiful creature, earning the meager living for the two of them as a governess in
a wealthy family.

Fiction and the studies of eminent women.—Equally impressive is the discovery and realization that in all the novels
of the study, with their 150 single-woman characters, there
is not even one who could be called truly representative of
the thousands of single women who have won "eminence."
There is not even one who could be called a "success," in the
ways that great numbers of single women in America have
been successful: the woman of character, attractive in person or personality, possessing skills in which she is highly
trained, following a vocation of trust and responsibility in
which she obtains self-expression and financial security, the
woman who commands admiration and the respect of her
associates, the woman whose achievement and influence are
comparable to her potentialities. Indeed, the investigator is
hard pressed to find one single-woman fiction character who
made even a commendable achievement.

This is highly significant because of its absence. That single women who combine many qualities which lead to success do exist and in great numbers is a matter of common observation; that many have been listed in the annals of distinguished Americans is shown by the analyses of *Who's Who* data in the previous research. It is even more surprising that the novelists studied have not recognized the important contribution which single women have made to American life or that they are seemingly unaware of the changed pattern of economic dependency. Dependency is, after all, only one of a number of factors in the larger pattern of success or the lack of it; the socioeconomic aspect of life, however fundamental it may be, is of less consequence than the larger aspects of success, as measured in terms of ambition, achievement, or personal fulfillment.

The *Who's Who* data, and the other studies of "eminence" reviewed under previous research, show convincingly that thousands of single women in America have made contributions to society of a caliber which earned citation for them in the most respected annals of society. Mention in these sources is a coveted attainment, and one may safely say that most of these citations are earned. One might even surmise that it may be a little more difficult for a woman to earn a place in these permanent annals than it is for a man, all other things being equal.

These eminent single women were "successful" women, were they not?

Or were they?

Fuller implications of these questions will be developed at a later point in the study. For the present, it is enough to say that one can only attribute this failure to portray the modern single woman on the part of novelists either to a lack of knowledge or a lack of appreciation—or a lack of conviction. Surely one would expect to find some writer of fiction concerned with creating a woman character whose work was her life.

Fiction and the "sociology of the novel."—In any case, the omission of these significant elements from the novelists' portrait of single women must be observed as a kind of cultural lag—but in reverse. Social thinking is generally found to be in advance of social fact, often with a considerable lag between. In fact, novelists and other creative thinkers are often prophetic, far ahead of present reality, and controversial issues are discussed in fiction long before they would be acceptable to many readers in their own lives. But here the social fact—the actual status and achievement of the single woman—is found to be in advance of the fictional picture. Here it is the novelist, the creative artist, who lags.

The novelist has not otherwise been insensitive to woman's changing role. In the fiction represented in this study, there are examples of many kinds of women which the history of America has witnessed and which the many studies in the analysis of previous research on the sociology of the novel brings to the fore. There is the urban woman such as Grey and Dunlap comment upon at length; the rural woman whom Hazard delineates; and the small-town single woman who appears in Herron's study. There is the woman exploited by business and industry, such women as Chamberlain and Flory and Regier discuss in their studies of economic criticism in the novel. There is the woman benefactor, the woman of wealth or position or influence, who gives of herself and her resources toward aiding her less fortunate sisters. There are examples of New England women, Southern women, women of the Midwest, the Great Plains, and the Far West. There are feminine women and feminist women; servants and gentlewomen; rich and poor. The present study seems to have caught something of everything which the social and literary historians have brought to light.

But where is the "successful" woman?

Needham's study of the "old maid" in English life and literature of the eighteenth century shows little discrepancy between the actual status of single women in that day and the fictional portrait of them. Though Needham was more concerned with how the elements of the unfortunate fiction portrait came into being than how or whether it had persisted, the study unmistakably points this emphasis. It seems unlikely that there should be in a progressive nation like America and in an enlightened era such as this a social lag greater than was found in England two centuries ago.

With regard to social lag, though not specifically to single women, Barnett's study on divorce as reflected in the American novel is revealing. In comparing social attitudes toward divorce as fiction reflected them with certain social facts pertaining to divorce, Barnett found that the nearer one came to the present, the less was social lag a factor. The time lag of from ten to twenty years in the early days of the present century between newspaper accounts of divorces and fictional portrayal decreased as one approached the present; the theme of post-divorce adjustment appeared in the novel as soon as it did in periodical literature. If a comparable situation were true of single women, "the new woman" who lives her life successfully without marriage should already have appeared in the novel. There has been ample time for her to have made her fictional debut.

4

WHAT DO OTHER AMERICAN
NOVELS SHOW?

*There is no dissatisfaction and unhappiness among these
people because of their restricted view of life, but it may be
that the lack of unhappiness constitutes the real tragedy.*
MARY E. WILKINS FREEMAN, Pembroke

The Enlarged Portrait

A QUESTION may arise at this point as to whether the composite portrait of the single woman in fiction would have been different if this investigation had not been delimited by precise definition of terms and the use of a sampling of American novels.

Is the stereotype more sharply revealed in the sampling than in other novels that a more general study would have included? May it be that the controls imposed upon the research throw the portrait out of focus and that single-woman characters are shown in a less favorable light than if a larger number of characters had been considered? In other words, if the study had dealt with the single woman without specifying that she must be "thirty years of age or older," and if pertinent material concerning her had been included wherever it might have been found, would the results have been markedly different? Would the tendency to stereotype have been more or less pronounced?

To be sure, a larger and more general survey will show some variations. A few, though a very few, highly individualized single-woman characters appear, characters which deviate considerably from the norm of the stereotype. These are generally women younger than thirty. The proportion of smaller groups within the larger group also varies; this, too, as might be expected. This is especially noticeable as one finds more women engaged in voluntary social service. Among themselves they show much similarity, and while they are somewhat more admirable than other single women, they differ from them in only small detail. In the larger range of American fiction one sees more and more varied opportunities for women, especially in business and the arts. "Career" begins to take on its modern meaning and offers its first real threat to marriage.

But this is not to say that the stereotype has been fundamentally altered. A few variations cannot change a pattern so deeply etched. In fact, in this larger survey a highly significant aspect of the stereotype is brought to light. If a woman is shown to be attractive, if she is clever and competent, if she has ambition and achieves it, the novelist "rewards" her before the end of the book by marriage. One would assume this is what the reader expects. She is not, of course, the single woman with whom the central study is concerned; she is "the woman who marries late." But in the novelists' delineation of her the stereotype of the woman who remains single is, by contrast, reinforced.

The sampling vs. the larger range of American fiction.— As will be recalled, the sampling this investigation used, i.e., the Dickinson list, began with James Fenimore Cooper, or about 1820, and ended in 1935. But the pruning process which reduced the original list to its most exclusively American novels ruled out the listed works of Cooper because they were either historical or stories of the sea, and established the actual beginning of this study some thirty years later, with Nathaniel Hawthorne. Before Hawthorne, during almost a century which the sampling covers, and also since 1935, were many other novels which the study has not considered, some containing notable delineations of single women.

Obviously, this brief survey of the larger range of American fiction, of novels marginal to the data of this study, cannot be and does not pretend to be exhaustive. It can merely cite certain other examples of single women which did not appear in the original data, and sketch in a few bold strokes to suggest the changes in sociological setting.

Since changes in fictional portraiture often anticipate or follow certain changes in social structure, this discussion will follow in general a chronological pattern, grouping the fiction into five broad divisions, but within each division the single-woman characters will be grouped around certain topics which the material suggests. Hawthorne marks the beginning of the study proper; hence the first division will deal with pre-Hawthorne fiction. The second division will include fiction marginal to the sampling, which appeared during the last half of the nineteenth century; the third, from 1900 to the close of the First World War, or about 1920; the fourth, from 1920 to 1935; and the fifth, the recent decade, will appraise the fiction published since 1935, the terminal point of the sampling. Each division will be summarized in terms of the new elements which extend the findings of the study as well as those which strengthen and support the stereotype.

THE PRE-HAWTHORNE PERIOD

If I refuse, from mere ends of personal ease, to enter into this orderly state [of marriage], I cannot be happy, and, of course, cannot enter into heaven.

T. S. ARTHUR, Married and Single

With few exceptions, the older unmarried woman in novels prior to Hawthorne was relegated to a minor place, and was presented in an unfavorable light. Most of the early novels America produced, such as William Hill Brown's *The Power of Sympathy* (1789), Susanna Rowson's *Charlotte Temple* (1794), and *The Coquette* (1797) by Hannah Webster Foster, were hardly more than feeble imitations of

English novels and showed only slight variations upon the Richardsonian theme of the triumph of virtue and the wages of sin. The characteristic plot revolves around the frail but virtuous heroine, the cruel villain who tries to seduce her, and the handsome lover who rescues her from a cruel fate.

In the minor plot, however, one frequently found that the heroine was under the guardianship or chaperonage of an older female relative, and this woman was often a maiden aunt—a vicious, scheming woman who seemed to derive sadistic satisfaction from her cruel domination of the young girl. Such a one was the spinster aunt, Miss Martha, who directed the life of the heroine in *The Asylum; or, Alonzo and Melissa* (1810) by I. Mitchell. This kind of fictional character is closely patterned after the English prototype and, as will be observed, persists in American fiction in several notable examples of a considerably later period.

Charles Brockden Brown, writing his novels of "Gothic terror" at the turn of the nineteenth century, offered some variation in his delineation of woman characters. His was an English influence also, but of a different kind: the radical theories of William Godwin and the rebel Mary Wollstonecraft then being voiced in England. Brown had been reared among Philadelphia Quakers, a religious group also English in its roots which had always proclaimed the spiritual equality of women. This combination of thought in Brown showed itself in his creation of such characters as Constantia Dudley in *Ormond* (1799), and Clara Wieland, sister of the hero in his novel *Wieland* (1798), who were unusually independent women of their day. His *Alcuin* (1798) sets forth the author's ideas on the education and rights of women. But suicide is still Constantia Dudley's only way out of difficulty, and with a number of his lesser characters Brown reverts to the prevailing fictional pattern. He emphasizes, for example, the element of gossip as a vicious but effective means by which one woman can dominate another, a device

which continues to be a familiar one in fiction. In his novel
Jane Talbot (1801), the villain is a gossiping little spinster.

Although a major novelist and generously represented in
the original Dickinson list, James Fenimore Cooper made no
contribution to this study. His materials are more American
than those of the earlier novelists, his masculine characters
are sturdy pioneers, but his heroines still follow the English
pattern and are anything but original. They are young and
beautiful, noble and chaste, and although subjected to such
harrowing experiences as to cause the strongest of women
to shudder, they follow a stilted decorum and remain genteel
to the point of what someone has called "virtuous vacuity."
However, to certain of his minor characters, those representing a lower level of society than his heroines, Cooper
grants greater freedom, and among these several well-
drawn single-woman characters are to be found. Most noteworthy, perhaps, in terms of this investigation, is Remarkable
Pettibone, the inquisitive and resentful housekeeper of the
mansion in *The Pioneers* (1823). She is a Yankee spinster,
but still the English shrew.

Up until the time of Hawthorne, therefore, the American
novelists' delineation of the older single woman conforms
closely to the English pattern as set forth by Needham in
her study of "the old maid" in English life and fiction of the
eighteenth century, previously cited: an unattractive, unpleasant, and often a villainish personality. In fact, it was in
this early period that this concept of spinsterhood was translated and took deep root in American fiction. Only one
novelist, Charles Brockden Brown, influenced by the radical
theories of Godwin, dared to present the unmarried woman
as somewhat admirable. But he too adopts the Richardsonian
suicide motif, and in some of his minor characters, makes
the gossiping spinster the villain.

There can be little doubt or question as to the social attitude toward single women in this early period of American

fiction. Herbert Ross Brown, in his recent study on the sentimental novel, observes that the "new woman" who entertained ambition outside the home was regarded as the moral horror of the time. He summarizes tersely the prevailing opinion: if happiness beyond the bonds of wedlock was criminal for a man, it was the unpardonable sin for woman.[1]

THE LATTER HALF OF THE NINETEENTH CENTURY

Her sister, Miss Watson, a tolerable slim old maid, with goggles on, had just come to live with her [the Widow Douglas]. . . . Then she told me about the bad place and I said I wished I was there. . . . She said it was wicked to say what I said; said she wouldn't say it for the whole world; she was going to live so as to go to the good place. Well, I couldn't see no advantage in going where she was going, so I made up my mind I wouldn't try for it.

MARK TWAIN, The Adventures of Huckleberry Finn

In the period from 1850 to 1900, the old and the new appear simultaneously. While the English pattern continues with little or no variation in some novels, elements which are new and essentially American begin to appear. Most of the latter, however, vary the old pattern only slightly. It becomes merely a matter of grafting new shoots upon an old stem.

Two of Hawthorne's major woman characters are of interest in this connection, though neither fulfills completely the accepted definition of single woman. Hester Prynne of *The Scarlet Letter* (1850) is actually an English woman, and in most respects her experience in America is not very different from what it might have been in England. Zenobia of *The Blithedale Romance* (1852) is a mature woman who has achieved a degree of emancipation, having identified herself with a socialistic colony resembling Brook Farm. She is a striking example of a woman caught between old and new ideologies; when the hero, Miles Coverdale, shows his preference for a younger and more traditionally feminine woman, Zenobia can see no way out of her disappointment except suicide, this again in keeping with the Richardsonian fiction formula. Hester and Zenobia were both said to have been married in their early youth—an attempt, perhaps, on the part of the novelist to romanticize his characters—but both lived among their contemporaries as single women.[2]

Still not far removed from the English prototype but yet an interesting variation is the character of Miss Ophelia St. Clare in Harriet Beecher Stowe's *Uncle Tom's Cabin* (1852). When Miss Ophelia goes from staid New England to the lackadaisical life of New Orleans, as housekeeper for her cousin Augustine (Little Eva's father), her conscience is under severe strain. The episodes in which she is involved not only point up differences in manners and mores, but also reveal amusing aspects of her prim personality.

A more daring theme and a more nearly unique character are found in Herman Melville's *Pierre; or, The Ambiguities* (1852). Isabel Glendinning, whose lot is one of misfortune from the moment of her illegitimate birth, finds herself the victim in an incestuous relationship with her half brother, the quixotic hero of this strange and depressing novel. Isabel, of course, is only the passive partner, and as such is hardly more than any other woman controlled by conditions she can neither comprehend nor remedy, but the couple become so distraught by their sense of guilt that self-inflicted death seems the only solution. Though the circumstances differed, one may note that suicide, for Isabel as well as for Hawthorne's Zenobia, was the only way of escape in that day for women (in fiction, at least) who dared to deviate from the conventional pattern of thought and action.

Louisa May Alcott came near contributing one of her best-loved heroines to this investigation in the character of Jo March in *Little Women* (1868), except for the technicality that Jo is not yet thirty and she agrees to marry the "aging" but kindly Professor Bhaer. Jo's reflections upon her independence, upon her struggle to become a writer (undoubtedly the experience and opinion of the author), her feelings as she sees the romantic hero Laurie marry her younger and prettier sister, form an excellent commentary upon the place of women in her day.

Little Women also contains the faithful domestic (perhaps a single woman) in the character of old Hannah, who is indispensable in the March household. She appears at intervals throughout this novel, but the reader is never told anything about her. Always it is her efficiency, her loyalty and devotion that are emphasized; never herself as a personality. She is middle-aged or older, is always called by her given name only, and no comment is ever made about her past life or her marital status. Old Hannah may be said to be a rather typical American version of the servant of the efficient and lovable sort, a woman—probably a neighbor—who is not altogether a servant, but is wholly subservient to her handiwork. This kind of domestic should be observed in contrast to the illiterate, immigrant woman, who appears somewhat later in American life and fiction.[3]

The rise of industry in America, which was accelerated after the Civil War, produced several distinguishable kinds of women who lived their lives apart from marriage. For some women, the development of industry created wealth; for others, it created poverty. In between was the emergent middle class, wherein many of the women turned to the humble trade of dressmaking, and otherwise served the households of those who had become rich enough to hire these services done by others. Actually, as commerce and industry expanded, all life and social intercourse changed. The opportunities thus afforded began to lure away the unmarried sisters and aunts who had been the mainstay of the colonial family. "Rich folks" employed cooks, maids of all work, nurses and governesses for their children, seamstresses and milliners to make their clothing, and, more often than not, these workers were women who had not married and established homes of their own. Other smaller groups also appear. Along with the women of wealth and the ones who worked for them were those who had neither wealth nor skill, neither work nor comfortable leisure, but who found themselves displaced or bereft by the changing character of life around them. These lived chiefly on their pride and their memories.

About this time there also began to appear in fiction numerous examples of the rich woman, the woman of social position and influence, who had somehow been awakened to the need of her less-fortunate fellow men. In 1888 appeared *Annie Kilburn* by a major novelist, William Dean Howells, in which the heroine, after living in luxury abroad, returned to her native New England village and thereafter devoted herself to "uplift" among the factory workers. Howells, however, realized the shortcomings of charitable enterprise, the folly of merely trying to relieve the distress instead of changing the social order which created them. He had already touched the same chord in *The Minister's Charge* (1887). In this novel, an eccentric maiden lady, Sibyl Vane, carries on a flower mission among those she calls "the deserving poor." Of her work her niece remarks, "Hundreds of bouquets are given away every day. They prevent crime."

The woman engaged in social service is also portrayed by lesser novelists of this period, generally in one of two ways. Some writers offer what might be called a practical suggestion for alleviating the lot of the workers. Such a woman is Miss Melinda Van Zenden of Helen Campbell's novel, *Miss Melinda's Opportunity* (1886), who decides to use the money she had been saving for foreign missions to help a group of working girls furnish a small apartment and set up housekeeping for themselves, thereby making it more nearly possible for them to exist on their miserable wage.

Other novelists in this day were more farseeing but less practical in advocating some kind of philosophical cure for the ills created by industry. Charles Sheldon's *In His Steps* (1897), an outstanding example, offered a kind of Christian socialism as a panacea, rooted in the belief that the principles of Christ, if properly implemented, would solve all human difficulties. In this novel Sheldon directed a related group of characters to follow in the Master's steps, and observed the outcome. Among them was the well-born Virginia Page who, after her conversion, decided to give all her wealth toward rehabilitating the slums in her city.

Such privileged women as these were apparently aware of the growing problems of industry, especially for other women, but most of their efforts, if we were to appraise them now, would be considered sincere but shortsighted. Few women of that earlier day were well enough informed to understand the tremendous social forces which were being let loose. If they could only think of something practical or convert a few persons in their little community to the Christian ideal, all other desirable things, they thought, would be added. It was not until later that social problems began to appear in all their complexity, and one begins to hear through novels the voice of the underlings, the victims of industrial oppression.

William Dean Howells was not only one of the first major novelists to present the older woman devoting her energies to social service instead of marriage, but he was also one of the first to present in fiction other "new" avenues of endeavor for women. Howells early foresaw the social conflict which career women were to face. In *Dr. Breen's Practice* (1881), as in Elizabeth Stuart Phelps Ward's *Doctor Zay* (1882), the heroine, a woman physician, is subjected to severe social censure, but at the end she "repents her ways" and decides to marry. Mark Twain and Charles Dudley Warner, in their joint work of fiction, *The Gilded Age* (1873), also present a young Quaker girl in Philadelphia who, in spite of all the criticism directed against her, succeeds in becoming a physician. But also like her predecessors, she decides to marry rather than struggle along in her profession alone. In brief, these three fictional women all have the courage to choose a career and the ability to achieve it, but still are made to "repent their ways" and follow the traditional pattern of marriage. These are the fictional beginnings of women in the professions.

Another major novelist, meanwhile, was dealing with the "progress" of women in still a different way. Because most of his novels are international in setting, Henry James yielded nothing to this investigation. In two of his novels, however, which are exclusively American in setting (but which were not included in the Dickinson list), he presents deftly drawn single-woman characters. In *The Bostonians* (1886) one finds the woman of means who had taken up the banner of Feminism, which in the opinion of its advocates was to become the hope of the world. Olive Chancellor is the elegant woman of Boston in the 1870's, involved in social functions and petty politics, drawing around her a coterie of like-minded women. Among the latter is little Miss Birdseye, about eighty, who had belonged at one time or another to "any and every league that had been founded for any purpose whatever, and was in love with only causes, and languished only for emancipations."

The plot of *The Bostonians* concerns Olive Chancellor's attempt to dominate the life of the young heroine in forcing her to participate in activities against her will, and in this recalls the fictional pattern of novels appearing much earlier. Parenthetically, two other even more marked examples occur in novels of S. Weir Mitchell, not mentioned elsewhere. One is the leading character of *Hepzibah Guinness*

and the other a woman (with the astonishing name of Oc-
topia Darnell) in Mitchell's better known *Roland Blake*
(1886). Both these women are vicious spinsters ruled by a
dominating passion to control the destiny of their young
wards.

Another spinster, Catherine Sloper, is a major character
in Henry James's *Washington Square* (1881). She too is
a woman of wealth, but takes little or no interest in social
betterment. When her father objects to her marrying the
man of her choice, she turns to a life of seclusion, becomes
narrow-minded and convention-bound, wholly content to
live in the old family mansion on Washington Square, itself
as dignified and elegant as its occupant.

Dealing with a vastly different locale and wholly different kinds of characters, Hamlin Garland presents several
women who, like Olive Chancellor and the women engaged
in social service, had caught the spirit of reform. Ida Wilbur,
a native of the Midwest, is an example of a strong, handsome, educated young woman, as she appears in the novel *A
Spoil of Office* (1892). Imbued also with the philosophy of
Feminism, she leaves teaching to devote herself to lecturing
toward agrarian reform. What Ida has to say and how her
message is received makes an interesting document, even
though it appears in a novel which is hardly more than a
social tract. Ida Wilbur is such a woman as might have made
a lifelong career for herself, but in line with the fictional
custom, the author has her agree to marry the hero, help
elect *him* to Congress, and thereafter turn her talents toward
furthering *his* career.

Writing also of rural people in a rural community is another grimly realistic novelist, Harold Frederic, who wrote
of his native upstate New York. In *Seth's Brother's Wife*
(1887) appear two single women who strongly support the
established stereotype. One is the uneducated, uncouth hired
girl, Alvira Roberts, with her "sallow, bilious visage," who

through her long years of servitude has become intricately involved in the affairs of the Fairchild family. Her mistress, Sabrina Fairchild, a proud and selfish woman (with her "bold, sharp, red face"), who spends most of her time reading her Bible, is a further example of the self-centered spinster who has by this time become a familiar figure of fiction.

To counterbalance these villainish women, Harold Frederic, in another of his novels, introduces a single-woman character who comes near being an original personality. She is Celia Madden, one of the four key characters in *The Damnation of Theron Ware* (1896), a novel which still remains controversial. The heroine of this novel calls herself a pagan priestess, and contributes to the undoing of the young clergyman with whom the novel is chiefly concerned. Celia Madden, unlike most of the single women previously considered, is the child of an immigrant Irish family which has grown rich. In her vivacity, her rich Catholic culture, her knowledge of music and the arts, she becomes a symbol of everything the Protestant clergyman had never known, which explains, partially at least, why he falls under her spell against his better judgment. How much of Celia Madden's strange appeal is attributed to her religion and how much to a kind of amoralism will depend upon the personal and religious bias of the reader. Celia is young, but has a remarkable maturity and declares with finality that she will never marry. Hers is a kind of secular monasticism.

Celia Madden is of special significance in this survey in that she is articulately Catholic, whereas all the earlier fictional women seem to have been of some definitely expressed or vaguely implied fundamentalism. She is also outstanding in that she is a woman of glowing beauty; this also in marked contrast to the women before her. Also, unlike most of the rich women of an earlier day, she is apparently less concerned than they with the needs of her community, nor is she impressed by the attitude of her neighbors toward her. Her life, withdrawn into a little world she has created, seems rich and full, and there is no evidence either of mute resignation or rebellion.

Other instances which reflect the growth and the spread of Catholicism in the latter half of the nineteenth century appear in two novels of William Dean Howells which were published about this time. In an involved plot, running through two of his major works and their sequels, he observes, though only in retrospect, that two of the important woman characters have become nuns. Kitty Ellison of *A Chance Acquaintance* (1873), who came from the Middle West to Boston, refuses to marry a man who considers her inferior. At the end of the novel, *Their Wedding Journey* (1872), which portrays the same characters in middle life, Kitty is seen standing upon a station platform, garbed in the habit of a religious order she has joined. Likewise, in *A Hazard of New Fortunes* (1890), Howells presents another of his heroines, Margaret Vance, who has been active in social work and whose lover is killed in a labor riot. In the last few pages of this novel, Howells uses a familiar fictional device of that day and takes a look into the future to see "what became" of the characters. In this brief glimpse of Margaret Vance in later life, she too has become a nun. She is seen in the drifting black robes of the sisterhood, and those who observed her "felt that the peace that passeth understanding had looked at them from her eyes."

Though the reader does not observe any part of the decision made by these women, he should note three points about them which are significant to this investigation. They are among the first major characters of a major novelist to come under the persuasion of Catholicism. Secondly, in them Howells implements the idea that suicide was not woman's only way out of difficulty—there was also a refuge in religion. Thirdly—and this is extremely important—that in taking the vows and the veil these women changed the attitude of their friends from pity to veneration.

One cannot adequately discuss American fiction of the latter part of the nineteenth century without taking at least passing notice of a little cluster of writers frequently referred to as writers of local color. Most of their work appeared originally in magazines, and they were, for the most part, writers of the short narrative. As such, they need not be mentioned here, except to note that in their writings one finds innumerable single-woman characters. Such stories and characters, for example, as Louisa Ellis in Mary E. Wilkins's "A New England Nun"; Miss Lucinda, 'Miny Todd, and the rebellious Celye Barnes in short tales of Rose Terry Cooke; and Sarah Orne Jewett's "The Dulham Ladies" and "Miss Tempy's Watchers" are known to every student of American literature. The tradition of the short, homely chronicle was carried on by such later writers as Zona Gale, Margaret Deland, Alice Brown, Alice French (Octave Thanet), and Dorothy Canfield Fisher, but these writers, as well as Mrs. Mary E. Wilkins Freeman, are represented in the major part of this investigation by some of their longer works of fiction. Mary Noilles Murfree, who wrote under the *nom de plume* of Charles Egbert Craddock, is often grouped with these writers, but she dealt with a different milieu, the Tennessee mountains, in which the spinster is a less familiar figure than in New England and the Middle West.

Occasionally, one finds in a long novel a short tale which is almost a unit in itself, and in one such instance appears one of the best-drawn single-woman characters in American fiction. Weaving through the lurid details of one of the grimmest pieces of realism ever penned, *McTeague* (1899) by Frank Norris, is a tender and wistful bit of autumn romance. It furnishes a striking example of restraint, in marked contrast to the primordial activities of the major characters. Little Miss Baker is a retired milliner who lives in the shabby San Francisco boardinghouse which figures in the plot. In the room adjoining hers lives an old bachelor, also friendless and alone, who is known only as Old Grannis. The two pass each other many times in the hallways or on the stairs, but never once do they raise their eyes or dare to speak. In fact, their very shyness creates such suspense that it is almost climactic when Miss Baker carries a cup of tea to the old gentleman and they muster enough courage to plan the rest of their days together.

Several distinguishable groups of single-woman characters begin to appear toward the latter part of the century, but they are more strikingly illustrated in novels which appear after 1900. Women engaged in labor activities, for example, and in certain forms of politics, seem more appropriately to be discussed in connection with later novels. The voice of the woman exploited by labor, though heard earlier, becomes a shriller cry during the era of the muckrake. The woman of talent likewise appears to better advantage at a later date. Such outstanding examples of these women as occurred previous to 1900 will be carried over into the next chronological division.

One such group, however, although represented also by later examples, seems to deserve mention at this point, chiefly because its most remarkable examples occur within this period. The reader of such fiction as has been discussed, both in the study itself and in this supplementary section, will almost certainly be impressed by the absence of humor. With few and mild exceptions, the single women in fiction take themselves seriously, and they are accepted in dead earnestness by their associates. The spinsters have been vicious and villainish, gaunt and homely, proud and selfish —or they have been devoting themselves admirably enough to good works on a small scale. The ridiculous aspects of spinsterhood, so much a part of the English fiction formula, seem not to have been emphasized by most novelists who have been considered. This does not mean, however, that these elements are lacking entirely, for they have already been emphasized by several important writers.[4]

The writings of Frank R. Stockton, two books in particular, offer amusing glimpses of single women. In his book *The Casting Away of Mrs. Lecks and Mrs. Aleshine* (1886), Elizabeth Grootenheimer, hired girl in Mrs. Aleshine's house, is described as "the dumbest of the dumbest family in town," and "won't do for marriage" because she is so stupid. *Rudder Grange* (1879) is still a readable tale of a fantastic family who take up their residence on a houseboat. In their ménage is an eccentric hired girl, Pomona, who reads romantic novels aloud and goes off into unexplained flights of fancy. Her age is never revealed, and she eventually marries an equally eccentric farmer, Jonas (to whom she gives the romantic name of Miguel), but she appears through most of her adventures as the single hired girl.

Much of the humorous writing of this day, in an attempt to catch the true flavor of the ridiculous, is written in a dialect in which the title "Mis' " is applied indiscriminately to all women, whether married or single. For this reason, the reader frequently finds it impossible to classify certain characters. One of the best of these chronicles in dialect is the series of fictional adventures of Josiah and Samantha Allen, of which probably the best known is *Samantha at Saratoga* (1887), by Marietta Holley. Though marital status is not always clearly indicated, from the context the reader can occasionally identify certain women as spinsters.

The most amusing, perhaps, of all portraits of spinsters appear in the immortal stories by Mark Twain, *The Adventures of Tom Sawyer* (1876) and its sequel *The Adventures of Huckleberry Finn* (1884). The reader has sufficient reason to assume that Tom's Aunt Polly is a spinster. In Huck's adventures, however, appears what is probably the classic description of the ridiculous but well-meaning spinster. Miss Watson is the sister of the Widow Douglas and the owner of Nigger Jim. Her effort to civilize Huck, described as Huck sees it, and quoted elsewhere in this study, is the fictional stereotype at its best, and worst.

In an effort to discover "new" elements which may arise in the "progress" of the American woman in her struggle toward emancipation and to determine whether or not marked variations occur in contrast to the findings of the central study, this brief survey of nineteenth-century fiction marginal to the data has included a number of characters who are not actually single women—these in contrast to the woman who remains single. Some are younger than thirty, or their age is never determined; many marry or plan to marry before the story ends. They are mentioned here because they too are marginal: they serve to illustrate certain forces, ideas, or trends which have a bearing upon the growing spirit of independence which so often moves in the direction of singleness. More of these "women who marry late" will appear in later fiction.

By way of summary, the half-century considered here gives fictional illustration of: (1) the rich woman turning her efforts toward social service; (2) women taking up the banner of Feminism and other kinds of reform; (3) women, thwarted in love, seeking refuge in monastic religion rather than in suicide; (4) a few women beginning to achieve some small recognition in the arts and the professions. Some of these are "new" elements in fiction, but so far as the older single woman herself is concerned, little has been added here to what the investigation has already brought to light. Almost all these kinds of women are represented in the study. What one does find is a certain difference in the proportion of women within the various gradations as more works of fiction are explored. Several of William Dean

Howells's characters, for example, were shown in the study as being engaged in social service, but the data derived from the Dickinson list seem not to have reflected the great numbers of this kind which appeared in lesser fiction of this period. The central data included only minor figures and missed a novel (a novel not nearly so well known) in which the heroine was such a woman. In another instance, this supplementary exploration brought to light two leading spinster characters in works of a major novelist, but again, in lesser-known novels. These are minutely drawn characters, but add nothing essentially new to the findings of the study.

To return to the more exclusive subject of the study, the woman who remains single: she is still tragic, pitiful, or amusing; still self-centered and domineering, or passive and colorless. Only one departs widely from the English fiction formula. She is an original character, but by no means admirable.

THE TWO DECADES 1900 TO 1920

A thousand times you have seen the . . . daughter devoting . . . all of her youth to a . . . mother. . . . Sweet she is, and pathetically hopeful . . . never quite reconciled to spinsterhood, though . . . often by her insistence that she is an "old maid," she makes the thought of her barren age embarrassing to others. The mother is sweet, too, and "wants to keep in touch with her daughter's interests," only her daughter has no interests. . . . They are all examples of the mother-and-daughter phenomenon, that most touching, most destructive example of selfless selfishness, which robs all the generations to come.

SINCLAIR LEWIS, The Job

The two decades, 1900 to 1920, witnessed a variety of fiction. Some novelists followed old patterns and old themes; others delved into new materials and expressed new points of view. These decades also saw a greatly increased output of fiction—many more novels by more and different authors.

The dominant note, of the first decade at least, is an exposé of the evils brought about by industry and commerce. Commonly referred to as the "era of the muckrake," this is the period in which Ida Tarbell, Lincoln Steffens, and others were bringing to the attention of the public startling facts about monopolistic finance and other forms of prostitution, and one finds fiction writers also adopting the same social themes in their novels. Such novelists as David Graham Phillips, Robert Herrick, and Winston Churchill were writing vigorous fiction attacking many of the social evils of the day.

The rich woman who found a use for her time and energy as well as an easing of her conscience and a justification of her wealth in a petty round of social service begins to be overshadowed by the woman exploited. The despairing voice of those who were victimized by the same industry which created the rich, a voice which began to be heard in fiction even before the Civil War, now becomes more insistent. It was not only wealth which created the social problem, which made the life of one woman different from another; it was not only the mere fact that one woman had to work for her living and the other did not; it was the social cleavage which the possession of wealth created. It was the subtle implication that the fact of having wealth made the one who had it a person superior to the one who did not have it. It was, in short, the intangible force of a system of social caste, created by the imbalance in the distribution of wealth, which brought to the fore a syndrome of social problems which challenged certain novelists. The possession of wealth, for example, set up a greater social difference between the mistress and the servant. The spirit of neighborliness, of one family helping another, gradually gave way to a spirit of subservience, and as the "hired girl" came to be replaced by the "servant," the latter often a woman unlearned and unacquainted with "American ways," all domestic help began to be judged as socially inferior. Also along with the luxury of wealth came such refinements as elaborate fashions for women, which further distinguished the mistress from those whom she employed. All this comes to light in fiction as well as in the more explicitly social documents of the day.

As early as 1850 the cry of social injustice was raised in novels of Sylvester Judd, Maria Cummins, and Susan Warner, and before another decade had passed, in even stronger novels by Rebecca Harding Davis and Elizabeth Stuart Phelps. From time to time the cry was heard, but until almost the end of the century, the world of industry was more often presented through the eyes of the rich and the privileged than from the point of view of the down-trodden. When the single woman appeared, she was more often the woman of wealth or some one of the women who served the wealthy.

In 1892 came Stephen Crane's *Maggie, a Girl of the Streets*, which told the tragic story of a child of the tenements drawn into prostitution, cast off from her filthy home, and finally ending her life in suicide. The public could hardly ignore conditions such as drove Maggie Johnson to her death.

The year 1900 established another landmark in Theodore Dreiser's *Sister Carrie*, which thrust upon an unready world a moving story and a "new" kind of heroine. Carrie Meeber also grew up in a poverty-stricken home and became the victim of a cruel society, but Carrie was made of sterner stuff and Dreiser's formula contained some new elements. His was a powerful indictment of the social order; here were forces much too vast for any single panacea such as the 1880's had offered. Here was a materialistic world beginning to run riot. But what was even more startling, here was a woman, "a fallen woman," who not only rose above her malefactors, but subsequently attained a measure of success in her own right. So powerful was this novel and so shocking the idea that a wicked woman could do anything but fail, that the book was immediately banned and almost lost sight of for more than a decade. In fact, not until 1911, when Dreiser's second novel, *Jennie Gerhardt*, was published, was the earlier book brought back to attention.

Several novels of this period, though by no means major works or by major writers, present significant points of view with regard to woman's increasing interest in such activities as labor, law, and politics. This may be said to be a kind of continuation or natural evolution of the woman engaged in social service, since these activities are, in their way, only more specialized forms of social service. Some of the women who take part in politics are well-born women who have the prestige of a family or family wealth to pave the way for their political career. Not all of them, however, are women of this kind; by this time a few begin to come up from the middle class.

Variations of the woman in social service had begun to appear in fiction before the close of the century. William Dean Howells's heroine, Margaret Vance, has already been cited as a woman whose social work brought her into close collaboration with labor activities. Ida Wilbur of Hamlin Garland's *A Spoil of Office* has been observed as a Middle-Western, middle-class girl who turned her efforts toward agrarian reform. A familiar figure of the 1870's was the lobbyist, of which Laura Hawkins of Mark Twain and Charles Dudley Warner's *The Gilded Age*, a novel already cited in another connection, was an outstanding example. Some critic has said that Laura was either "a victim or a dupe," and while she was an unsympathetic and even a tragic figure, she represents, in general, the characteristics of the female lobbyist: always subordinate to some mascu-

line leader and often used to further the schemes of un-
scrupulous politicians.

In Mary E. Wilkins Freeman's novel, *A Portion of Labor*,
published in 1902, Ellen Brewster, a factory girl, leads a
successful labor strike, but later decides to marry her stanch
collaborator, also a worker.

A novel by Brand Whitlock, *Her Infinite Variety*, published two years later, introduced Maria Burley Greene,
a Chicago attorney and counselor-at-law, who persuades
her fiancé to sponsor a bill for woman suffrage in the state
senate, and in so doing alienates his affection for her. Miss
Greene is described as a woman of admirable qualities, handsome rather than beautiful, but is made to appear somewhat
ridiculous because of her being a female lawyer. Her associates call her "Burlaps."

A similar but less substantial novel is Helen M. Winslow's
A Woman for Mayor (1909) which tells the fictional story
of the well-born Miss Gertrude Van Deusen, "the first
woman to sit in a mayor's chair in America," in "a town
going to the demagogues." She and her ally, Miss Mary
Snow, find themselves in such a political muddle that only
a self-arranged kidnapping can catch the culprits, but on the
whole her administration is successful. At the end of her
term, however, she refuses to run for office again and decides
to marry the most heroic of the politicians. "Say what you
will," she exclaims, "woman was not meant for this kind of
thing."

Angela's Business (1915) by Henry S. Harrison is in most
respects a pleasing romantic tale, but it brings to light in
connection with its heroine, some sidelights upon the woman
who aspires to political place. Mary Wing is assistant principal of a "great city high school," a position arrived at
"after eight years' incessant battling upward," and also an
officer in the state branch of the National League for Education Reform. She refuses a higher position when she de-

cides, like Mayor Van Deusen, to marry and to leave the ranks of single women. Also in this novel is the elder Miss Hodger, who lectures on Women's Rights and the New Ego. She is described as "a tall figure, bony but commanding; she had a flat chest, a tangled mane of sorrel hair and a face somewhat like a horse's." Miss Hodger remains single.

Carrying on the tradition of reform were two novels in which major characters appear for a time as single women. Winston Churchill in *The Inside of the Cup* (1912) presented a strong and attractive woman in Alison Parr, who rebels against the narrow restrictions in the life of a minister's daughter. She finally attains her ambition as a landscape architect, a profession newly opened to women, and agrees to marry her suitor, but only after she has converted his social thinking into channels similar to her own.

Deborah Gale, elder daughter in *His Family*, a novel by Ernest Poole which won the Pulitzer Prize in 1917, is a fine, sturdy character who devotes herself to teaching and social work in the New York City slums. Like Alison Parr, she achieves her professional goal, but also like Alison, marries a man who shares her spirit of social reform, and they plan to go on with their work together.

Appearing simultaneously with novels which deal with reform, exposé, and social indictment were the novels of romance, as far removed as Graustark from the realities of life. Begun with themes of court intrigue and chivalric valor, this romantic pattern moved to American setting in such novels as Paul Leicester Ford's *Janice Meredith* (1899) and Maurice Thompson's *Alice of Old Vincennes* (1900), both historical novels presenting captivating heroines.

On the side of romance was Owen Wister's still popular novel, *The Virginian* (1902), which dealt with an entirely different milieu: the cowboy West, where life required courage and ingenuity, but where the antagonistic forces were of a wholly different kind from those the muckrakers were bringing to light. The heroine, who eventually marries the Virginian, is younger than thirty, but she aptly illustrates the group of adventurous women who were not content to stay behind when the men went West—this in contrast to the women whose barren lives were chronicled by Sarah Orne Jewett, Mary E. Wilkins Freeman, and others.

One episode in *The Virginian* is significant for the point of view expressed. When the heroine, Molly Stark Wood, of Bennington, Vermont, writes to state her wish to become the schoolmarm of Bear Creek (Wyoming), she signs her letter, "Your very sincere spinster." The recipient guesses from this that she must be "about forty," but the Virginian concluded she must be considerably younger, for, said he, "your real spinster don't speak of her lot that easy." Molly's great-aunt, not sufficiently identified to have been included in the story proper, is, nevertheless, a forceful character and figures strongly in Molly's decision to go West and later to marry the "uncouth" Virginian. She defends her niece against the false pride and criticism of her New England family, recalling a similar experience of her own, in which she followed the family wishes and gave up her lover. Both are noteworthy points of view in connection with spinsterhood.

Light romantic fiction,[5] apparently unaware of the pressing social problems of the day, was carried on notably by Gene Stratton-Porter, Harold Bell Wright, John Fox, Jr., and probably reached its culmination in the series of Pollyanna stories by Eleanor H. Porter, the first of which appeared in 1913. In these saccharine stories, which enjoyed an enormous vogue, the little girl Pollyanna and her "glad" philosophy dominated all else. Even her Aunt Polly Harrington, with whom the child lived, was a sour "old maid" until her little niece converted her and she agreed to forgive an old suitor and marry him.

Two novels by major American novelists, appearing in

1905 and 1906, respectively, present single women in un-common roles. Both books have a metropolitan setting, and their heroines are daughters of the privileged class, but they are less concerned with social service than with problems of their own: problems growing out of the mores peculiar to their class, rigid rules of conduct, matters of family prestige, and jealousies set in motion by wealth and inordinate family pride.

Lily Bart, heroine of Edith Wharton's *The House of Mirth* (1905), is a tragic figure, and her story is a powerful document. Unable to effect a marriage satisfactory to her-self and her family, she goes abroad to the French Riviera, and finally escapes what has become an intolerable existence through her self-inflicted death. *The Wheel of Life* (1906) is an early and atypical work of Ellen Glasgow's, but it presents an interesting single-woman heroine in Angela Wilde, a pallid, poetic, ultrarefined woman who lives an exclusive and sheltered life in New York City. Both Lily Bart and Angela Wilde are women of wealth, but they are less concerned with social "uplift" than most of the wealthy women in fiction of preceding decades.

While some women were being exploited by industry, submerged in the slum life of cities it had helped to create, others were finding in the world of commerce and in those same cities, greater opportunities than women had ever known. By the second decade of the new century, the muck-rake pattern of fiction began to make way for novels which were essentially the experiences of an individual woman. Not all women were destined to fail: some, like Dreiser's Sister Carrie, would succeed, in spite of every handicap. Some were women with artistic talent, some had only aver-age abilities of which they made the most. But the advent of their stories in fiction marks another classification.

A transitional novel which followed somewhat tardily in the muckrake tradition but which also told a story of the success of a remarkable woman was *Susan Lenox: Her Fall and Rise*, written by David Graham Phillips and published in 1917. This two-volume novel was chiefly an exposé of the victims of prostitution in metropolitan New York, but its heroine was a woman capable of rising above her environment, who finally won acclaim as an actress. Susan fled from an early marriage and preferred to live unconventionally rather than to marry again.

The cumulative fictional story of the woman of talent in America, however, began much earlier. One of the first novels which presents such a heroine was Hamlin Garland's *Rose of Dutcher's Coolly*, published in 1895. Like Ida Wilbur of Garland's earlier novel, *A Spoil of Office*, Rose was a farm girl from the Middle West who rebelled against her impoverished life. She came to Chicago, worked her way through a university, and showed promise as a writer. She shunned all offers of marriage from farm swains, but at the end of the book she decided to marry.

Elia W. Peattie's novel, *The Precipice* (1914), though it deals with social service in its higher and broader categories, seems more properly considered as the story of a woman who reaches phenomenal success in this field. This novel, though now dated in many respects, still presents as moving a fictional contrast as one will find between the feminine and the Feminist points of view. The heroine, Kate Barrington, like the Garland heroines, grows up in a small community, graduates from a Chicago university, goes into settlement work at Hull House, finally becomes head of the National Bureau of Children in Washington. Kate refuses several offers of marriage but finally agrees to marry a Westerner who owns and operates Western mines, and on rather unusual terms: that she will go on with her work and he with his own. Also in this fictional treatise is the pathetic character of Lena Vroom who impoverishes herself and finally becomes mentally unbalanced over the strain of attaining the degree of Doctor of Philosophy. This is a striking example of an early social attitude toward the woman who did not marry but turned toward scholarly habit and ambition.

Telling another success story is McGovern's novel *Burritt Durand*, published in 1890, which follows the fortunes of Marion Rutherford, as she rises from a small-town singer to a famous opera star. A later and more famous novel traced along similar patterns is Willa Cather's *The Song of the Lark* (1915). Its heroine, Thea Kronborg, also reaches the highest pinnacle of fame, that of the opera singer acclaimed on two continents. But Willa Cather is more concerned with Thea Kronborg's struggle as an artist than with her ultimate achievement. When Thea marries, after a long unconventional courtship, it is with the idea that the man she marries, a wealthy patron of the arts, will help further her career.

It was not only in the arts that women were making progress. Business and commerce were also offering new opportunities. Three novels of this period, published within a few years of each other, tell stories of women who made an unusual success in the business world. Exceedingly popular were the Emma McChesney stories by Edna Ferber, most of them short and published serially, but later compiled into several novel-length books. They set forth the adventures of a traveling saleswoman for the T. A. Buck Featherloom Petticoat Company. Emma was a widow with a son to rear, a situation which furnished both her need and her incentive, but she represented a woman-on-her-own so far as her work-world was concerned. *Fanny Herself*, another novel of Edna Ferber's, published in 1917, was essentially the chronicle of the Brandeis family, but the up-and-coming daughter Fanny is highly successful in the millinery business before she decides in favor of love. Her decision is finally made as she gazes upon the epitaph of a rough slab marker high in the mountains—this is the grave, it said, of "an old maid who died alone."

An early and little-known novel by Sinclair Lewis entitled *The Job* also appeared in 1917, in which he presents a remarkable study of what he calls "an average girl." Una Golden and her widowed mother come from a small Pennsylvania town to New York, and she finally becomes successful in the large-scale development of real estate. Lewis's commentaries on the woman in business are pointed and, in many respects, still timely. Una first takes marriage to escape "the job"; later she gladly takes "the job" to escape marriage!

In a somewhat different sphere are two major heroines of two major novelists. Of all the women of talent and achievement, Alexandra Bergson of Willa Cather's *O Pioneers!* (1913) is perhaps the strongest and most nearly original. Like Thea Kronborg, Alexandra is among the first American fictional heroines who are not of native stock. Alexandra is the child of pioneering Scandinavian parents and succeeds admirably in developing the virgin lands of the Nebraska plains. Alexandra loves the land and is stronger than the forces with which she wrestles—a wholly self-sufficient and "triumphant" kind of person. When in middle life she plans to marry a neighbor less successful than she herself, it is merely for companionship and none of the other things which marriage has traditionally stood for.

Because they are so similar in so many respects and together so unlike most of the other heroines of fiction, Dorinda Oakley of Ellen Glasgow's *Barren Ground* should be mentioned along with Alexandra Bergson. Dorinda Oakley is of Scotch-Irish Calvinist heritage, lives in Virginia instead of the Middle West, and is forced to live down an unfortunate romantic attachment in her youth—all differing strongly from the early experiences of Alexandra Bergson; yet both women become successful farmers and on the same land on which their fathers failed. Both are tall, sturdy, and strong, both capable and efficient, both magnanimous and forgiving. Both women marry or plan to do so; but only as a matter of convenience or companionship and not for romance in the usual fictional sense of the word.

Several other individual heroines and novelists should also be noted at this point. When considered along with narratives of remarkable achievement, the quiet, pathetic little story of *Miss Lulu Bett* by Zona Gale, which appeared in 1920, seems slightly anachronistic. It still remains, however, probably the best fictional study of the unmarried sister, the poor relation, who has become the indentured slave in the household of well-to-do relatives. It is not so much the physical drudgery as the emotional dependence it creates which makes Lulu Bett the memorable and pitiful creature she is. The fact that Lulu marries, not once but twice, in no wise challenges her preeminent position in American fiction as the symbol of bullied spinsterhood.

Sherwood Anderson, like Zona Gale, contributed several single-woman characters to the body of this investigation, but while exploring the fiction marginal to the study, one can hardly fail to mention Kate Swift, the spinster schoolteacher of *Winesburg, Ohio* (1919), who figures poignantly at one time in the life of the hero. Kate is glimpsed only briefly, but few portraits of single women in fiction are more startling and memorable than hers: secretly desired by one who dared not reveal his passion and driven to desperate behavior by the realization that "even in Winesburg there are those who must live and die alone." [6]

The spinster as a humorous figure, a fictional portrait such as those established by Mark Twain, Frank Stockton, David Noyes Westcott, and others, is presented again in this period by at least one vigorous exponent: Mary Roberts Rinehart in the unpredictable adventures of *Tish* (1912). Tish (Letitia Carberry) is a lovable but utterly ridiculous spinster, and she and her two timid cronies, Lizzie and Aggie, form a trio of "irrepressible old maids" whose adventures have been set forth to date in no less than four volumes. The women travel in much the same manner as the Josiah Allens of Marietta Holley's earlier adventure series, showing up at unexpected places and events. They are present, for example, at the English Coronation, and on one of their jaunts, when bent upon seeing America, they find themselves the inspiration of a new version of the national anthem, "My Country Tish of Thee."

To summarize the first two decades of the twentieth century, few of the women mentioned in the fiction of this period live their lives entirely apart from marriage. They marry early or they marry late; hence they do not belong in the body of this study. But they are, nevertheless, related to the pattern of singleness and strengthen the stereotype of the single woman by the contrast they afford. With them marriage has taken on a new meaning; in marriage they have begun to control their own destiny and are no longer merely victims of men and circumstance. These women are significant as marginal and contrasting figures. They represent the "growing spirit of singleness" in contrast to the earlier attitude that marriage must be the focal point of a woman's life.

THE INTERVAL BETWEEN THE WARS

She became more and more like the typical old maid: precise, methodical, absorbed in trifles, and attaching an exaggerated importance to the smallest social and domestic observances.

. . .

The worst of suffering such as hers was that it left one sore to the gentlest touch.

EDITH WHARTON, The Old Maid

The years following the end of the First World War and the beginning of the Second World War, or more narrowly seen here as the decade and a half from 1920 to 1935, still project the old patterns along with the new. But the new is carried apace during this period, particularly in the direction of the unconventional. Whether this is woman's "new freedom" moving toward its inevitable conclusion, as some would maintain, or merely the fictional reflection of the breakdown of the mores generally attributed to the disintegration of war, need not be determined here or for present purposes. However, it is interesting to observe how many of the women who have forged their lives and careers apart from marriage have become major characters. In almost every title some such woman is named or reference is made to her. In short, here are more stories of "successful women"—if the reader reserve the right to define the adjective.

In 1921 Edna Ferber devoted a full-length novel, entitled *The Girls*, to three generations of spinsters within a well-to-do Chicago family: the elderly Aunt Charlotte who had sacrificed love to preserve the family pride; Lottie, the Red Cross worker, to whom the war offered a new solution to an old problem; and young Charlie who is drawn toward a career in the arts. This brisk novel contrasts effectively the social attitudes toward spinsterhood among three generations, but it is Lottie who presents the new angle. She brings back from France a war orphan she claims to have adopted, but presently she admits the child is her own.

The year 1924 brought forth two works of fiction which are significant in connection with any study of single women. One is Edith Wharton's *The Old Maid* and the other, Louis Bromfield's *The Green Bay Tree*. The former is hardly a full-length novel, being one of a series of four vignettes of the New York of an earlier day, and the Bromfield novel is the first of a trilogy; hence neither properly belongs in the main body of this investigation. But the prominent characters of both these novels deserve more than passing mention. Charlotte Lovell, the old maid, has the misfortune to fall in love with the wrong man—a man not socially acceptable to her family. When her devotion to a group of underprivileged children reveals that her main object of interest is her own child, whom she has managed to conceal in the orphanage, her securely married sister, the only one of her family to learn of Charlotte's transgression, adopts the child and rears her with her own children. This situation, in an original turn of plot, forces the child's real mother into the role of the old-maid aunt, in order to preserve for the child a possibility of a suitable marriage. Charlotte Lovell's poignant punishment points up strikingly the force of social attitude in a socially exclusive group.

Bromfield also presents a new turn in social attitude in his portrayal of the sisters, Lily and Irene Shane. Lily is the "wicked one" who flourishes as the Biblical "bay tree" from which the novel takes its name; while Irene, mortally ashamed of the disgrace her sister has brought upon the family, turns to the life of a *religieuse*. According to the fiction formula of the past, the woman who devotes herself to religion has been an admirable figure, but in this novel it is Lily who is portrayed as the strong personality, living according to her convictions, and Irene is the selfish, narrow-minded, warped personality who merely takes refuge in religion.

This iconoclastic point of view may be said to pave the way for Sharon Falconer, the woman evangelist of Sinclair Lewis's *Elmer Gantry*, which appeared in 1927. Sharon, misrepresenting her humble origin, imagines herself to be the reincarnation of Catherine of Siena, and there are times when she appears to be sincere in her burning desire to save souls. But as in other instances one could name, she is not able to distinguish clearly between the things of the spirit and the things of the flesh. She is portrayed as a "glamorous" woman who becomes ignominiously linked with the shoddy Elmer Gantry, and her life comes to a tragic close. In the details of that liaison there is nothing particularly unique, but in relation to this study, Sharon Falconer must be observed as a far from worthy character. As presented by a major satirist, the woman engaged in religious pursuits is no longer portrayed as an admirable person.

Ann Vickers, another novel by Sinclair Lewis, which appeared five years later, in 1932, illustrates a similar point with regard to women in social service. The dominant character of this novel begins as a social worker and eventually becomes famous as a penologist. Actually, she becomes one of the most successful women in fiction, as success is extrinsically measured. The fact that she is made merely the vehicle of many of Lewis's ideas on reform one may disregard for the moment. The important point here is that Ann Vickers, though engaged in what has always been considered an admirable work, is by no means an admirable woman. Her first emotional alliance leads to an abortion; her subsequent marriage terminates in divorce; and her later relationship with a political gangster is anything but worthy.

The story of Ann Vickers is similar in many respects to that of another "successful" woman who appears in fiction of this period. Clara Barron, leading character of the novel by the same name, by Harvey O'Higgins and published in 1926, is another woman who attains outstanding success in her profession, but fails miserably in her life. Like Ann Vickers, Clara Barron comes to New York from a small village. Both women have been well educated, both bring a small amount of inherited money to tide them over in the city until they can get a start. Both are drawn into "reform," but in their private lives, their patterns differ markedly. Ann fails, one may say, from being too much of a woman; Clara, from not being woman enough. Ann is uninhibited by any kind of religious or moral conscience; Clara brings a narrow fundamentalism into all she does. Clara organizes "a gang of sociological Calvinists," and projects this attitude into all her efforts toward reform. When the World War frustrates her high hopes, when she loses her stanchest admirer to a younger, more "womanly" girl, and her pet cat is dead, Clara suddenly and mysteriously disappears. Her ultimate fate is not known, but she had found life intolerable and sought some kind of escape.

The year 1932 brought another fictional study of women in the metropolitan world—this time in the world of business—in Christopher Morley's *Human Being*. This novel is primarily the story of a man, a half-real, half-allegorical figure named Richard Roe. But associated with him in his successful little business are three women whose destinies are inextricably linked with his. The one most loyal, most indispensable to Richard, is Minnie Hutzler, his private secretary who has fashioned her own career upon Richard's success. Not only are the business lives of these two interwoven, but their personal lives as well, and each finds complete fulfillment in the other. Minnie never attains the heights of success as did Ann Vickers and Clara Barron; hers is always subordinate to "her boss." But Minnie is far happier than they, going along quietly and efficiently, "mothering" the two younger girls in the office, and meeting Richard on the only terms he, a married man, could offer. The delineation of these women in their relation to each other and to their business makes an interesting study, and especially in that they seem to lead to *Kitty Foyle*, a far more widely read novel by the same author, which was to appear in 1939.

As women become more "successful," more independent, and hence farther removed from marriage, some are not only forced to derive their affectional satisfactions from association with men whom they cannot marry, but others turn to forms of behavior which are even less socially acceptable. In a novel entitled *Labyrinth*, published in 1923, Helen Hull presented in the minor character of Amy, one of the first implications in American fiction that a woman may prefer a homosexual relationship to marriage.[7] Presently, this theme appears again. Among the strange array of women with whom Ann Vickers becomes associated in her devious career are two who have entered into such a relationship, this of a more bold and objectionable kind. The dominant one is a professional woman, Belle Herringdean, Ph.D., a woman of supposedly superior intellectual ability. Ann is drawn into the affair in the interests of the "victim," Eleanor Crevecoeur, whom Ann had known in her earlier days of crusading for woman suffrage—but not in time to save the younger girl from death by suicide. This "new" development in women's relationships, this "new" substitute for marriage, continues to be a concern of the novelist in the next decade, 1935 to 1945, in which several works of fiction will be found to be devoted to this as a major theme.

Another "new" idea of much sociological significance receives fictional illustration in a novel by Margaret Ayer Barnes entitled *Edna, His Wife* (1935): the idea that "the other woman" (often a single woman, but not always) is a more worthy person than the wife. In this novel, Katherine Boyne, who has for many years been the mistress of Paul Jones, is presented as a more sympathetic and more desirable person than Edna, his wife. Miss Boyne, a sculptress, is called "a lady," and is an attractive, warm-hearted, generous woman. In the past, fiction has portrayed "the other woman" as cheap, crass, scheming, and vulgar; here, she has none of those derogatory characteristics.

To return to the theme of "success," it should be observed that not all the fictional women of this period succeeded. Lucy Gayheart, for example, heroine of a novel by the same name by Willa Cather which also appeared in 1935, tells the tragic story of a wistful, appealing, small-town girl who has the soul of an artist but not quite the talent or the stamina or the ingenuity to succeed as did Thea Kronborg in the author's earlier novel *The Song of the Lark*. Lucy has the misfortune to fall in love with her teacher, a professor of music, who is not free to marry, and when he goes abroad, she is forced to return to her gossiping home town, her insensitive and improvident family, and she finally ends her life. This novel is not a major work of its author, but sociologically, it is a moving study of one of the thousands of girls who aim for the artistic heights but never achieve that pinnacle of success—girls who must return to the small community from which they came, with the stigma of failure in their hearts. Some marry and settle down to a comfortable life; few solve their problems in the way Lucy Gayheart solved hers, but on the whole, theirs is an unhappy lot.

Two fictional lives of women who followed more conventional patterns appear in novels published within a year of each other. *Miss Bishop* (1933) by Bess Streeter Aldrich and *Mary Peters* (1934) by Mary Ellen Chase are full-length portraits of schoolteachers, among the first American novels of consequence in which teachers are major characters. One may say both these women succeeded, in the way in which teachers are apparently meant to succeed. Both are unusually sympathetic characters, but in both lives runs a minor chord of tragedy. Mary Peters rebuilt her life with her practical-minded courage after her brief and unworthy marriage ended in tragedy; Ella Bishop, having lost her lover to "a cozy little kitten of a girl," devotes her life to teaching, and is shown as she retires, quietly triumphant (much in the same manner as the English schoolmaster, Mr. Chips) after a life career as professor in the little Middle Western university from which she herself had graduated as a young girl.

Most of the novels and characters mentioned up to this point as having been published since 1920 have illustrated some essentially new element, either in the portrayal of the single woman herself or in the point of view of the novelist toward her. Not all of these elements, however, are wholly new. Ella Bishop, Edith Wharton's *The Old Maid*, Aunt Charlotte Payson in Edna Ferber's *The Girls*, Irene Shane in Bromfield's *The Green Bay Tree*, all have in them familiar elements of the old stereotype. Moreover, in a number of other novels of this period, the old pattern, with little or no change, persists.

Another novel by Edna Ferber, *American Beauty* (1931), presents the queer-looking, bad-tempered Judith Oakes, whom the author calls "the cosmic comic—the middle-aged virgin." This character also resembles the shrewish Parthenia Ann Hawkes in Miss Ferber's better known *Show Boat* (1926) who is said to have lived "a barren spinster life" before she married Cap'n Andy.

A similar derogatory attitude is also the basic pattern in *The Perennial Bachelor* (1925) by Anne Parrish, in which three sisters are also perennial spinsters. Maggie, May, and Lily Campion remain single in order to "look after" their young brother, thwarting his life as well as their own. They are all given to romantic illusions, and one commits suicide. Cora Truesdale, an important character in Margaret Ayer Barnes's chronicle of a closely knit family, *Within This Present* (1933), is in many respects a remarkable woman, but she is variously called "the family slave" and "one of those interfering old maids," and physically, at least, is "absurdly thin and angular and gawky . . ." Leda Perrin, heroine of Zona Gale's novel *Faint Perfume* (1923), true to the familiar pattern, is destined to live her life with only the "faint perfume" of a lost romance and never the full fruition of love.

In some ways the most remarkable story in which a single woman plays a prominent role is a novel published in 1935, *Miss Marvel* by Esther Forbes. This novel, which gives evidence of much psychological insight, tells the story of two sisters, Angelica and Gwendolyn Marvel, the former occupying the major place in the plot. As the child of the "best people" in the New England village, where her father owned the largest factory, Angelica wrote mysterious letters to an imaginary lover—yearned for love but shunned marriage. As the years went by, she retired more and more into her dream world, and became known merely as "the Marvel." Several times a year she emerged from her solitude to attend concerts in all her one-time elegance; finally, at the end of her long life, she piled all her thirty-six evening gowns on the guest room bed and "died on top of them." Her chief bequests beside her personal apparel were more than a bushel of letters to her imaginary "Best Beloved" and a faded miniature of herself when young.

The Decade from 1935 to 1945

Molly and me had a talk one time about the White Collar Woman. . . . Jesusgod, I read about the guts of the pioneer woman and the woman of the dustbowl and the gingham goddess of the covered wagon. What about the woman of the covered typewriter? What has she got, poor kid, when she leaves the office?

CHRISTOPHER MORLEY, Kitty Foyle

In surveying the notable fiction of the decade 1935 to 1945—1935 being the terminal point of the Dickinson list—one is impressed by the great number of novels which are not American in any sense of the word. Many are foreign in their setting, others are foreign in their authorship, and an unusual number of those which use American materials are long historical novels covering several generations or a much earlier period of American life; hence they are not well adapted to a study of this kind.

Another small group of novels are those which deal with

the so-called "underlings" of society, who in the hands of their fictional interpreters rise to something near heroic stature. These are wholly American, but the segment of society they portray is not, sociologically, the kind of culture in which women remain unmarried.

Subtracting these several varieties of fiction from the most widely read novels of this decade leaves a surprisingly small body of material in which one may find anything pertinent to a study of single women in America. But in this comparatively small group of novels, which conform in general though not specifically to the definition of the investigation, several interesting single-woman characters are delineated.

One finds here certain variations on the old themes, a further extension of some of the newer ones, but also a persistence of the stereotype with little or no variation. Old professions receive new prominence, and certain new professions appear. The stories of "successful" women run to greater lengths and greater detail, and some novelists begin to show greater insights in evaluating moral standards. Facts and situations which seemed rather shocking in past decades become commonplace in recent fiction, and the whole period may be said to be characterized by sophistication.

Undoubtedly the best known woman character of this decade is Christopher Morley's Kitty Foyle, the lovable and amusing heroine of the novel of the same name which appeared in 1939. Kitty is not quite thirty when she finally makes up her mind to encourage her latest suitor in the direction of marriage, but in her previous adventures she is the best fictional example of the white-collar girl who "makes good" in the big city. Kitty follows in the tradition of Una Golden in Sinclair Lewis's *The Job* (1917) and *Ann Vickers* (1932), and particularly of Minnie Hutzler and her co-workers in Morley's earlier novel, *Human Being* (1932), but Kitty supersedes them all in her humorous, frank, first-person account of her experiences. She falls in love with the scion of a Philadelphia Main Line family, but refuses to marry him or to bear his child when she discovers the family's condescending attitude toward her. She prefers to make her way alone and achieves success in the cosmetic business—a new kind of business venture in fiction. Kitty will be remembered for making articulate, with remarkable insight and courage and in a colorful vernacular, what thousands of girls, by 1940, had experienced, observed, or imagined.

Another working girl who finds her life inextricably interwoven with the affairs of a family socially superior to her own is Mary Rafferty in Marcia Davenport's three-generation novel *The Valley of Decision* (1943). Like Kitty Foyle, Mary is an Irish girl, daughter of a mill-working Pennsylvania family, and falls in love with the elder son of the family in whose home she works. Though more favorably accepted by the Scott family than Kitty had been by the Staffords of Philadelphia, Mary realizes that Paul will be handicapped by marrying "beneath" him, and it is she who refuses to marry him. Paul marries another, a girl more socially acceptable (as did also Wyn Stafford), but Mary, in spite of herself, is further drawn into the family affairs. She refuses all other offers of marriage, continues to serve the family through her long life, finally saves much of the family fortune for the man she loves. Mary Rafferty is a remarkable woman, and her story is told in great detail and in memorable terms, but she is the domestic and the seamstress—a combination of types who appear again and again throughout American fiction.

Another variation of the same basic theme is Hannah Parmalee, dominant character of the popular *White Banners* by Lloyd C. Douglas, published in 1936. It is Hannah who epitomizes the author's religious thesis in much the same manner as it was delineated in his earlier novel, *The Magnificent Obsession*. Hannah enters a household as a servant, and by her philosophy completely transforms the family life. The later intricacies of the plot in which Hannah's earlier life is revealed, her association with a prominent well-to-do family and her efforts to save her son his birthright, are merely an interesting embellishment. Hannah is still the domestic—the single woman as domestic—still but a variation upon an old theme.

In several of her novels which follow the fortunes of sturdy Maine families, Mary Ellen Chase presents domestics who are strong, lovable, loyal characters, but few of them are described in detail concerning their earlier life. In a novelist who so consistently emphasizes the wholesome and constructive values of life, it is rather surprising to find in her novel *Uplands* (1935) as near a villain type as she ever portrays: the spinster, Miss Abby Wickham, aristocratic, selfish, and proud. Though she is practical nurse and midwife in the country community and later joins and marries a traveling evangelist, both rather uncommon professions for a New England spinster, she is in almost every personal characteristic the familiar fictional stereotype.

Two novels by Josephine Lawrence bring something of a new insight to the life of women in business. In the earlier *But You Are Young* (1940), in the story of Kelsie Wright, manicurist, the author touches upon some of the elements of what this investigation has called "the new dependency," but Kelsie is still young when she determines to break the economic bond which her improvident family has fastened upon her, and decides to marry. The later novel is perhaps more pertinent there, in that it is among the first to emphasize what might be called the positive values in gainful employment, this in contrast to the earlier idea that such work for women was always an unfortunate necessity. The title, *Tower of Steel* (1943), implies that to each of the four young women with whom the plot is concerned, her job is such a tower of strength. To one it means adventure; to another, an escape from her fears of having a child; to the girl, newly married to her soldier across the seas, the courage to await his return. But to Fran, now twenty-nine years old and studying law in night school, the office is a place she can shut herself away "from the indecent demands made upon her spiritual privacy." These demands are particularly at the hands of her impractical, thrice-married mother and an indigent uncle, both of whom look to Fran for support. They have concluded that Fran will never marry, and as the novel ends there seems little hope for her to do so.

The schoolteacher and librarian appear in major roles in three novels of this period, the first time a librarian has so appeared in the fiction under consideration.[8] Two of these novels by the same author, Sophia Belzer Engstrand, are chronicles of interesting, but somehow colorless women. *Wilma Rogers* (1941) tells the story of a librarian, well trained for her work and with five years' experience in a New York university library, who accepts a position in a Mid-Western town. As she rides along on the train, she remembers how her mother had discouraged her from becoming a librarian, saying "librarians never marry and they never die." Her fate, however, is not quite so mournful. She manages to extricate herself from an emotional alliance which would have undermined her position, struggles with the complacency and mediocrity of an unliterary community, to say nothing of the antagonism of the older, more amateur librarian in charge, finally marries the son of her foreign landlady, a man much younger than herself, but who shares her spirit of uplift and social idealism.

Miss Engstrand's earlier novel of a schoolteacher, *Miss Munday*, won the Dial Award in 1940, and in many respects it is an unusual story. Helen Munday is thirty-one, "a thirsting school teacher . . . yearning for something beyond her life" in a small-town high school somewhere near Lake Michigan. She is the ordinary teacher (she had studied one summer at Columbia) in the ordinary community, meeting many of the ordinary problems a teacher must face. She meets them, however, in a rather individual manner. A poor but honest fisherman offers her marriage, but she refuses because she believes she can neither bring him up to her intellectual and social level nor adjust herself happily to his. She declares her teaching has unfitted her for any other life than that to which she has become accustomed, and she will remain, as she puts it, "still . . . a repressed school teacher."

A more dramatic delineation of a teacher appears in the leading character of Lydia Walsh in Elizabeth Janeway's *The Walsh Girls* (1943). Following the familiar fictional pattern, Lydia, the unmarried, is the older and less attractive of the Walsh daughters of a prominent New England family. It is she who stays with the father until his death, she who lives in the old house until her mismanagement and her unwillingness to ask help or advice from her friends cause her to lose the property. Lydia is prim, prudish, outspoken, troublemaking, queer, and queer-looking. Though devoted to Lydia, Helen, the married sister, says of her, "She can't help being warped, an old maid—but those words were cruel, and she didn't want to be cruel."

The teacher will appear again presently when minor characters from the novels already mentioned and others will be cited, but one must observe at this point in the two major characters above how many of the characteristics of the stereotype persist.

New England spinsters in a contemporary setting also appear as dominant characters but consistent with the recurring stereotype in three notable novels. The conventional plot is somewhat varied and modernized in Olive Higgins Prouty's *Now Voyageur* (1941) in which Charlotte Vale, neurotic daughter of a neurotic mother, living in the faded elegance of Back Bay Boston, is transformed with the aid of an understanding psychiatrist from a homely recluse to a socially poised and attractive woman. She falls in love with a man already married, but "saves" and "shares" his adolescent daughter whose emotional problem is similar to her own. This novel brings much psychological insight into its portrayal, in the manner of the earlier *Miss Marvel* by Esther Forbes, but its basic theme is not unfamiliar. Some readers will consider Charlotte Vale an improvement over most of the fictional spinsters which precede her; others will question whether the change is altogether for the better.

In Jean Stafford's more recent *Boston Adventure* (1944) the Boston spinster of the more traditional variety comes again into prominence in the character of Lucy Pride. The circumstances differ, to be sure, and the treatment of the plot is modern, but the way in which Miss Pride dominates the life of the young Russian-German girl who tells the story recalls Henry James's *The Bostonians*, published more than a half-century ago.

In 1946 *The Sudden Guest*, a novel by Christopher La Farge, was distributed to a large audience, among them the membership of the Book-of-the-Month Club, and was well received by critics and readers alike. It presented as its dominant and dominating character a spinster of sixty, living alone with her pride and her prejudices. The action of this novel deals with two New England hurricanes, episodes founded in fact, but it is the psychological study of the pride-ridden Celia Leckton which furnishes the motif of this unusual novel.

Another novel of this period imposed upon a factual setting is Augusta Tucker's *Miss Susie Slagle's* (1939). Miss Susie was a pleasant, motherly sort of woman who for many years kept the boardinghouse where many of the medical students of Johns Hopkins University lived. True to "type," Miss Susie had taken care of "papa and mama" while they lived, inherited the old house, and continued to live and earn her living there. Her "boys" loved and respected her in spite of her petty, prudish interference in their personal affairs, but when she fell ill of a malady from which all their skill could not save her, she became a pitiful figure.

In still a different setting and presenting a single woman in a role both old and new is *The Women on the Porch* (1944) by Caroline Gordon. Miss Willy Lewis, one of the women in the title, lives on an old, run-down plantation with an invalid mother, a queer cousin, and one old Negro servant. Although engaged in the rather uncommon role of a horse breeder—the tragic note of the novel is the death of her stallion which she had hoped would bring her the prize money at the fair—Miss Willy is otherwise a provincial and stereotyped character. She is "thin and pale" and "had never thought of anybody as being particularly fond of her."

The element of humor in portraying the spinster personality continues right up to the door of the present in such slight but popular novels as Theodore Pratt's *Miss Dilly Says No* (1945), a thoroughly amusing story of a forty-eight-year-old Hollywood secretary, named Sophronia Dilly, who after years of trying, finally writes a successful scenario. Her unexpected shrewdness in dealing with the producers furnishes insight into Hollywood methods, but it is herself as a person and her own adventures which are of special interest here. Her love affair, especially, with Eliphalet Horatio, a shy little man with a Van Dyke beard, who has never been able to succeed in anything except being a financier, is about as ridiculous as romance could be. Miss Dilly's far more experienced young protégée coaches her in how to get the shy Horatio to kiss her, and when her efforts turn out more successfully than she had anticipated, she doesn't know "whether to feel guilty or thrilled." It should be added, however, in Miss Dilly's behalf, that "she didn't dry up as the years went by"; she was "neither fat nor skinny, but filled out about as a decent human female should be."

Bringing the schoolteacher once more to the fore but with his characteristic humor, James Thurber includes in *The Thurber Caravan* (1945) a nostalgic piece which he calls "Here Lies Miss Groby." It is his reminiscence of a teacher of English composition, and offers not only a summary, but also something of a prophetic note. Thurber remembers the "quick little hen-like turns of her head," and how diligently she hunted for Topic Sentences and Figures of Speech "forever climbing up the margins of books and crawling between their lines." Then turning to the reader, he says, "You remember her. You must have had her, too. Her influence will never die out of the land."

The portrayals of single women cited up to this point in fiction of the last decade can hardly be said to be flattering to spinsterhood, but even the most liberal reader will probably agree that more derogatory delineations are yet to come. These are the still more sophisticated novels, though all of them are fairly substantial works by well-known novelists. It is in these, as one might expect, that certain tendencies of a moralistic kind may be observed, all with much significance in their relation to the single woman and social attitudes regarding her.

Several novels of the last decade deal more openly with the theme of homosexuality among women, one of them so obviously that its dramatic version upon the liberal Broadway stage met with censorship. This novel, entitled *Trio* (1943), by Dorothy Baker tells of a relationship between an attractive and intelligent professor of French in a Mid-Western university, Pauline Maury, who intimidates and dominates one of her students, Janet Logan, in a vicious manner. When Janet finally musters courage to declare her intention to marry and the professor's motive is revealed, the older woman commits suicide. This novel not only presents the woman homosexual as a major character and an arch-villain, but in one of its episodes shows a social attitude also relevant to the present theme. In a desperate effort to turn the young man against the girl, and thus keep her under her control, the professor leads him to believe the girl had been promiscuous and at one time had undergone an abortion. The lover is an ultraliberal, and although he is somewhat startled by this bold announcement, he brings himself to accept it and the girl in spite of it; but the discovery of her relationship with the older woman moves him much more deeply.

A substantial novel in which a homosexual relationship is implied though less explicitly stated is Marcia Davenport's story of the life of an opera singer, *Of Lena Geyer* (1936). As an immigrant girl Lena Geyer had borne an illegitimate child, but had wrested herself away from an adverse environment and ultimately reached great heights in her musical career, the latter similar in some respects to that of Willa Cather's heroine, Thea Kronborg, in *The Song of the Lark.* Although Lena Geyer in her mature life became the mistress of a duke, she believed that marriage would interfere with her career. She was willing, however, to enter into a continuing relationship with a well-born, wealthy woman, Elsie deHaven, who shared her interest in music. It is Miss de-Haven who as private secretary and constant companion helps to piece together the story of her life after the singer's death.

Fannie Hurst's *Lonely Parade* (1942) follows the fabulous careers of three women of widely different background and talents who share a manner of living considerably out of the ordinary. Together they maintain in a fashionable section of New York City a kind of salon for art lovers and others of Bohemian tastes and habits. Kitty Mullane eventually marries a wealthy old man for his money; Sierra Baldwin "distilled a serum out of her own loneliness and used it to cure others" by devoting herself to social work; but it is Charlotte Ames, the mouthpiece of the novel and the most dominant one of the three who is *the* character. She had cut herself off from "her class," crusaded for woman suffrage in her younger days, but the reader finds her as she has come to look "like a cross between a Tammany alderman, a baby-elephant, and a Buddha," and in her "forthright and foursquare" manner giving utterance to some startling statements. She smokes cigars, knits for a hobby, and declaring herself as "having missed the supreme carnal satisfactions," she intends "to fatten on the lesser ones" and finally dies, dramatically but philosophically, as the result of her intemperance. In her words, "Here were three women who had missed those centrifugal compensations that make the female world go round. Whatever furtive compensations, if any, they had found in sex, they had not known its open-and-above-board securities. . . . Here were three women in a busy design for living that had no bright thread through its center."

A novel similar to *Lonely Parade* in its brusque sophistication and also in its story of three "successful" women in Manhattan is Dawn Powell's *A Time to Be Born* (1942). The three women had grown up together in Lakeville, Ohio, eventually migrated eastward, where the heroine became a columnist of world affairs, aided by the fact that she married the man who owned the newspaper syndicate. Like Ann Vickers, Amanda Keeler became "Woman of the Year" and achieved a place in *Who's Who*, but also, like Lewis's heroine, made less of a success of her private life. Ethel Carey, who moves the plot along, "was thirty-two but she looked like a woman of forty so well-preserved that she could pass for thirty-two," a woman "grown pinched and desperate-eyed in the frantic effort to keep up." She finally went to Washington. It is chiefly the third, Vicky Haven, however, who presents two points of view—views from the world of urban sophistication—which are significant to a study of single women. In the words of the author: "Again Vicky felt guilty. She should never have confessed the sordid fact of her chastity to Ethel. Nowadays you didn't dare tell a thing like that to your own mother, or she'd have you analyzed to see what made you so backward." When Vicky entered into an affair with a man Amanda had cast off, that fact made no difference to her. "You had to take the leavings, if you didn't get served the first time," she tells herself, and adds, significantly, "You had to fight for even those." These remarks may be said to indicate a considerable change in the social evolution of spinisterhood: here nonchastity takes precedence over chastity, and here is unabashed testimony to the competition for men.

Up to this point, this brief summary of fiction of the decade 1935 through 1946 has cited only major characters: women who have either been single women or who have expressed points of view relevant to singleness. Most of the books mentioned have been best sellers or novels widely read and discussed; all have received attention and comment (though not always favorable, of course) from eminent critics and reviewers.

In these same novels or certain other novels of a similar classification, appearing in that decade, are numbers of other single women who are unusual personalities or who express certain attitudes worthy of brief mention. For example, Scarlet O'Hara's Aunt Pitty in Margaret Mitchell's widely read *Gone with the Wind* (1936) will be remembered as being dainty and lovable, protected and provided for silently by her family, but inefficient and ineffectual, swooning away at the sight of a crisis. In Henry Bellaman's *Kings Row* (1940) are the hero's schoolteachers: Miss Sally Venable, who characteristically "rapped on her desk with a brass-bound ruler, and stretched her abnormally long fingers out in a gesture of admonition," and her successor, Miss Martha Colt, in whom "the children were quick to recognize her bad temper and unfairness." One of the characters in Margaret Ayer Barnes's *Edna, His Wife* (1935) remembers a teacher as being "a grey-haired desiccated spinster, with a funny little tic that twitched her left eye-brow, and a mole on her upper lip. . . . she went stark crazy." Also in this novel are the maiden sisters who were dressmakers, the Misses Slade, one "iron-grey and angular and forbidding, with a smile that would sour cream," and the other "yellow-grey and soft and deprecating," who "lived in mortal fear of her sister."

Francie Nolan, the little heroine of Betty Smith's *A Tree Grows in Brooklyn* (1943), also recalls her teachers. There was Miss Briggs, "whose voice was gentle when she spoke to those fortune-favored few, and snarling when she spoke to the great crowd of unwashed." Miss Pfeiffer, "a bleached blond teacher with a high giggle," was reported among the pupils as engaging in rather astonishing sex activities during school hours, as was also the lady principal, "a hard-bitten, heavy cruel woman of middle years who wore sequin-decorated dresses and smelled always of raw gin . . ." Only Miss Bernstone was "sweet and tender," but she was much disliked by the other jealous-hearted teachers. In this widely read novel were also the two Miss Tynsmores, Miss Lizzie and Miss Aggie, who lived in an apartment under the Nolans and taught voice and piano. These spinster sisters, while struggling to keep up the appearance of elegance, actually derived their main sustenance from the cup of tea and a few crackers they got from their pupils as a gesture of hospitality.

Kitty Foyle (1939) also made a few comments on teaching in general and one teacher in particular. In a large Chicago department store Kitty meets Miss Bascom, dean of the college Kitty attended for one week. "Dean Bascom was going to some conference of college deans—what a riot that must be—and fixing herself fit to be ravished." "But she's really an old sweetheart," Kitty declares, after she had sold her a generous amount of cosmetics, "You never get to know how human folks can be until you meet them away from their job. But how's about a job that lets you be human at the same time?"

In William Saroyan's *The Human Comedy* (1943) is "old Miss Hicks," said to be one of the "best teachers in Ithaca High School" and more human and understanding than she first appears. However, her class of ancient history (a subject she has been teaching for thirty-five years), in which the hero and his friends appear in one important episode, is a burlesque of strained formality.

Brief but pointed references occur either in describing certain single women or as an expression of an attitude toward them. Gladys Dunham, a teacher and spinster friend of the heroine in Sophia Engstrand's *Miss Munday* (1940), is described as "tall and spare—her voice as thin as her body." Among the friends of the major characters in *Miss Marvel* (1935) by Esther Forbes are the banker's daughters, Josephine and Eunice Whipple, "bright, lean spinsters—with asthma and horsey teeth." In *Kings Row* (1940) by Henry Bellaman, a man says a woman of the town is "a . . . regular bean pole. She looks like somebody's old-maid aunt. . . . I'd as soon get into bed with a stepladder."

A variety of "reluctant virgins" appear as friends of the three major characters in Fannie Hurst's *Lonely Parade* (1942), all described in the blatant, forthright manner characteristic of this novel. Friends of Sierra Baldwin, her associates in settlement work, include Elma Watson, a woman many years older than Sierra, who is "flat-footed, flat-waisted, gray-eyed, gray-haired, ascetic in her pattern of behavior, lush in her suppressed instincts." Miss Gertrude Blackesley, though recognized as a "shrewd, and inspired combination of humanitarianism, business-man, and executive," is referred to as a "virgin by preference and no choice." Miss Marian Dickens, formerly a dean of women at a Midwestern college who becomes head of a certain settlement house, is "statistical and efficient," but so absent-minded that she is "unable to identify one in ten of the residents by name." But Erna, the poor relation, who serves in a variety of ways the fabulous trio of women, is perhaps the most pitiful of all. Wrenched away from her poor but simple life into a life of luxury, she finds she cannot return to the former and is driven into an affair with an unworthy man. After Erna had turned away from her humble suitor who pursued her to New York, her Aunt Charlotte says, "I wish to God I had been firmer with you that time when Tommy Adenoids was wooing you. Fourteen kids in a boxcar, even with female trouble thrown in, has its points."

So one might go on and on, in the newest fiction as in the old, citing examples of single women who conform in large measure to the familiar stereotype: more schoolteachers, more domestics, more pairs of maiden sisters, more women of whatever vocational pursuit or profession whose chief "business" is gossip, whose chief activity is motivated by an inordinate concern with other people's affairs. Add to these the continuing numbers of lovable but ridiculous spinsters in humorous fiction and the increasing numbers of women who substitute for normal marriage some kind of unconventional sex relationship, and the social investigator is forced to recognize that the fictional portrait of the single woman in the American novel—in the larger range of fiction as well as in the more limited sampling of the study proper— can hardly be said to have improved with the passing of time. Certain details have changed in accordance with the situation in real life, but one finds even in the last decade many of the same elements of the stereotype which were familiar in fiction nearly a century ago. So far as the single woman is concerned, the fictional pattern, like history, seems endlessly to repeat itself.

With regard to what has been called the negative conclusions of the study, one must observe that in some respects the discrepancy between fiction and fact is less noticeable.

Recent fiction shows a greater concern among novelists for the psychological rather than the moralistic interpretation of character, and with this modern approach, deviational behavior is made to seem more understandable and more nearly commonplace. Homosexuality appears more frequently and more obviously as a theme of fiction, and the woman who follows this pattern is still the highly intellectual and well-educated woman; this still in accord with the factual clinical studies cited earlier. One novelist at least shows an awareness of the emotional concomitants of the new dependency, though this theme has not yet challenged a major novelist in a major novel. Since women have been more economically successful, in a few instances they have also attained eminence, but these are chiefly the women who are younger than thirty or those who marry late. And may not one still question the true quality of that success? In new fiction as in the older the woman who attains economic success is still something of a sensational figure; the woman who follows quietly, competently, and happily, a worthy profession has not yet appeared as a major character. The discrepancy between fiction and fact is less marked, but only a little less. One may still ask without much hope of answer: where are the successful women who build their lives apart from marriage?

For women in general, a considerable change has taken place, especially in the last half-century. The change has come slowly, but as one approaches the present one finds in fiction, as in life, several changed situations. Most noticeable, perhaps, is that women are engaging in a greater variety of occupations and are better trained for the work they do. There are fewer poor relations emotionally and economically dependent upon more affluent members of their families. At the other extreme, there are also fewer women of wealth and leisure who voluntarily turn their efforts toward social uplift. The social attitude toward such work has changed as social work has become more of a profession and less motivated by religion. Women of artistic talent are gaining acclaim, and the world of commerce is offering new opportunities to women.

To meet these new demands and opportunities, the women of recent fiction seem to be healthier, somewhat more attractive physically, and more able to cope with the practical problems of life. They are less likely to take refuge from responsibility in invalidism, to find a haven in cloistered religion, or to take the ultimate escape in suicide. They are more independent in thought and action, and, one may also add, of marriage. There is a greater spirit of adventure, and likewise a greater ability to deal with the physical consequences adventure sometimes necessitates. They seem not to have gained, however, a comparable ability to deal with the psychological consequences of that independence.

A woman today is a little more likely to say what she thinks, to take matters into her own hands, to grapple with fate. Her economic freedom has made her more articulate and often more rebellious against the mores which tend to restrict her. She has gained enough freedom and mustered enough courage to leave her small community and migrate to larger, urban centers where she imagines, at least, she will find a greater opportunity. In the city she finds the door swings wider. She finds greater vocational advantage—or certainly a greater diversity—but she also finds a greater range of freedom in her personal life with which she sometimes is less able to deal satisfactorily. In her eagerness to "live life," to attain a fulfillment which she believes to be denied her in her smaller community, she innocently, or with full awareness of the probable consequences, takes freedom where she finds it, only to find herself enslaved by a new kind of emotional bondage.

With regard to this new freedom and the new kind of

success some women attain, it should be reemphasized that those women who are portrayed by novelists as being most "successful" are generally those who marry at some time, even though they may live and work as women-on-their-own. Either they have married prior to the outset of the novel or they plan to marry as the novel ends. They are also, for the most part, somewhat younger than thirty years of age. It should be noted also that those women who advance the farthest vocationally are women in the arts and in business, and they achieve their ultimate success in the large city. Furthermore, if those women who have transgressed the social code in their youth eventually succeed, it is generally in the arts, seldom in those professions subject to strong social control.

Concerning the woman who remains single, the situation has not kept pace. As one approaches the present, one finds in fiction fewer humble seamstresses, post office clerks, and itinerant workers, fewer indentured household slaves, fewer who are economically and emotionally dependent upon relatives. They more often remain in their small communities, grow up and grow old within the same milieu. They seldom step beyond what one might call the commonplace professions, and with only few exceptions are they the most worthy examples of women within those professions. Except for minor changes, the older single woman in the larger range of the American novel is the same person who emerged from the analysis of the more limited sampling. Lydia Walsh, Abby Wickham, Lucy Pride, Celia Leckton, all appearing as major figures in important fiction of the last dozen or so years, are the same petty, proud, dominating women who have long been familiar in the American novel.

The persisting stereotype of the older single woman—the spinster in American fiction—is undoubtedly the significant discovery this study has brought to light. It is not within the present province to trace its etiology or to determine its function in the intangible social structure, but it is pertinent to raise the question as to why the stereotype of the spinster continues in its basic pattern, whereas so many other stereotypes have completely vanished from fiction and quite possibly have been dispelled from the social mind.

There have been many stereotypes in American fiction. The mustachioed, high-booted villain, the barroom drunkard, the business baron; the invalid wife, the pretty girl who always marries the boss's son, the scarlet woman wearing obviously the symbol of her profession—all these were once familiar stereotypes, now all but passed from the pages of fiction. The spirit of villainy is still abroad in the land, but the fiction villain has become the problem drinker or the psychological misfit. Wives are still troubled and troublesome at times, but they are less often invalids. If the heroine marries, it is not always to the junior boss, and she does not always live happily ever after. With these as with many other stereotypes one could mention, the fictional pattern has changed with the times.

That any stereotype should persist is all the more impressive when one realizes the vast change in attitude toward almost every other kind of character and human relationship, and how unmistakably that change is reflected in fiction. That social attitudes do change and that fiction is a sensitive index of the change, there cannot be the slightest doubt. Barnett has illustrated in his study the change in social attitude toward divorce over a period of some eighty years. One can easily trace in fiction the changing attitude toward smoking and drinking, especially among women. How changed is the attitude of parents toward their children and of children toward their parents; of wives toward their husbands and of husbands toward their wives. How different the attitude toward marriage! So great has been the change it is almost impossible to believe it is the same old world of even half a century ago. All the more startling, therefore, is the discovery that the attitude toward the older single woman as expressed in fiction has not kept pace, either with changes such as those noted above, or even with the facts concerning her actual status in American life.

What persists is not so much the details of the portrait, for, as has been shown, many of the details have changed. As the portrait is enlarged in consideration of the larger scope of the American novel, many of the smaller details become less visible, but the bold strokes of the outline stand out just as clearly. The woman who does not marry is still essentially the same woman she always has been. Occasionally, she is a more important individual, but her dilemma is hardly better understood and appreciated than it was years ago. Because of the emptiness in her own life, she still concerns herself unduly with criticism of others who live their lives more fully.

Noticeably persistent is the social attitude toward the single woman, though often reflected through implication rather than by explicit statement. She may be praised for her good deeds and her personal characteristics, but it is seldom unqualified praise. What the novelist seems repeatedly to say is that regardless of the nature of her occupation, or how much she earns, or the social value of the work she does, her work is somehow not satisfying nor wholly commendable. Sometimes the novelist expresses his attitude directly. Sometimes he expresses it in neighborhood gossip. Sometimes, though less often, he puts it into the woman's own words and lets her declare that she has a right to be a woman even though the world requires her also to do a man's work and take a man's responsibility. Or the novelist may only imply a deep loneliness, a nagging dissatisfaction, or a nameless unrest. Almost without exception, the novelist contrives to evoke the reader's pity for the woman, if, indeed, he is willing to save her from ridicule.

The final conclusion one must inevitably reach, therefore,

is that the social attitude toward the woman who remains single, as expressed by the novelist in America, is far more derogatory than otherwise. She is at best, as the novelist sees her, an unfortunate member of society. She may be useful in her small sphere, but in a humble way. She may be loved and respected, but she is likewise pitied or ridiculed.

Ever conscious of the educational implications of this study, the investigator has at every point defined "admirable" to mean "worthy of emulation." So, in closing, it is with that same interpretation that one supports the statement that it is almost impossible to find among all the single-woman characters women who are wholly admirable. If their overt activities are above reproach, if they are decorous and conventional, they are sad or bitter or dull or queer or utterly resigned to a life of pettiness. Where is there one a young girl would want to emulate?

5

WHAT DO THE DATA MEAN?

As she the girl grows she is taught domestic, so-called feminine, duties. She plays with toy washtubs and kitchen utensils. She is given dolls to nurse and care for in imitation of her mother. Her fairy tales always end "And they lived happily ever after." Her stories, novels and movies present the joy of feminine surrender. All society extolls the sacredness of motherhood. The married woman is presented to her as financially secure and socially acceptable. The Old Maid is presented as lonely, sour and ridiculous.

GEORGE H. PRESTON, M.D. The Substance of
Mental Health

SIGNIFICANCE OF THE STEREOTYPE

WHAT is the significance of this stereotype of the single woman?

Why does the stereotype linger when its prototype has all but passed out of society?

What are the implications for the education of women?

There are no absolute answers to these questions, but several possible answers may be suggested. First, the stereotype has already been partly attributed to a social lag but in reverse to that generally found, which indicates that the novelists may yet catch up with the facts. This is undoubtedly an element, though Barnett and Needham found no such wide discrepancy between social fact and the fictional portrait. Second, one may mention again that the single women are, for the most part, minor characters in the novels, and not drawn in detail by the novelists. If the writers had drawn their characters more fully, they might have softened the lines and the result would have been a more favorable picture. Yet, as has been stated, the very fact that so many of the single women in these novels are such minor characters carries, in itself, considerable cultural significance. Only a few of the major characters, for that matter, depart from the stereotype; though highly individualized, many of them are hardly more admirable than the minor ones. Neither the novelists' lag nor the fact that the characters are minor can fully account for the stereotype.

What the persisting stereotype must mean—if one grant the basic assumption that fiction is a valid index of how people think and feel and act—is that the woman who lives her life apart from the traditional pattern of marriage, and, indeed, against the very current of life itself, is not, or not yet, at least, a convincing figure in the social mind. Perhaps the thoroughly emancipated woman is so new a creature in the long history of the world that she has not yet gained a permanent place either in literature or in life. This may be considered a third possible answer to the questions raised above. Or, one may go beyond the social into philosophical roots and suggest, as a fourth possibility, that the element of selfish pride, so evident among the fictional women, may carry more than a little significance. While the social reasons for singleness may be all that have been emphasized earlier in this investigation, it must be admitted that some women deliberately evade the responsibilities of living: that they guard too closely their own way of life and treasure too highly such values as family pride and social prestige. Not only do these women not deserve social commendation, but they actually make the way more difficult for other women who do not marry for less selfish reasons. To live a self-centered life is the direct antithesis of the giving and sharing required in successful marriage and parenthood, and perhaps society is reluctant to realize that the single life can be anything but a selfish existence.

The matter of psychological identification may be suggested as a fifth possible factor in the stereotype. The hero and the heroine persist (though the patterns change) because the reader identifies himself with them and their presumably heroic characteristics. By imagining that he is the hero or the heroine, as the case may be, the reader not only escapes a less desirable reality for the time, but also shares their heroic experiences vicariously. But why is the heroine so seldom a single woman and why is it so difficult for the feminine reader to become identified with her? Is it that the novelist, being something of a clairvoyant of society, does not wish (or dare) to make the single woman so attractive that the reader would wish to identify herself with her? If he made the single woman too desirable a figure, too easy for the reader to become identified with, would this, if carried to its final purport, work toward the ultimate undoing, if not the complete disintegration, of the very structure of society itself? Must the woman reader still imagine herself to be the nubile heroine who is sought after, won, and finally married, "to live happily ever after"? The occasional novelist may dare to depart from the norm in his delineation of character, but it would seem that the majority of novelists must conform to the traditional pattern of life, meeting not only the emotional and psychological needs of the reader, but also making their contribution toward the perpetuation of society itself. Other social and fictional stereotypes may come and go without affecting the basic pattern of life. Is the single woman still presented as unattractive and undesirable because she does not symbolize a way of life that can safely be emulated, except, perhaps, by a very few?

Can this be the fundamental reason why the fictional stereotype persists? If it is and if it cannot be changed, then the novelist is nearer "right" than the sociologist, and the implications are simple and obvious. More women must marry.

IMPLICATIONS FOR SOCIETY

The cumulative evidence of this investigation does not imply that the single woman today is like this stereotype; in fact, it has striven to show that the very opposite is more nearly true. Whatever the reasons may be why women do not marry; whatever may be the reasons why the stereotype persists; certainly much of the constructive work of the world is being carried on by single women. What the evidence of this study does imply is that if single women are like the fictional stereotype, if they are not so efficient nor so well adjusted as they should be, surely the social attitude toward them is one of the reasons. If these women could be freed from this kind of subtle pressure by which nature and society try to force them into marriage, their lives could be lived far more effectively than is now possible. If society must lose by not having the children these women might have borne, it should gain by increasing their efficiency in work of social value. Society is shortsighted indeed if it cannot draw from millions of its able-bodied and superior women something over and above their own minimum of existence.

One might suggest that some of the frustration single women occasionally feel may be of biological rather than social origin, attributable to the fact that the physical and nervous organism, designed and endowed through unbroken generations toward reproducing its kind, if denied that maturing experience may react in emotional disturbances of one kind or another. The drive toward reproduction is one of the most powerful forces of life, and if not given normal expression, some kind of unfavorable reaction might be expected. As the single woman approaches the climacteric, the feeling of biological frustration, of the lack of continuity and purpose in life, may increase and make itself evident in certain more or less obvious symptoms. Concerning this biological phase of the single woman's existence, little can be done, perhaps, except to treat the symptoms directly; unless society, in the interest of race survival, can bring itself to legitimize polygamy, to subsidize the illegitimate child, or accept the child born out of wedlock as the social equal of the child of marriage—no one of which is likely to come about suddenly or soon. Evidence would seem to indicate that mere sex license or promiscuity apart from marriage does not provide a permanently satisfying emotional security for most women.

If the need were sufficiently felt, however, it would be within the realm of the possible for medicine, psychiatry, and other allied fields to isolate the symptomology of biological frustration peculiar to single women. By analyzing morbidity and mortality records, as well as by observation and experimentation, it would be possible to learn a good deal more than is now known about the pathology of singleness. To date, most of the studies, such as those of Davis, Strakosch, and Landis, in which single women are an identifiable group, have been more concerned with the range of normality than with singleness per se. But in the original data of these investigations, much pertinent material lies latent. Medical and hospital files, sociopsychological case studies, pathological records, such as are already available to qualified research workers, could furnish much meaningful data on this subject. The symptoms of biological frustration among single women, therefore, could be made the subject of future research.

By comparison, the "social symptoms" of singleness are far more elusive, and far more difficult to treat, than the individual symptoms. Yet the present investigator, sensitized by analyzing its various components as expressed or suggested by the novelist, firmly believes that this, too, can be gradually accomplished. Public-opinion polls, which apparently are becoming more skillful and accurate with experience, could sample and measure social attitudes toward single women, to discover to what extent the attitudes expressed in fiction are actually held by society and in which social areas they are strongest. Social studies which set out to interview an entire community could likewise include a well-worded item of this kind on their schedules. By questionnaire or interview, controlled or otherwise, some of the less personal aspects of social attitude toward single women could be derived.

The more personal aspects—determining how the individual single woman herself has sensed and reacted to the attitudes society has expressed toward her—are, admittedly, still more difficult to obtain, but this also can be accomplished, once the favorable climate for it has been provided. This investigator believes that single women will discuss their singleness more freely if or when a situation can be structured in which anonymity can be preserved and the element of censure reduced to a minimum. Under the leadership of a skilled and understanding person, a two-way group discussion, impersonally focused upon characters of fiction or biography, real or hypothetical case studies, can be made a valid instrument for research. Group discussions of this kind, incidentally, can also be therapeutic, in the sense that by a direct discovery of the commonality, if not the universality, of experience, one's own emotional tensions often find release.

good summary

The primary function of this study, as the investigator has conceived of it, is to set forth and point up certain of the social aspects of singleness among women in fiction as expressed in the stereotype, in the hope that these factors may offer a clue, though it may be only a clue, as to what may be a similar situation in real life. It uses fiction, the embodiment and expression of social attitudes held or sensed by the novelist, to the end that those aspects of singleness may be brought into the conscious awareness and understanding of those qualified to study further or implement its implications. One recalls once again the words of Chekhov quoted earlier: that the function of literature is not to solve the problems of humanity, but to state them more clearly. At most and at best, this pioneer study can offer only such a statement, variously expressed.

It is not necessary, however, to wait until the clue has been traced or the hypothesis further proved to do something about making known the discrepancy between the actual facts concerning the status of single women and the fictional stereotype. Sufficient evidence already exists and more will be accumulated as more persons become sensitive to whatever conditions actually exist. As has been shown in this investigation, society has a great deal to learn about this important social problem, and, this investigator maintains, society can be taught. It can be taught either in the mass, or through work with individuals.

Many organizations already exist in which social information of this kind could be disseminated. The many and varied women's clubs and organizations, as well as the similar ones for girls and younger women, would have an interest in this matter. Parents and teachers, charged with the education of children, would certainly welcome such discussion, if authoritatively presented. Such movements as that of adult education might find it a topic for occasional consideration in their programs. Now that churches are seeing the importance of wholesome relationships in their religious pattern, some information of this kind might aid in their understanding. In short, any organization which is concerned with morale building or good citizenship might well be brought to realize that the optimum adjustment of women is a basic factor in any community. Ideas recurrently expressed in the moving picture, on the radio, the stage, in the press, and in the dozens of periodicals of every kind and variety, to say nothing of the enormous quantities of fiction constantly outpouring, eventually take hold upon the social mind. Any or all of these may become the vehicle of social change, not only in attitudes but in behavior. The content of these media of communication, therefore, is highly important if that change is to be in a favorable direction.

This investigator would not go so far as to agree wholly with the idea that the creative artist has a social obligation to revise the stereotypes he has helped to create, but recalling the unfortunate manner in which some groups are portrayed in the fiction studied, she can reasonably understand that point of view. Whether the creative artist is consciously aware of a social obligation or not, there is no denying that he wields a power for good or ill upon the social mind.

IMPLICATIONS FOR EDUCATION

The dynamic of this study, however, does not lie either in awakening the creative artist to his social responsibility or in the more direct approach to adult society. It expresses its hope in the direction of the education of the young, especially the education of girls and young women at the secondary school and college levels.

Without considering such matters as the problems involved in differentiating the curriculum to meet the specific needs of the sexes, or the arguments for or against coeducation, all, admittedly, a part of the practical problem, the findings of this investigation seem to indicate that the aims and purposes in the education of women be reviewed and revised to meet more effectively their needs in the present-day world. The problems peculiar to the single woman and those social problems aggravated by the great numbers of single women in the population must be recognized. Education must not only be more efficient in its training of women but it must be more honest and forthright. When the needs are fully felt, the curriculum will provide for the changing emphasis just as it has repeatedly done in the past. But first, education must be brought to see the matter clearly, and, perhaps one might add, dramatically.

The idea of educating women for the single life immediately meets with resistance. One can almost hear the protest against such a proposal: "We don't want to educate our girls to be single, we want to educate them for marriage!" And certainly, if marriage were to be possible for all women, there would be no question as to that being the more desirable goal. So deeply intrenched is the romantic element with regard to marriage in the Western world that even intelligent adults strongly resist, if they do not actually resent, the idea of viewing marriage realistically or providing consciously for it. Especially would they oppose anyone's suggesting to the adolescent girl that she might not marry. "She's only young once—let her keep her romantic dream," comes the shout in unison. "Let her assume that she will marry, and let us educate her for that."

The writer of these paragraphs would be the last to deprive any girl of her romantic dream. Dreams should be always cherished and respected. But it is to be seriously doubted whether any kinds of realistic data can disrupt irreparably anything so perennial and persisting as the adolescent dream of romance. Come statistics, graphs, or studies galore, it will still live! One might raise a further question as to whether the suggestion that a girl may have to live her life without marriage would bring about any more of a traumatic experience than meeting certain other kinds of disillusionment now accepted almost as commonplace. One may question whether it is any more cruel on the part of one's elders to disturb the dream of romance than to leave it to a slow and painful awakening. The writer offers her judgment of a not infrequent observation that the gradual realization that this dream one has cherished without ever a doubt ("I always took it for granted I would marry" seems to be almost a universal expression among women) will remain unfulfilled, can be even more emotionally disturbing than if one had taken it equally for granted, even in adolescence, that one might not marry, and had fashioned one's life accordingly.

The element of romance in marriage, for all its positive and enduring values, is, under present sociological conditions, a cause of confusion in many individuals. In fact, the confusion in ideology with regard to marriage is widespread and deep-rooted. One moment women feel that they must deliberately and aggressively take matters into their own hands, place themselves in a favorable social environment, devote much time, money, and attention to such matters as dress, grooming, and that abstract something called "personality development," in a desperate effort to keep themselves "in circulation"; the next, they passively resort to the dictum that marriages are made in heaven, and if they but trust in the gods and keep their hope alive, some day their Prince will come! Either method might possibly lead to marriage, but a blend of the two often yields nothing but vacillation and disillusionment.

The author does not mean to advocate or suggest that the romantic element in marriage be eliminated or even diminished, but rather that it be recognized for exactly what it often is, a source of confusion. Neither does the writer maintain that women should be trained deliberately for singleness. But what she does advocate—and this with emphasis—is that society should educate women to face the possibility of singleness, of having to live their lives without marriage, and to have them take into account, and at an early age, what differences this might make in their plans for life. If education can bring specific aid to the adolescent in the choice of vocation, or can train specifically for marriage and family life, both of which have been provided for in the curriculum of many schools, certainly an equally important body of fact regarding the statistical chances of marriage, the art of sublimation, and the solid satisfactions of life could appropriately be incorporated into any course of study which deals with human relationships. It is not perhaps so much a new subject matter that is called for, but rather a new understanding, a new emphasis, and a new interpretation.

The purpose of including such a body of fact and making the new approach, as pointed up by the findings of this study, would be threefold: first, to inform the general public of the actual facts about the place and importance of single women in contemporary society and to show the discrepancy between those facts and the prevailing stereotype; second, to impress those directly engaged in education that they can proceed to implement the data, revise the curriculum, and provide for differentiation between the sexes wherever and however it may seem feasible to do so; and third, to bring to girls and young women, especially, such facts and information and such dramatic interpretation of those facts as can be found in fiction, drama, biography, and other of the arts, to the end that they may more clearly distinguish between social pressures and biological needs and to recognize the frustration and futility these demands combine to produce in the individual.

Most women want to marry, and society wants them to marry. If in an earlier day only the unfit and the unattractive remained single, it was also a day when life offered nothing to women except marriage. Then there may have been some reason why women were considered failures if they did not follow the traditional pattern. But in the modern world, when the reasons why women cannot and do not marry have become so numerous and so varied and so often beyond the control of the individual, the state of being single should no longer carry with it an implication of failure or disapprobation. Women should not have their vocational efficiency reduced or their personal adjustment affected by being made to feel that if they have not married, something must be the matter with them. The fault, more often than not, is not that they are underlings; if it is not quite so far away as the stars, it is at least beyond their immediate ken.

Marriage will continue to be the dream and the reality for most women; but in a world such as the world today and the world which will continue through many tomorrows, there will be much worthy work for women to do quite apart from marriage, and in the doing of it there can be deep satisfaction. It is only necessary that society be brought to alter its attitudes and release the pressures by which it subtly drives women into marriage; that people be brought to think of woman's role in terms of something greater than tradition; and that women themselves can be brought to lift their vision to see a new and different world beyond the horizon. Women must be trained for and society must be brought to value those larger opportunities rather than to focus the whole attention upon something that is denied.

The ultimate aim is a more accepting and acceptable society in which a girl can grow into wholesome and effective maturity, either with marriage or without. Regardless of what life may bring to any individual, the best way to achieve a balanced and integrated personality is to anticipate what things may come, to plan for them as intelligently as one can, and *then* leave the rest to the gods.

APPENDICES

Appendix A: The Dickinson Lists

THE comprehensive list of American fiction which follows combines all titles appearing in the three Dickinson lists from which the data of the study are derived. All works of a given author are grouped and arranged alphabetically by author's name.

LEGEND

a Action takes place, wholly or in part, outside the boundaries of the United States.

b Novel fits every definition of the study but contains no identifiable single-woman character.

c Collection of short stories or sketches; not a full-length novel.

d Deals chiefly with Negro, Indian, or Chinese life, or members of some other than the white race.

e Fantasy or allegory; not sufficiently realistic.

f Historical, wholly or in part; not contemporary with lifetime of author.

g One of a series of novels; sequel, trilogy, or quartet.

h Retained for study proper.

Louisa May Alcott	*h* Little Women
Thomas Bailey Aldrich	*c* Marjorie Daw
	h The Story of a Bad Boy
Hervey Allen	*f* Anthony Adverse
James Lane Allen	*b* The Choir Invisible
	b The Kentucky Cardinal
	h The Mettle of the Pasture
Sherwood Anderson	*h* Marching Men
	h Poor White
	c The Triumph of the Egg
	h Windy McPherson's Son
	c Winesburg, Ohio
Gertrude Atherton	*f* The Conqueror

Mary Austin   *a* A Woman of Genius
Ray Stannard Baker   *c* Adventures in Contentment
                             c Adventures in Friendship
                             c The Friendly Road
                             c Great Possessions
Margaret Ayer Barnes   *f* Years of Grace
Rex Beach   *a* The Barrier
                             a The Iron Trail
                             a The Spoilers
Archie Binns   *a* Lightship
James Boyd   *f* Drums
                             f Marching On
Thomas Boyd   *a* Through the Wheat
Louis Bromfield   *g* Early Autumn
                             g A Good Woman
                             g Possession
Alice Brown   *c* Homespun and Old Gold
                             c Country Neighbors
                             c County Road
                             h The Prisoner
Pearl Buck   *d* The Good Earth
                             d The Mother
                             d Sons
Frances Hodgson Burnett   *a* A Fair Barbarian
                             a The Shuttle
                             a T. Tembarom
                             a That Lass O' Lowrie's
Struthers Burt   *h* The Interpreter's House
James Branch Cabell   *c* The Certain Hour
                             e Cords of Vanity
                             e Cream of the Jest
                             e Domnei
                             e Figures of Earth
                             e Jurgen
                             e The Rivet in Grandfather's
                                Neck
George Washington Cable   *h* The Cavalier
                             h Dr. Sevier
                             f The Grandissimes
                             b Lovers of Louisiana
                             c Old Creole Days

Abraham Cahan	*a* The Rise of David Levinsky
Gladys Hasty Carroll	*h* As the Earth Turns
Willa Cather	*f* Death Comes for the Arch-bishop
	b A Lost Lady
	h Lucy Gayheart
	h My Ántonia
	b O Pioneers!
	c Obscure Destinies
	a One of Ours
	h The Professor's House
	a Shadows on the Rock
	h The Song of the Lark
Robert W. Chambers	*f* Cardigan
	b The Fighting Chance
Mary Ellen Chase	*h* Mary Peters
A. B. Chrisman	*d* Shen of the Sea
Winston Churchill	*f* Coniston
	f The Crisis
	f The Crossing
	h A Far Country
	h The Inside of the Cup
	a A Modern Chronicle
	h Mr. Crewe's Career
	f Richard Carvel
Samuel L. Clemens (Mark Twain)	*a* Joan of Arc
	g Huckleberry Finn
	c The Mysterious Stranger
	a The Prince and the Pauper
	g Tom Sawyer
Humphrey Cobb	*a* Paths of Glory
Irvin S. Cobb	*c* Old Judge Priest
Ralph Connor	*a* The Man from Glengarry
James Fenimore Cooper	*f* The Deerslayer
	f Last of the Mohicans
	f The Pathfinder
	a The Pilot
	f The Spy
Francis Marion Crawford	*a* Mr. Isaacs
	a Saracinesca
James Oliver Curwood	*a* The Valley of Silent Men

Margaret Deland   *c* Around Old Chester
                                   g The Awakening of Helena
                                        Richie
                                   c Dr. Lavender's People
                                   g The Iron Woman
                                   h The Rising Tide
Mazo De la Roche   *a* Jalna
Floyd M. Dell   *g* The Briary-Bush
                                   g Moon-Calf
Brian Oswald Donn-Byrne   *a* Blind Raftery
                                   a Messer Marco Polo
John Dos Passos   *g* 1919
                                   a Three Soldiers
Theodore Dreiser   *h* An American Tragedy
                                   g The Financier
                                   h The "Genius"
                                   h Jennie Gerhardt
                                   g The Titan
                                   c Twelve Men
Edward Eggleston   *h* The Hoosier School Boy
                                   h The Hoosier Schoolmaster
Leonard Ehrlich   *f* God's Angry Man
John Erskine   *f* The Private Life of Helen of
                                        Troy
Edna Ferber   *h* Cimarron
                                   f The Girls
                                   c Half Portions
                                   f Show Boat
                                   f So Big
Rachel Field   *f* Time Out of Mind
Dorothy Canfield Fisher   *a* The Bent Twig
                                   g The Brimming Cup
                                   a The Deepening Stream
                                   a Her Son's Wife
                                   c Hillsboro People
                                   g Rough-Hewn
                                   h The Squirrel-Cage
Paul Leicester Ford   *h* The Honourable Peter Stir-
                                        ling
                                   f Janice Meredith
John Fox, Jr.   *h* Heart of the Hills

	f The Little Shepherd of Kingdom Come
	b The Trail of the Lonesome Pine
Mary E. Wilkins Freeman	*c* A Humble Romance
	c A New England Nun
	b The Portion of Labor
Alice French (Octave Thanet)	*b* The Man of the Hour
Zona Gale	*b* Birth
	b Faint Perfume
	c Friendship Village
	c The Loves of Peleas and Etarre
	b Miss Lulu Bett
Hamlin Garland	*f* Captain of the White Horse Troop
	a The Long Trail
	c Main-travelled Roads
Katherine Fullerton Gerould	*a* Conquistador
	c The Great Tradition
	c Vain Oblations
Ellen Glasgow	*b* Barren Ground
	f The Battleground
	b The Deliverance
	b Life and Gabriella
	b The Miller of Old Church
	b The Romance of a Plain Man
	b The Romantic Comedians
	b The Sheltered Life
	b They Stooped to Folly
	b Vein of Iron
	b Virginia
	b The Wheel of Life
Zane Grey	*f* Riders of the Purple Sage
Edward Everett Hale	*c* The Man without a Country
Arthur Sherburne Hardy	*a* But Yet a Woman
Joel Chandler Harris	*d* Uncle Remus and His Friends
	d Uncle Remus—His Songs and His Sayings

Henry S. Harrison	*b* Angela's Business
	b Queed
	b V. V.'s Eyes
Francis Brett Harte	*c* The Luck of Roaring Camp
	c Tales of the Argonauts
Charles Boardman Hawes	*a* The Dark Frigate
	a The Great Quest
	a The Mutineers
Nathaniel Hawthorne	*b* The Blithedale Romance
	b The House of the Seven Gables
	a The Marble Faun
	c Mosses from an Old Manse
	f The Scarlet Letter
	c Twice-told Tales
Ernest Hemingway	*a* Farewell to Arms
	a Men without Women
Joseph Hergesheimer	*f* Balisand
	a The Bright Shawl
	c The Happy End
	f Java Head
	b The Lay Anthony
	b Linda Condon
	b Mountain Blood
	c San Christobal de la Habana
	f Three Black Pennys
Robert Herrick	*a* Clark's Field
	a The Common Lot
	b Master of the Inn
	b Memoirs of an American Citizen
	b Together
DuBose Heyward	*d* Mamba's Daughters
Alice Tisdale Hobart	*a* Oil for the Lamps of China
Josiah Gilbert Holland	*b* Sevenoaks
Oliver Wendell Holmes	*b* Elsie Venner
	b The Guardian Angel
Emerson Hough	*f* The Covered Wagon
	f The Mississippi Bubble
William Dean Howells	*g* A Chance Acquaintance
	b A Hazard of New Fortunes

	a The Kentons
	b The Leatherwood God
	h A Modern Instance
	h The Rise of Silas Lapham
Jay William Hudson	*a* The Abbe Pierre
Fannie Hurst	*c* Humoresque
Helen Hunt Jackson	*b* Ramona
Henry James	*a* The Ambassadors
	a Daisy Miller
	a The Golden Bowl
	a Portrait of a Lady
	a The Wings of the Dove
Sarah Orne Jewett	*c* Deephaven
	f The Tory Lover
Josephine W. Johnson	*b* Now in November
Owen Johnson	*b* Stover at Yale
Mary Johnston	*f* Audrey
	f Lewis Rand
	f The Long Roll
MacKinlay Kantor	*f* Long Remember
Basil King	*a* The Inner Shrine
	a The Street Called Straight
	a Wild Olive
Peter B. Kyne	*a* Kindred of the Dust
Oliver La Farge	*d* Laughing Boy
Sinclair Lewis	*a* Arrowsmith
	b Babbitt
	a Dodsworth
	b It Can't Happen Here
	h Main Street
	b Work of Art
Joseph C. Lincoln	*h* Cap'n Eri
	h Dr. Nye
	h Galusha the Magnificent
	h Mary 'Gusta
	b Mr. Pratt
	h Partners of the Tide
	b The Portygee
	b Rugged Water
Jack London	*a* Burning Daylight
	a Call of the Wild

Jack London	*a* Martin Eden
	a The Seawolf
	a Smoke Bellew
	a White Fang
George Barr McCutcheon	*e* Graustark
Herman Melville	*a* Moby Dick
	a Omoo
	a Typee
S. Weir Mitchell	*a* Adventures of François
	b Constance Trescot
	f Hugh Wynne, Free Quaker
	f The Red City
	b Westways
Christopher Morley	*e* The Haunted Bookshop
	e Parnassus on Wheels
	e Thunder on the Left
	e Where the Blue Begins
John Muir	*a* Stickeen
Robert Nathan	*b* Autumn
Meredith Nicholson	*b* A Hoosier Chronicle
	b The House of a Thousand Candles
	a The Port of Missing Men
Charles G. Norris	*b* Brass
Frank Norris	*b* McTeague
	g The Octopus
	g The Pit
	b Vandover and the Brute
Kathleen Norris	*a* Mother
	b Saturday's Child
Marie Conway Oemler	*b* Slippy McGee
Martha Ostenso	*b* Wild Geese
Thomas Nelson Page	*a* Gordon Keith
	c In Old Virginia
	b Red Rock
Anne Parrish	*f* The Perennial Bachelor
Julia Peterkin	*d* Black April
	d Scarlet Sister Mary
Edgar Allen Poe	*c* Tales of the Grotesque and Arabesque
Ernest Poole	*b* Beggar's Gold
	b The Harbor

	b His Family
Eleanor H. Porter	*g* Pollyanna
William Sydney Porter	*c* Cabbages and Kings
(O. Henry)	*c* The Four Million
	c The Gentle Grafter
	c The Heart of the West
	c The Trimmed Lamp
	c The Voice of the City
	c Whirligigs
Herbert C. Quick	*g* Hawkeye
	g The Invisible Woman
	g Vandemark's Folly
Alice Hegan Rice	*h* Mrs. Wiggs of the Cabbage Patch
Grace S. Richmond	*h* Red Pepper Burns
Mary Roberts Rinehart	*h* The Circular Staircase
	h K
Elizabeth Madox Roberts	*f* The Great Meadow
	b The Time of Man
Elizabeth Robins	*a* Come and Find Me
	a The Magnetic North
Robert Rylee	*d* Deep Dark River
Carl Sandburg	*c* Rootabaga Stories
Anne Douglas Sedgwick	*a* A Fountain Sealed
	a The Little French Girl
	a The Old Countess
	a Tante
Ernest Thompson Seton	*c* Lives of the Hunted
Upton Sinclair	*a* The Jungle
	b King Coal
F. Hopkinson Smith	*c* Arm Chair at the Inn
	h The Fortunes of Oliver Horn
	b Kennedy Square
	h Peter
	c Wood Fire in No. 3
Mrs. C. D. Snedeker	*a* The Spartan
Wilbur Daniel Steele	*c* Land's End
Charles David Stewart	*h* The Fugitive Blacksmith
Frank Stockton	*a* The Casting Away of Mrs. Lecks and Mrs. Aleshine
	b The Lady or the Tiger

Frank Stockton	*b* Rudder Grange
Harriet Beecher Stowe	*f* The Minister's Wooing
	f Oldtown Folks
	d Uncle Tom's Cabin
Gene Stratton-Porter	*g* Freckles
	g A Girl of the Limberlost
	h The Harvester
Ruth Suckow	*h* The Folks
Booth Tarkington	*b* Alice Adams
	b The Conquest of Canaan
	h Gentle Julia
	h The Gentleman from Indiana
	h The Magnificent Ambersons
	b The Midlander
	a Monsieur Beaucaire
	g Penrod
	g Penrod and Sam
	h Seventeen
	b The Turmoil
Carl Van Vechten	*a* Peter Whiffle
Lew Wallace	*a* Ben Hur
Mary S. Watts	*a* The Boardman Family
	h From Father to Son
	h The Legacy
	a Nathan Burke
	a The Rise of Jennie Cushing
	a Van Cleve
Glenway Wescott	*f* The Grandmothers
Edward Noyes Westcott	*h* David Harum
Edith Wharton	*a* The Age of Innocence
	a The Children
	a The Custom of the Country
	h Ethan Frome
	b The Fruit of the Tree
	b The Glimpses of the Moon
	a The House of Mirth
	a Madame de Treymes
	a The Mother's Recompense
	c Old New York

	a The Reef
	b Summer
	a The Valley of Decision
	c Xingu and Other Stories
Edward Lucas White	*a* Andivius Hedulio
	a El Supremo
Stewart Edward White	*g* The Blazed Trail
	g Gold
	g The Gray Dawn
	g Riverman
	g The Rose Dawn
	g The Rules of the Game
	a The Silent Places
William Allen White	*b* A Certain Rich Man
	b In the Heart of a Fool
Kate Douglas Wiggin	*b* Rebecca of Sunnybrook Farm
Thornton Wilder	*a* The Bridge of San Luis Rey
	b Heaven's My Destination
	a The Woman of Andros
Harry Leon Wilson	*b* Merton of the Movies
	a Ruggles of Red Gap
Theodore Winthrop	*a* John Brent
Owen Wister	*b* Lady Baltimore
	c Lin McLean
	b The Virginian
Harold Bell Wright	*b* The Winning of Barbara Worth
Thomas Wolfe	*a* Of Time and the River
Elinor Hoyt Wylie	*a* Jennifer Lorn
Anzia Yezierska	*c* Hungry Hearts
Stark Young	*f* So Red the Rose

APPENDIX B: THE SINGLE-WOMAN CHARACTERS

Listed below are the 150 single-woman characters which fit the definition set forth in Chapter 1, as they appear in each of the novels "retained for the study proper"; that is, as classified under *h* in Appendix A. The novels below are now arranged in chronological order, in an effort to show the expected progression or evolution of the stereotype.

Date	Title and Author	Single-Woman Characters
1. 1851	The House of the Seven Gables Nathaniel Hawthorne	1. Hepzibah Pyncheon
2. 1852	The Blithedale Romance Nathaniel Hawthorne	none
3. 1861	Elsie Venner Oliver Wendell Holmes	none
4. 1868	Little Women Louisa May Alcott	2. Miss Crocker 3. Miss Norton
5. 1868	The Guardian Angel Oliver Wendell Holmes	4. Cynthia Badlam 5. Miss Byloe
6. 1869	The Story of a Bad Boy Thomas Bailey Aldrich	6. Abigail Nutter 7. Dorothy Gibbs 8. Dame Jocelyn
7. 1871	The Hoosier Schoolmaster Edward Eggleston	9. Miss Nancy Sawyer
8. 1879	Rudder Grange Frank Stockton	none
9. 1881	A Modern Instance William Dean Howells	10. Anna Halleck 11. Louisa Halleck
10. 1883	The Hoosier School-Boy Edward Eggleston	none

Date	Title and Author	Single-Woman Characters
11. 1884	The Rise of Silas Lapham William Dean Howells	12. Miss Kingsbury
12. 1884	Dr. Sevier George Washington Cable	13. "Sister Jane"
13. 1884	Ramona Helen Hunt Jackson	none
14. 1894	The Honourable Peter Stirling Paul Leicester Ford	14. Miss Anneke DeVoe
15. 1894	The Kentucky Cardinal James Lane Allen	none
16. 1897	The Choir Invisible James Lane Allen	none
17. 1898	David Harum Edward Noyes Westcott	15. "Sairy" 16. "Old maid Allis" 17. Miss Knapp
18. 1898	Red Rock Thomas Nelson Page	18. Miss Thomasia Gray
19. 1899	The Gentleman from Indiana Booth Tarkington	19. Selina Tibbs
20. 1901	The Cavalier George Washington Cable	20. Miss Martha Harper
21. 1901	Mrs. Wiggs of the Cabbage Patch Alice Hegan Rice	21. Miss Hazy
22. 1901	The Portion of Labor Mary E. Wilkins Freeman	22. Miss Higgins
23. 1902	The Fortunes of Oliver Horn F. Hopkinson Smith	23. Miss Lavinia Clendenning 24. Miss Ann Teetum 25. Miss Sarah Teetum

Date	*Title and Author*	*Single-Woman Characters*
24. 1902	The Virginian Owen Wister	none
25. 1903	The Mettle of the Pasture James Lane Allen	26. Anna Hardage
26. 1903	Rebecca of Sunnybrook Farm Kate Douglas Wiggin	27. Miranda Sawyer 28. Jane Sawyer 29. The Burnham sisters
27. 1904	The Deliverance Ellen Glasgow	30. Cynthia Blake 31. Saidie Fletcher
28. 1904	Cap'n Eri Joseph C. Lincoln	32. Miss Melissa Busteed 33. Miss Mary Emma Cahoon
29. 1905	Memoirs of an American Citizen Robert Herrick	none
30. 1905	Partners of the Tide Joseph C. Lincoln	34. Priscilla Allen 35. Temperance Allen
31. 1905	Constance Trescot S. Weir Mitchell	36. Miss Bland 37. Miss Althea Le Moine
32. 1905	The House of a Thousand Candles Meredith Nicholson	38. Sister Theresa Evans
33. 1905	The Fugitive Blacksmith Charles David Stewart	39. Mary Ann McBride
34. 1905	The Conquest of Canaan Booth Tarkington	none
35. 1905	The Man of the Hour Octave Thanet (Alice French)	40. Miss Tina Miller 41. Miss Ally Miller
36. 1906	The Fighting Chance Robert W. Chambers	none
37. 1906	The Wheel of Life Ellen Glasgow	42. Angela Wilde
38. 1906	Mr. Pratt Joseph C. Lincoln	none

Date	Title and Author	Single-Woman Characters
39. 1906	Lady Baltimore Owen Wister	43. Miss Eliza St. Michael 44. Miss Josephine St. Michael
40. 1907	The Fruit of the Tree Edith Wharton	none
41. 1907	The Port of Missing Men Meredith Nicholson	none
42. 1908	Mr. Crewe's Career Winston Churchill	45. Euphrasia Cotton
43. 1908	The Trail of the Lonesome Pine John Fox, Jr.	none
44. 1908	The Master of the Inn Robert Herrick	none
45. 1908	Together Robert Herrick	none
46. 1908	The Circular Staircase Mary Roberts Rinehart	46. Rachel Innes 47. Liddy Allen
47. 1908	Peter F. Hopkinson Smith	48. Felicia Grayson
48. 1909	The Romance of a Plain Man Ellen Glasgow	49. Miss Matoaca Bland 50. Miss Mitty Bland
49. 1909	A Certain Rich Man William Allen White	51. Miss Hendricks
50. 1911	The Miller of Old Church Ellen Glasgow	52. Kesiah Blount
51. 1911	Queed Henry S. Harrison	none
52. 1911	Stover at Yale Owen Johnson	none
53. 1911	The Harvester Gene Stratton-Porter	none

Date	Title and Author	Single-Woman Characters
54. 1911	Kennedy Square F. Hopkinson Smith	none
55. 1911	The Winning of Bar- bara Worth Harold Bell Wright	none
56. 1911	The Legacy Mary S. Watts	53. 'Lizbeth Hurd
57. 1911	Jennie Gerhardt Theodore Dreiser	54. Jennie Gerhardt
58. 1911	Ethan Frome Edith Wharton	55. Mattie Silver
59. 1912	The Inside of the Cup Winston Churchill	56. Sally Glover
60. 1912	The Squirrel Cage Dorothy Canfield Fisher	57. Flora Burgess 58. Anastasia O'Hern
61. 1912	The Heart of the Hills John Fox, Jr.	59. St. Hilda
62. 1912	A Hoosier Chronicle Meredith Nicholson	60. Mary 61. Miss Waring 62. Miss Featherstone
63. 1913	V. V.'s Eyes Henry S. Harrison	none
64. 1913	Westways S. Weir Mitchell	none
65. 1914	Vandover and the Brute Frank Norris	63. Turner Ravis 64. Flossie
66. 1914	The Lay Anthony Joseph Hergesheimer	none
67. 1914	Saturday's Child Kathleen Norris	65. Miss Thornton 66. Virginia Lancaster 67. Emily Saunders 68. Ella Saunders 69. Lydia Lord 70. Mary Lord
68. 1914	K Mary Roberts Rine- hart	71. Harriett Kennedy

Date	Title and Author	Single-Woman Characters
69. 1914	A Far Country Winston Churchill	72. Miss McCoy 73. Miss Allsop
70. 1915	The Song of the Lark Willa Cather	74. Tillie Kronborg
71. 1915	The "Genius" Theodore Dreiser	75. Miriam Fitch 76. Norma Whitmore 77. Miss De Sale
72. 1915	Mountain Blood Joseph Hergesheimer	78. Clare Makimmon 79. Meta Beggs
73. 1915	The Harbor Ernest Poole	80. Old Belle
74. 1915	The Turmoil Booth Tarkington	none
75. 1916	The Prisoner Alice Brown	81. Amabel Bracebridge
76. 1916	The Rising Tide Margaret Deland	82. Marie Spencer 83. Eliza Graham 84. Mary Graham
77. 1916	Life and Gabriella Ellen Glasgow	85. Miss Polly Hatch 86. Miss Amelia Peterborough 87. Miss Jemima Peterborough 88. Miss Lancaster 89. Miss Smith 90. Miss Danton
78. 1916	The Leatherwood God William Dean Howells	none
79. 1916	Mary 'Gusta Joseph C. Lincoln	91. Priscilla Cabot 92. Hortense Cabot 93. Letitia Pease 94. Mary Underwood
80. 1916	Windy McPherson's Son Sherwood Anderson	
81. 1916	Seventeen Booth Tarkington	none

Date	Title and Author	Single-Woman Characters
82. 1917	Slippy McGee Marie Conway Oemler	95. Sally Ruth Dexter
83. 1917	Marching Men Sherwood Anderson	96. Edith Carson
84. 1917	King Coal Upton Sinclair	none
85. 1917	Summer Edith Wharton	97. Miss Hatchard
86. 1918	Birth Zona Gale	98. Rachel Arrowsmith 99. Bonniebell Clauson
87. 1918	My Ántonia Willa Cather	100. Lena Lingard 101. Tiny Soderball
88. 1918	The Magnificent Ambersons Booth Tarkington	102. Fanny Minafer
89. 1919	Linda Condon Joseph Hergesheimer	103. Miss Skillern 104. Judith Feldt 105. Elouise Lowrie 106. Amelia Lowrie
90. 1919	From Father to Son Mary S. Watts	107. Clara Stillman 108. Miss Parker 109. Miss Stannifer
91. 1920	Poor White Sherwood Anderson	110. Rose McCoy 111. Kate Chanceller 112. Elsie Hunter
92. 1920	Main Street Sinclair Lewis	113. Ella Stowbody 114. Miss Villets
93. 1920	The Portygee Joseph C. Lincoln	none
94. 1921	Autumn Robert Nathan	115. Miss Beal
95. 1921	Brass Charles G. Norris	116. Beckie Meriweather 117. Mary Rowland
96. 1921	Beggar's Gold Ernest Poole	none
97. 1921	Alice Adams Booth Tarkington	none

Date	Title and Author	Single-Woman Characters
98. 1921	Galusha the Magnificent Joseph C. Lincoln	118. Marietta Hoag
99. 1922	Babbitt Sinclair Lewis	none
100. 1922	Gentle Julia Booth Tarkington	119. Cousin Virginia
101. 1922	Merton of the Movies Harry Leon Wilson	120. Miss Tessie Kearns
102. 1923	A Lost Lady Willa Cather	none
103. 1923	Faint Perfume Zona Gale	none
104. 1923	Doctor Nye Joseph C. Lincoln	121. Althea Bemis 122. Marietta Lamb 123. Olinda Pepper
105. 1924	The Interpreter's House Struthers Burt	124. Octavia Hiatt
106. 1924	Rugged Water Joseph C. Lincoln	none
107. 1925	The Professor's House Willa Cather	125. Augusta
108. 1925	An American Tragedy Theodore Dreiser	126. Zillah Saunders
109. 1925	Barren Ground Ellen Glasgow	127. Seena Snead 128. Texanna Snead 129. Tabitha Snead
110. 1925	Wild Geese Martha Ostenso	130. Althea Bjarnasson
111. 1926	The Romantic Comedians Ellen Glasgow	131. Amanda Lightfoot
112. 1926	The Time of Man Elizabeth Madox Roberts	none

Date	Title and Author	Single-Woman Characters
113. 1929	They Stooped to Folly Ellen Glasgow	132. Louisa Goddard 133. Aunt Agatha Little-page
114. 1929	Virginia Ellen Glasgow	134. Miss Willy Whitlow 135. Miss Priscilla Batte
115. 1930	Cimarron Edna Ferber	136. Mother Bridget 137. Dixie Lee
116. 1932	The Sheltered Life Ellen Glasgow	138. Etta Archbald
117. 1934	Mary Peters Mary Ellen Chase	139. Miss Tapley 140. Miss Crosby
118. 1934	Now in November Josephine Johnson	none
119. 1934	Work of Art Sinclair Lewis	none
120. 1934	The Folks Ruth Suckow	141. Margaret Ferguson 142. Essie Bartlett 143. Ida Chisholm 144. Vanchie Darlington 145. Marcella Potter 146. Mary Lou
121. 1935	As the Earth Turns Gladys Hasty Carroll	147. Miss Esther Kingsley
122. 1935	Lucy Gayheart Willa Cather	148. Pauline Gayheart
123. 1935	Vein of Iron Ellen Glasgow	149. Aunt Meggie Fincas-tle
124. 1935	It Can't Happen Here Sinclair Lewis	none
125. 1935	Heaven's My Destina-tion Thornton Wilder	150. Miss Simmons

Appendix C: Basis for Classification

Following are the twenty categories which formed the basis for classifying each single-woman character, the results of which are summarized in "The Analysis" of Chapter 3. Under each category are ranged the possible elements which might be anticipated in any fictional characterization, set up, wherever feasible, according to a scale. Also in each category provision was made for those instances in which no comment was made on a given point or if the comment were something other than what was anticipated. By checking the individual item under each category which most nearly described a character, and recording the code letters on a chart, it was possible to arrive at a simple analysis. Several copies of the original chart are on file in the Library of Teachers College, Columbia University.

THE SINGLE-WOMAN CHARACTER

1. *Approximate Age-Span*
   a) Early childhood through age of thirty and beyond
   b) Adolescence through age of thirty
   c) Early maturity through age of thirty
   d) Beyond thirty when the story opens

2. *Prominence in Plot*
   a) Title carries name
   b) One of three major characters
   c) Minor character; influences major characters
   d) Minor character; little or no influence
   e) Pivot in plot
   f) Adds local color
   g) Furnishes comic relief
   y) Another than those mentioned

AMBITION AND ACHIEVEMENT

3. *Central Ambition*
   a) For love—husband, children, and home of her own
   b) To get ahead in her career
   c) To become financially secure
   d) To extricate herself from frustrating circumstances
   e) To help someone else achieve his or her goal

   f) To improve her community
   g) To become socially important in her community
   h) To be "accepted" socially
   i) To help family or relatives
   x) No comment
   y) Another than those mentioned

4. *Nature of Frustrating Circumstances*
   a) Lacks sufficient money to achieve ambition
   b) Cannot or does not get necessary education or training
   c) Adult domination prevents achievement
   d) Is not physically able
   e) Has one or more dependents
   f) Social position deters her
   g) Is held back by tradition, family or otherwise
   x) No comment
   y) Another than those mentioned

5. *Nature of Her Success*
   a) Advances in her career
   b) Becomes financially independent and secure
   c) Is relieved of frustrating circumstances
   d) Derives happiness from seeing someone else succeed
   e) Achieves place in the community to which she aspires
   x) No comment
   y) Another than those mentioned

6. *Nature of Her Failure*
   a) Wishes to marry but does not achieve marriage
   b) Fails in her vocation
   c) Cannot get along happily with those she lives with
   d) Becomes financially dependent
   e) Becomes ill, lonely, or otherwise distressed
   x) No comment
   y) Another than those mentioned

7. *Her Interest in Her Community*
   a) Holds public office, a place of respect and influence
   b) Is active in community affairs
   c) Wishes to be active, but held down by frustrating circumstances

d) Limits interest only to family group, an individual, or home
e) Is completely self-centered
f) Longs to leave where she is and go elsewhere
x) No comment
y) Another than those mentioned

8. *Adult Vocation*
a) Important position demanding superior ability
b) Ordinary position requiring no special skill or training
c) Modest position
d) Humble position of its kind
e) No vocation; social "parasite"; not fitted for any vocation
f) Entirely dependent upon someone else
x) No comment
y) Another than those mentioned

HUMAN RELATIONSHIPS-ADULT

9. *Quality of Human Relationships* (in general)
a) Popular; everybody likes her
b) Gets along well with most people
c) Gets along with all except one or two
d) Has trouble with those nearest her
e) Quarrels with everybody—nobody likes or understands her
f) Lives to herself—has no commerce with anybody
x) No comment
y) Another than those mentioned

10. *Sources of Tension* (Specific)
a) With one or both parents
b) With brothers or sisters
c) In school—with teachers or pupils
d) With her elders
e) With her contemporaries
f) With boys or men
g) With other girls or women
h) With her superiors
i) With her inferiors
x) No comment
y) Another than those mentioned

11. *Nature of Heterosexual Relationships* (Adult)
   a) Natural relationships
   b) Has no opportunity to form relationship
   c) Devoted to man who returns affection but cannot marry
   d) Loves a man who does not return affection
   e) Forms a liaison without marriage
   f) Bears child out of wedlock
   g) Promiscuous
   h) None
   x) No comment
   y) Another than those mentioned

ATTITUDES

12. *Her Attitude toward Her Vocation*
   a) Finds much pleasure in her work
   b) Finds it pleasant but not altogether absorbing
   c) Enjoys her work, but hopes life holds something more for
        her
   d) Has unpleasant relations in connection with work
   e) Intensely dislikes work and all connected with it
   x) No comment
   y) Another than those mentioned

13. *Her Attitude toward Marriage* (in general)
   a) Believes a woman should marry
   b) Believes any marriage preferable to no marriage
   c) Believes no woman's life can be complete without marriage
   d) Believes marriage is the social badge of success
   e) Indifferent to marriage
   f) Believes some women should not marry
   g) Believes marriage is not "everything" in life
   h) Believes no marriage is preferable to an unhappy marriage
   i) Believes a woman need not feel a sense of failure if she does
        not marry
   x) No comment
   y) Another than those mentioned

14. *Her Attitude toward Her Own Life*
   a) Believes her life has been good and successful without mar-
        riage
   b) Believes life has been good but marriage would have en-
        riched it

    c) Believes life would not have been good, even with marriage
    d) Indifferent
    e) Believes she has succeeded even though society may not think so
    f) Believes she has failed in this but is otherwise successful
    g) Believes life is an utter failure because she did not marry
    x) No comment
    y) Another than those mentioned

15. *Characteristics for Which Others Admire Her*
    a) Her beauty or physical appearance
    b) Her goodness of character
    c) Her achievement—vocational, social, or otherwise
    d) Her altruism, devotion, loyalty, or sacrifice
    e) Her courage, endurance, or patience
    f) Her handiwork or manual skill
    g) Her disposition
    h) Her efficiency
    x) No comment
    y) Another than those mentioned

16. *Characteristics for Which Others Do Not Admire Her*
    a) Her appearance
    b) Her faulty character
    c) Her disposition
    d) Her selfishness
    e) Her "peculiarity"
    f) Her inefficiency
    x) No comment
    y) Another than those mentioned

17. *Attitude of Other Characters (or the Author) toward Her*
    a) Admiration for her courage, strength of character, or goodness
    b) Appreciation of real circumstances which prevented marriage
    c) Indifference toward her
    d) Pity for her
    e) Ridicule for her as an "old maid" or queer personality
    f) Envious of her freedom, independence, and lack of responsibility

g) Contempt or scorn because she has avoided family responsibility
x) No comment
y) Another than those mentioned

FACTORS IN NONMARRIAGE AND ADJUSTMENT

18. *Her Own Reasons for Not Marrying*
   a) Could not leave parents or other family obligations
   b) Could not leave her job, needs what she earns
   c) Accustomed to higher standard of living than marriage offers her
   d) Could not adjust herself to prospective husband's social group
   e) Believes it is a mistake to marry late in life
   f) "Right man" cannot marry her
   g) Lover died; cannot marry another
   h) Cherishes "ideal" rather than real person
   i) Fears marriage, childbearing
   j) Believes herself ill, unable to marry
   x) No comment
   y) Another than those mentioned

19. *Reader's Judgment as to Why She Did Not Marry*
   a) Physically unattractive
   b) Unpleasant disposition
   c) Not adapted to marriage, homemaking, rearing children
   d) Peculiar or queer character
   e) A wholly "unromantic" person
   f) Factors beyond herself control her life
   x) No comment
   y) Another than those mentioned

20. *Her Adjustment at the Time She Leaves the Story*
   a) She is apparently happy and successful in her work
   b) She adopts a child, or devotes herself to children
   c) She finds solace in religion
   d) She is philosophically adjusted to "things as they are"
   e) She is miserable, wretched, and unhappy
   f) She dies without seeing her wishes fulfilled
   x) No comment
   y) Another than those mentioned

NOTES

NOTES TO CHAPTER I

1. Robert Latou Dickinson and Lura Beam, *The Single Woman*.

2. Katherine Bement Davis, *Factors in the Sex Life of 2200 Women*.

3. Frances M. Strakosch, *Factors in the Sex Life of 700 Psychopathic Women*.

4. *Ibid.*, pp. 89–90.

5. *Ibid.*, p. 88.

6. Carney Landis and co-authors, *Sex in Development*.

7. *Ibid.*, p. 205.

8. *Ibid.*, p. 234.

9. Carney Landis and M. Marjorie Bolles, *Personality and Sexuality of the Physically Handicapped Woman*.

10. *Ibid.*, p. vii (Preface).

11. *Ibid.*, p. 97.

12. Cora Sutton Castle, "Statistical Study of Eminent Women," *Archives of Psychology*, XXI, 1–91.

13. *Ibid.*, p. 50.

14. Amanda Carolyn Northrop, "The Successful Women of America," *Popular Science Monthly*, LXIV, 239–244.

15. H. D. Kitson and Lucille Kirtley, "The Vocational Changes of One Thousand Eminent American Women," *School and Society*, XIX, 110–112.

16. Emilie Hutchinson, "Women and the Ph.D.," *American Association of University Women Journal*, XXII, 19–22.

17. Luella Cole Pressey, "The Women Whose Names Appear in *American Men of Science* for 1927," *School and Society*, XXIX, 96–100.

18. This matter of "age" and the unwillingness of women to divulge their age will be referred to at several points later in this study. In the judgment of the writer, this tendency carries with it considerable significance, reflecting a cultural assumption that a woman no longer "young" is likewise no longer desirable as a wife. Is youth, and its presumed concomitants of

personal attractiveness, sexual vigor, and potential childbearing, the only basis for a sound and satisfying marriage?

19. Éva M. Pletsch, "A Study of Certain Characteristics of Women in *Who's Who in America*," abstracted in *Who's Who in America*, XVII, 26.

20. Kathleen Hergt and J. R. Shannon, "Marriage vs. Careers —Fame," *Occupations*, XVI, 848–851.

21. This study shows pointedly what is said to be a continuing trend toward a higher percentage of marriage among eminent women.

22. It should be observed that all the investigations reported above deal exclusively with American women except one. Castle's study, covering forty-two nations and several centuries in time, showed a much higher marriage rate. Of those discussed by Castle, only 16.3 per cent were single. This may be partly explained by the variety of cultures represented, and also by the fact Castle points out, that in the past, many women married eminence. In America, feminine achievement has been almost entirely a matter of individual attainment.

23. Amy Hewes, "Dependents of College Teachers," *Journal of the American Statistical Association*, XVI, 502–511.

24. Theresa P. Pyle, "The Teacher's Dependency Load," *Teachers College Contributions to Education*, No. 782.

25. Hutchinson, *op. cit.*

26. A. R. Mead, "A Study of Teachers' Dependents in Florida," *Educational Administration and Supervision*, XXI, 703–709.

27. National Education Association, "The Teacher's Economic Position," *Research Bulletin*, XIII, 167–267.

28. David W. Peters, "Status of the Married Woman Teacher," *Teachers College Contributions to Education*, No. 603.

29. United States Department of Labor, Women's Bureau Bulletins: No. 30, *The Share of Wage-earning Women in Family Support;* No. 75, *What the Wage-earning Woman Contributes to Family Support;* No. 155, *Women in the Economy of the United States of America.*

30. The present investigator has been impressed by the fact that among all the studies made and reported by the numerous bulletins of the Women's Bureau, not one has been devoted to the economic problem peculiar to the single woman. They re-

flect, instead, the absorbing concern during the past two decades with the status and problems of the married woman who works and the possible effect upon home and family welfare.

31. Bulletins of the Metropolitan Insurance Company are widely advertised and easily available.

32. Gwendolyn B. Needham, *The "Old Maid" in the Life and Fiction of 18th Century England.*

33. George A. Dunlap, *The City in the American Novel 1789–1900.*

34. Lennox Bouton Grey, *Chicago and "The Great American Novel."*

35. Lisle Abbott Rose, *A Descriptive Catalogue of Economic and Politico-economic Fiction in the United States 1902–1909.*

36. C. C. Regier, *The Era of the Muckrakers.*

37. John Chamberlain, *Farewell to Reform.*

38. Claude R. Flory, *Economic Criticism in American Fiction 1792–1900.*

39. Walter Fuller Taylor, *The Economic Novel in America.*

40. Ima Honaker Herron, *The Small Town in American Literature.*

41. Lucy Lockwood Hazard, *The Frontier in American Literature.*

42. Lillie D. Loshe, *The Early American Novel.*

43. Herbert Ross Brown, *The Sentimental Novel in America 1789–1860.*

44. Mary Sumner Benson, *Women in Eighteenth-Century America.*

45. James Harwood Barnett, *Divorce and the American Divorce Novel 1858–1937.*

Notes to Chapter 2

1. Kimball Young, *Personality and Problems of Adjustment*, p. 572.

2. Asa Don Dickinson, *One Thousand Best Books; The Best Books of Our Time 1901–1925;* and *The Best Books of the Decade 1926–1935.*

3. The list of American fiction used in this investigation is Dickinson's own list as it appears in each volume—with one exception: in the latest volume the investigator detected what appeared to be an error and made the correction. This added some dozen or more titles to the printed list.

4. Lennox Bouton Grey, *Chicago and "The Great American Novel,"* pp. 14–15.

5. Gwendolyn B. Needham, *The "Old Maid" in the Life and Fiction of 18th Century England,* p. 174.

6. Elizabeth Margaret Kerr, *The Twentieth Century Sequence Novel.*

7. The comprehensive Dickinson list of American novels, arranged alphabetically by authors' names, appears in the Appendix. Legend indicates whether a given book was retained for the study, or, if not, for what reason it was eliminated.

8. All items of the cross section classification, herein explained, will be found in the Appendix.

NOTES TO CHAPTER 3

1. Nathaniel Hawthorne, *The House of the Seven Gables,* p. 59.

2. *Ibid.,* p. 40.

3. *Ibid.,* p. 209.

4. *Ibid.,* pp. 55–56.

5. *Ibid.,* p. 344.

6. *Ibid.,* p. 57.

7. *Ibid.,* p. 66.

8. *Ibid.,* p. 344.

9. *Ibid.,* p. 56.

10. *Ibid.*

11. *Ibid.*

12. *Ibid.*

13. *Ibid.,* p. 104.

14. *Ibid.,* p. 257.

15. *Ibid.,* p. 125.

16. *Ibid.,* p. 111.

17. *Ibid.,* p. 104.

18. *Ibid.,* p. 127.

19. *Ibid.,* p. 59.

20. *Ibid.,* p. 66.

21. *Ibid.,* p. 51.

22. *Ibid.,* p. 50.

23. *Ibid.,* p. 74.

24. *Ibid.,* p. 48.

25. *Ibid.,* p. 163.

26. *Ibid.,* pp. 163–164.

27. *Ibid.*, p. 164.

28. *Ibid.*, p. 165.

29. *Ibid.*

30. *Ibid.*, p. 377.

31. Theodore Dreiser, *Jennie Gerhardt*, p. 16. From edition published by Constable & Co., Ltd., London, 1911; copyright 1926 by Theodore Dreiser and reprinted by permission of Mrs. Theodore Dreiser.

32. *Ibid.*, p. 34.

33. *Ibid.*, p. 55.

34. *Ibid.*, p. 56.

35. *Ibid.*, p. 174.

36. *Ibid.*, p. 126.

37. *Ibid.*, p. 128.

38. *Ibid.*, p. 144.

39. *Ibid.*, p. 367.

40. *Ibid.*, pp. 132–133.

41. *Ibid.*, p. 93.

42. *Ibid.*, p. 131.

43. *Ibid.*, p. 136.

44. *Ibid.*, pp. 98–99.

45. Edith Wharton, *Ethan Frome*, p. 65. Copyright 1911 by Charles Scribner's Sons and reprinted with their permission.

46. *Ibid.*, pp. 32–33.

47. In the stage version, as played by such artists as Pauline Lord, Ruth Gordon, and Raymond Massey, this last revelation was made in a brief epilogue. The impact upon the audience, as the curtain rose on this scene, was an unforgettable moment in the theater. For its sheer dramatic power, it should be compared with Galsworthy's *The Apple Tree*, which, according to the editor's prophecy, will someday make a "million-dollar movie."

48. Wharton, *op. cit.*, p. 188.

49. *Ibid.*, p. 194.

50. Joseph Hergesheimer, *Mountain Blood*, pp. 134–135.

51. *Ibid.*, p. 211.

52. *Ibid.*, p. 210.

53. Meta Beggs's appraisal of "virtue" should be compared with Dreiser's defense of Jennie Gerhardt.

54. Hergesheimer, *op. cit.*, p. 195.

55. *Ibid.*, p. 209.

56. *Ibid.*, p. 251.
57. *Ibid.*, p. 259.
58. *Ibid.*, pp. 258–259. Copyright 1915 by Alfred A. Knopf and reprinted with their permission.
59. *Ibid.*, p. 246.
60. Ruth Suckow, *The Folks*, p. 19.
61. *Ibid.*, p. 11.
62. *Ibid.*, p. 27.
63. *Ibid.*, p. 32.
64. *Ibid.*, p. 312.
65. *Ibid.*, p. 315.
66. *Ibid.*, p. 318.
67. *Ibid.*, p. 320.
68. *Ibid.*, p. 323.
69. *Ibid.*, p. 325.
70. *Ibid.*, p. 328.
71. *Ibid.*, p. 330.
72. *Ibid.*, p. 332.
73. *Ibid.*
74. *Ibid.*, p. 315.
75. *Ibid.*, p. 307.
76. *Ibid.*, p. 394.
77. *Ibid.*, p. 355.
78. *Ibid.*, p. 398.
79. *Ibid.*, p. 439.
80. *Ibid.*, p. 473.
81. *Ibid.*, p. 454.
82. *Ibid.*, p. 520.
83. *Ibid.*, p. 521.
84. Mary Roberts Rinehart, *The Circular Staircase*, p. 9. Copyright 1908; copyright renewed 1935 by Mary Roberts Rinehart and reprinted with her permission.
85. *Ibid.*, p. 15.
86. *Ibid.*, p. 26.
87. *Ibid.*, p. 56.
88. *Ibid.*, p. 11.
89. *Ibid.*, pp. 56–57.
90. *Ibid.*, p. 125.
91. *Ibid.*, p. 54.
92. *Ibid.*, p. 20.
93. *Ibid.*, p. 29.

94. *Ibid.*, p. 160.
95. *Ibid.*, p. 41.
96. *Ibid.*, p. 26.
97. *Ibid.*, p. 11.
98. *Ibid.*, p. 30.
99. *Ibid.*, p. 32.
100. *Ibid.*, p. 79.
101. *Ibid.*, p. 85.
102. *Ibid.*, p. 22.
103. *Ibid.*
104. *Ibid.*, p. 21.
105. *Ibid.*, p. 16.
106. *Ibid.*
107. *Ibid.*, p. 40.
108. *Ibid.*, p. 117.
109. *Ibid.*, p. 16.
110. *Ibid.*
111. *Ibid.*, p. 300.
112. *Ibid.*
113. *Ibid.*
114. Kate Douglas Wiggin, *Rebecca of Sunnybrook Farm*, p. 23.
115. *Ibid.*, p. 33.
116. *Ibid.*, p. 63.
117. *Ibid.*, p. 64.
118. *Ibid.*, p. 35.
119. *Ibid.*, p. 34.
120. *Ibid.*, p. 34.
121. *Ibid.*
122. *Ibid.*, p. 35.
123. In this connection, it is of interest to note that Margaret Mead, writing on "Patterns of Culture Affecting the Physical Fitness of Men and Women" (unpublished report of the Women's Commission of the Committee on Physical Fitness of the United States Federal Security Agency, pp. 14–15), observes that in almost every culture more prestige is attached to what men do than what women do. This is largely explained by the fact that society expects women to find their satisfactions in reproduction and men in various forms of social achievement. It is not surprising, therefore, to discover similar evidence in fiction that women show less interest in achievement, since

it is to activities "distinctly masculine" that society attaches the greater prestige.

124. The women who have considerable means, presumably inherited, are largely the same group, as those women who engage in some self-appointed charitable enterprise. These women work, but are not paid for their work; hence their activity is not defined as a vocation.

125. The tendency on the part of novelists to call up some lover of the past, seemingly to enhance the character or to invoke sympathy for her, would bear a more thorough analysis than this investigation can devote to it. A notable example appears in Hawthorne's *The Blithedale Romance*, in which he explains that Zenobia had been married in her early youth. This investigator took this statement as fact, and therefore did not consider her a single woman.

126. This finding recalls and supports a pertinent comment made by Warner and Lunt in their Yankee City study. Their statistical data are supplemented by a number of "profiles" of persons typical of many found in the New England community. The second of these personality sketches is entitled "All the Men Have Left," and reveals the dilemma of a girl twenty-eight years old who laments the lack of marriageable men. It is a confidential report of a commonly prevailing situation, and she ends her confession thus: "Nothing like being well-behaved and maintaining your reticence." These words might provide an appropriate text for this study of single women in American fiction.

127. The list of domestics in the study would have been much longer if it were not for the fact that many household workers were not described in enough detail for their marital status to be determined. Many were referred to by a given name only. Negro servant women, of whom there were some dozen or more, would have extended the list still further, but these, for reasons already explained, were not included. Another vocational group which the investigator took account of but could not enumerate for similar reasons were the nurses. Though one might suppose their social status to be somewhat above that of the domestics, the nurses were frequently without names by which they could be identified. Often they were referred to merely as "nurse" or "the nurse," so could not be classified. Even less than the other vocational groups, the nurse's position is not

clearly delineated. As a practical nurse, she is also a house-worker. As a governess, she is perhaps more appropriately called a teacher than a nurse. The professional nurse appears rarely in fiction and, one might add, not too commendably. The stereo-type of women in the several professions here named deserves a much more extended investigation than has been possible herein.

128. Miss Miranda Sawyer is one of the seven major charac-ters of the study and she, as well as her sweet, shy sister Jane, is described in much detail in the earlier chapter.

129. The tendency to stereotype may be further emphasized in that the miscellany of characters which do not conform to any of the three vocational groups mentioned add up to a smaller group than any of the three. This miscellany includes: one lecturer and philanthropist; three stenographers or secre-taries; two librarians; two who work in dry-goods stores or dress shops; three musicians of sorts; one society reporter; one writer and editor; one who owns a paper; four prostitutes or men's mistresses; one sculptress; one assistant to a retired minister engaged in slum work; one spirit-medium; two poetesses; and one who dabbles in real estate. Though this shows a rather wide variety within a comparatively small group, actually many of these women who follow different pursuits resemble the others in most of the recurring characteristics noted above.

130. This novel was published in 1914.

Notes to Chapter 4

1. Herbert Ross Brown, *The Sentimental Novel in America 1789–1860*, p. 286.

2. It should be observed that Hepzibah Pyncheon, major character of Hawthorne's *The House of the Seven Gables* (1851), with which the study proper begins, is in almost every detail the English "old maid" transported to an American set-ting. The theme of this novel may be said to grow out of its locale, and the element of witchcraft creates its sense of gloom; but old Hepzibah, with her gross inefficiency, her gaunt un-gainliness, and her family pride, would have been quite as fa-miliar a figure in an English village as in old Salem.

3. The colored woman as servant has appeared by this time in representative American novels, a notable example in *Elsie Venner* (1861), but since Negro women have a different origin

and a different cultural significance, they were not included or analyzed in this investigation. They deserve a whole study of their own.

4. An outstanding humorous novel, *David Harum* (1898) by Edward Noyes Westcott, appears in the study and contributes several varieties of the humorous, small-town spinster.

5. *Rebecca of Sunnybrook Farm* by Kate Douglas Wiggin, which furnished a major character to this study, should be re-called as an example.

6. It should be recalled that Sherwood Anderson, in his novel *Poor White*, presented an example of an intellectual woman who apparently preferred a homosexual relationship to mar-riage. *Winesburg, Ohio* is a series of related episodes, most of them complete as short stories; hence it cannot, in the truest sense, be called a novel.

7. The central study found its first, as it happens, its only delineation of a woman of homosexual tendencies in the char-actor of Kate Chanceller in Sherwood Anderson's *Poor White*, a novel published in 1920.

8. Several characters in the central study are librarians but are not prominently so. Margot Ferguson, one of the seven major characters appearing in Ruth Suckow's *The Folks*, worked in her home-town library, but only for a short time.

BIBLIOGRAPHY

THE following are selected references which have a direct bearing upon the subject of single women, the sociological interpretation of the American novel, or the method of the present investigation. Other writings which have furnished background have been mentioned by title and author at various points in the Introduction and the study proper, but are not included in the selective bibliography which follows.

SELECTED REFERENCES

Barnett, James Harwood. Divorce and the American Divorce Novel 1858–1937; a Study in Literary Reflections of Social Influences. Philadelphia: Privately printed, 1939. 168 pp.

Benson, Mary Sumner. Women in Eighteenth-Century America. New York: Columbia University Press, 1935. 345 pp.

Brown, Herbert Ross. The Sentimental Novel in America 1798–1860. Durham, N.C.: Duke University Press, 1940. 407 pp.

Castle, Cora Sutton. "Statistical Study of Eminent Women." *Archives of Psychology*, XXI (August, 1913), Columbia University Contributions to Philosophy and Psychology, 1–91.

Chamberlain, John. Farewell to Reform. The Rise, Life, and Decay of the Progressive Mind in America. New York: The John Day Company, 1932. 333 pp.

Davis, Katherine Bement. Factors in the Sex Life of 2200 Women. Study for the Bureau of Social Hygiene. New York: Harper and Brothers, 1929. 430 pp.

Dickinson, Asa Don. One Thousand Best Books. New York: Doubleday, Page and Company, 1924. 416 pp.

—— The Best Books of Our Time 1901–1925. New York: Doubleday, Doran and Company, 1928. 405 pp.

—— The Best Books of the Decade 1926–1935. New York: H. W. Wilson Company, 1937. 194 pp.

Dickinson, Robert L., and Lura Beam. The Single Woman; a Medical Approach. Volume II of study under auspices of National Committee on Maternal Health. Baltimore: Williams and Wilkins, 1934. 469 pp.

Dunlap, George Arthur. The City in the American Novel 1789–1900; a Study of American Novels Portraying Contemporary Conditions in New York, Philadelphia, and Boston. Doctoral dissertation, Department of English, University of Pennsylvania. Philadelphia: Privately printed, 1934. 187 pp.

Flory, Claude R. Economic Criticism in American Fiction 1792–1900. Doctoral dissertation, Department of English, University of Pennsylvania. Philadelphia: Privately printed, 1936. 261 pp.

Grey, Lennox Bouton. Chicago and "The Great American Novel." A Critical Approach. Unpublished doctoral dissertation, Department of English Language and Literature, the University of Chicago, 1935.

Hazard, Lucy Lockwood. The Frontier in American Literature. New York: Thomas Y. Crowell, 1937. 308 pp.

Hergt, Kathleen, and J. R. Shannon. "Marriage vs. Careers—Fame." Occupations, XVI (June, 1938), 848–851.

Herron, Ima Honaker. The Small Town in American Literature. Durham, N.C.: Duke University Press, 1939. 477 pp.

Hewes, Amy. "Dependents of College Teachers." Journal of the American Statistical Association, XVI (December, 1919), 502–511.

Hutchinson, Emilie. "Women and the Ph.D." American Association of University Women Journal, XXII (October, 1928), 19–22.

Kerr, Elizabeth Margaret. The Twentieth Century Sequence Novel. Unpublished doctoral dissertation, the University of Minnesota, 1942.

Kitson, H. D., and Lucille Kirtley. "The Vocational Changes of One Thousand Eminent American Women." School and Society, XIX 1924, 110–112.

Landis, Carney, and M. Marjorie Bolles. Personality and Sexuality of the Physically Handicapped Woman. New York: Paul B. Hoebner, Inc., 1942. 171 pp.

Landis, Carney, and co-authors. Sex in Development. Study under the auspices of the Committee for Research in the Problems of Sex of the National Research Council, Washington, D.C. New York: Paul B. Hoebner, Inc., 1940. 329 pp.

Loshe, Lillie D. The Early American Novel. New York: Columbia University Press, 1907. 131 pp.

Mead, A. R. "A Study of Teachers' Dependents in Florida."

Educational Administration and Supervision, XXI (December, 1935), 703–709.

National Education Association. "The Teacher's Economic Position." Research Bulletin, XIII (September, 1935), 167–267.

Needham, Gwendolyn B. The "Old Maid" in the Life and Fiction of 18th Century England. Unpublished doctoral dissertation, Department of English, the University of California, Berkley, 1938. 322 pp.

Northrop, Amanda Carolyn. "The Successful Women of America." *Popular Science Monthly*, LXIV, (January, 1904), 239–244.

Peters, David W. "Status of the Married Woman Teacher." Teachers College Contributions to Education, No. 603. New York: Teachers College, Columbia University, Bureau of Publications, 1934. 97 pp.

Pletsch, Eva M. "A Study of Certain Characteristics of Women in Who's Who in America." (1932–33 ed.) Thesis at Teachers College, Temple University, Philadelphia. Abstracted in Who's Who in America, XVII, 26.

Pressey, Luella Cole. "The Women Whose Names Appear in American Men of Science for 1927." *School and Society*, XXIX (January, 1929), 96–100.

Pyle, Theresa P. "The Teacher's Dependency Load." Teachers College Contributions to Education, No. 782. New York: Teachers College, Columbia University, Bureau of Publications, 1939. 111 pp.

Regier, C. C. The Era of the Muckrakers. Chapel Hill, N.C.: University of North Carolina Press, 1932. 254 pp.

Rose, Lisle Abbott. A Descriptive Catalogue of Economic and Politico-Economic Fiction in the United States 1902–1909. Unpublished doctoral dissertation, Department of English Language and Literature, the University of Chicago, 1935.

Strakosch, Frances M. Factors in the Sex Life of 700 Psychopathic Women. Utica, N.Y.: State Hospitals Press, 1934. 102 pp.

Taylor, Walter Fuller. The Economic Novel in America. Chapel Hill, N.C.: University of North Carolina Press, 1942. 378 pp.

United States Department of Labor, Women's Bureau Bulletin No. 30. The Share of Wage-earning Women in Family Support. Washington, D.C.: Government Printing Office, 1923. 170 pp.

—— Women's Bureau Bulletin, No. 75. What the Wage-earning Woman Contributes to Family Support by Agnes L. Peterson. Washington, D.C.: Government Printing Office, 1929. 20 pp.

—— Women's Bureau Bulletin, No. 155. Women in the Economy of the United States of America; a Summary Report by Mary Elizabeth Pidgeon. Washington, D.C.: Government Printing Office, 1937. 137 pp.

United States Federal Security Agency, Women's Commission, Committee on Physical Fitness, Physical Fitness of Girls and Women. Report in progress. 1945.

Warner, W. Lloyd, and Paul S. Lunt. The Social Life of a Modern Community. New Haven: Yale University Press, 1941. 460 pp.

Young, Kimball. Personality and Problems of Adjustment. New York: F. S. Crofts and Company, 1940. 868 pp.

NOVELS USED IN STUDY PROPER

Alcott, Louisa May. Little Women. New York: A. L. Burt, 1868. 424 pp.

Aldrich, Thomas Bailey. The Story of a Bad Boy. Boston: Houghton Mifflin Co., 1869. 261 pp.

Allen, James Lane. The Mettle of the Pasture. New York: The Macmillan Co., 1905. 448 pp.

Anderson, Sherwood. Marching Men. New York: John Lane Co., 1917. 314 pp.

—— Poor White. New York: B. V. Huebsch Inc., 1920. 371 pp.

—— Windy McPherson's Son. New York: John Lane Co., 1916. 347 pp.

Brown, Alice. The Prisoner. New York: The Macmillan Co., 1916. 471 pp.

Burt, Struthers. The Interpreter's House. New York: Charles Scribner's Sons, 1924. 445 pp.

Cable, George Washington. The Cavalier. New York: Charles Scribner's Sons, 1901. 311 pp.

—— Dr. Sevier. New York: Charles Scribner's Sons, 1883. 473 pp.

Carroll, Gladys H. As the Earth Turns. New York: The Macmillan Co., 1935. 339 pp.

Cather, Willa. Lucy Gayheart. New York: Alfred A. Knopf, 1935. 231 pp.
—— My Ántonia. New York: Houghton Mifflin Co., 1918. 419 pp.
—— The Professor's House. New York: Alfred A. Knopf, 1925. 283 pp.
—— The Song of the Lark. London: Jonathan Cape, 1915. 490 pp.
Chase, Mary Ellen. Mary Peters. New York: The Macmillan Co., 1934. 377 pp.
Churchill, Winston. A Far Country. New York: The Macmillan Co., 1914. 509 pp.
—— The Inside of the Cup. New York: The Macmillan Co., 1912. 513 pp.
—— Mr. Crewe's Career. New York: The Macmillan Co., 1908. 490 pp.
Deland, Margaret. The Rising Tide. New York: Harper and Bros., 1916. 293 pp.
Dreiser, Theodore. An American Tragedy. New York: Horace Liveright Inc., 1925. 840 pp.
—— The "Genius." New York: John Lane Co., 1915. 736 pp.
—— Jennie Gerhardt. London: Constable and Co., Ltd., 1911 (Copyright 1926 by Theodore Dreiser). 367 pp.
Eggleston, Edward. The Hoosier Schoolmaster. New York: Orange Judd Co., 1871. 218 pp.
Ferber, Edna. Cimarron. New York: Grosset and Dunlap, 1930. 388 pp.
Fisher, Dorothy Canfield. The Squirrel Cage. New York: Henry Holt and Co., 1912. 371 pp.
Ford, Paul Leicester. The Honourable Peter Stirling. New York: Henry Holt and Co., 1894. 417 pp.
Fox, John, Jr. The Heart of the Hills. New York: Charles Scribner's Sons, 1912. 396 pp.
Freeman, Mary E. Wilkins. The Portion of Labor. New York: Harper and Bros., 1901. 563 pp.
Gale, Zona. Birth. New York: The Macmillan Co., 1918. 402 pp.
Glasgow, Ellen. Barren Ground. New York: Doubleday, Page and Co., 1925. 511 pp.
—— The Deliverance. New York: Doubleday, Page and Co., 1904. 543 pp.

Glasgow, Ellen. Life and Gabriella. New York: Doubleday, Page and Co., 1916. 529 pp.

—— The Miller of Old Church. New York: Doubleday, Page and Co., 1911. 432 pp.

—— The Romance of a Plain Man. New York: The Macmillan Co., 1909. 464 pp.

—— The Romantic Comedians. New York: Doubleday, Page and Co., 1926. 346 pp.

—— The Sheltered Life. New York: Doubleday, Doran and Co., 1932. 395 pp.

—— They Stooped to Folly. New York: Doubleday, Doran and Co., 1929. 351 pp.

—— Vein of Iron. New York: Harcourt, Brace and Co., 1935. 462 pp.

—— Virginia. New York: Doubleday, Doran and Co., 1929. 478 pp.

—— The Wheel of Life. New York: Doubleday, Page and Co., 1906. 474 pp.

Hawthorne, Nathaniel. The House of the Seven Gables. Boston: Houghton Mifflin Co., 1851. 423 pp.

Hergesheimer, Joseph. Linda Condon. New York: Alfred A. Knopf, 1919. 304 pp.

—— Mountain Blood. New York: Alfred A. Knopf, 1915. 368 pp.

Holmes, Oliver Wendell. The Guardian Angel. Boston: Houghton Mifflin Co., 1868. 431 pp.

Howells, William Dean. A Modern Instance. Boston: Houghton Mifflin Co., 1881. 514 pp.

—— The Rise of Silas Lapham. Boston: Houghton Mifflin Co., 1884. 515 pp.

Lewis, Sinclair. Main Street. New York: Grosset and Dunlap, 1920. 451 pp.

Lincoln, Joseph C. Cap'n Eri. New York: A. L. Burt Co., 1904. 397 pp.

—— Doctor Nye. New York: D. Appleton and Co., 1923. 423 pp.

—— Galusha the Magnificent. New York: D. Appleton and Co., 1921. 407 pp.

—— Mary 'Gusta. New York: Grosset and Dunlap, 1916. 411 pp.

—— Partners of the Tide. New York: A. L. Burt Co., 1905. 400 pp.

Mitchell, S. Weir. Constance Trescot. New York: The Century Co., 1905. 384 pp.

Nathan, Robert. Autumn. New York: McBride and Co., 1921. 198 pp.

Nicholson, Meredith. A Hoosier Chronicle. Boston: Houghton Mifflin Co., 1912. 606 pp.

—— The House of a Thousand Candles. Indianapolis: Bobbs-Merrill Co., 1905. 382 pp.

Norris, Charles G. Brass. New York: E. P. Dutton and Co., 1921. 452 pp.

Norris, Frank. Vandover and the Brute. New York: Doubleday, Doran and Co., 1914. 311 pp.

Norris, Kathleen. Saturday's Child. New York: Doubleday, Page and Co., 1914. 531 pp.

Oemler, Marie Conway. Slippy McGee. New York: The Century Co., 1917. 405 pp.

Ostenso, Martha. Wild Geese. New York: Dodd Mead and Co., 1925. 356 pp.

Page, Thomas Nelson. Red Rock. New York: Charles Scribner's Sons, 1898. 586 pp.

Poole, Ernest. The Harbor. New York: The Macmillan Co., 1915. 387 pp.

Rice, Alice Hegan. Mrs. Wiggs of the Cabbage Patch. New York: The Century Co., 1901. 153 pp.

Rinehart, Mary Roberts. The Circular Staircase. New York: Grosset and Dunlap, 1908. 301 pp.

—— K. New York: Grosset and Dunlap, 1914. 410 pp.

Smith, F. Hopkinson. The Fortunes of Oliver Horn. New York: Charles Scribner's Sons, 1902. 461 pp.

—— Peter. New York: Charles Scribner's Sons, 1908. 482 pp.

Stewart, Charles David. The Fugitive Blacksmith. New York: The Century Co., 1905. 321 pp.

Suckow, Ruth. The Folks. New York: The Literary Guild, 1934. 727 pp.

Tarkington, Booth. Gentle Julia. New York: Doubleday, Page and Co., 1922. 375 pp.

—— The Gentleman from Indiana. New York: Doubleday, Page and Co., 1899. 504 pp.

—— The Magnificent Ambersons. New York: Doubleday, Page and Co., 1918. 516 pp.

Thanet, Octave. The Man of the Hour. Indianapolis: The Bobbs-Merrill Co., 1905. 477 pp.

Watts, Mary S. From Father to Son. New York: The Macmillan Co., 1919. 310 pp.

—— The Legacy. New York: The Macmillan Co., 1911. 394 pp.

Westcott, Edward Noyes. David Harum. New York: D. Appleton and Co., 1898. 392 pp.

Wharton, Edith. Ethan Frome. New York: Charles Scribner's Sons, 1911. 195 pp.

—— Summer. New York: D. Appleton and Company, 1917. 291 pp.

White, William Allen. A Certain Rich Man. New York: The Macmillan Co., 1909. 434 pp.

Wiggin, Kate Douglas. Rebecca of Sunnybrook Farm. New York: Houghton Mifflin Co., 1903. 327 pp.

Wilder, Thornton. Heaven's My Destination. New York: Harper and Bros., 1935. 304 pp.

Wilson, Harry Leon. Merton of the Movies. London: Jonathan Cape, 1922. 288 pp.

Wister, Owen. Lady Baltimore. New York: The Macmillan Co., 1906. 405 pp.

INDEX